VALUE INVESTING TODAY

Charles H. Brandes

Third Edition

McGraw-Hill

New York   Chicago   San Francisco   Lisbon   London
Madrid   Mexico City   Milan   New Delhi
San Juan   Seoul   Singapore
Sydney   Toronto

The **McGraw·Hill** Companies

6 7 8 9 0   DOC/DOC   1 5 4 3 2

ISBN 0-07-141738-9

This publication is designed to provide accurate and authoritative information in regard to the subject matter covered. It is sold with the understanding that neither the author nor the publisher is engaged in rendering legal, accounting, futures/securities trading, or other professional service. If legal advice or other expert assistance is required, the services of a competent professional person should be sought.

—From a Declaration of Principles jointly adopted by a Committee of the American Bar Association and a Committee of Publishers

McGraw-Hill books are available at special quantity discounts to use as premiums and sales promotions, or for use in corporate training programs. For more information, please write to the Director of Special Sales, Professional Publishing, McGraw-Hill, Two Penn Plaza, New York, NY 10121-2298. Or contact your local bookstore.

Library of Congress Cataloging-in-Publication Data

Brandes, Charles H.
    Value investing today / by Charles H. Brandes.—3rd ed.
        p.   cm.
    Includes index.
    ISBN 0-07-141738-9 (hardcover : alk. paper)
    1. Stocks.   2. Investments.   I. Title.
  HG4661.B68   2003
  332.67'8—dc21
                                 2003006914

To L. F. B.

Contents

Preface   ix

Introduction   xi

Part 1. What Is Value Investing and Why It Makes Dollars and Sense   1

1   What Is "Value Investing"?   3

2   Behavioral Biases: Why Value Investing Works   17

3   The Value Pedigree and the Rewards of Value Investing   31

Part 2. How to Find Value Companies   47

4   Characteristics of Value   49

5   Narrowing Your Focus   61

6   Gathering Company Information   71

7   Corporate Governance and the Value Investor   79

Part 3. Learning to Think Globally   95

8   Why Go Overseas?   97

9   How to Invest in Companies Worldwide   119

10   Unique Aspects of Global Investing   139

Part 4. Value Investing and You   157

11   Managing Risks and Your Value Portfolio   159

12   Are Stocks an Intelligent Investment?   173

13 Staying the Course 185

14 Above All, Be Patient 203

Epilogue 207

Index 209

Preface

"Intelligent investing."

In many ways, the global investment landscape is far different than it was in 1989 when I wrote the first edition of this book. Today's environment also has changed quite a bit from when the second edition was published in 1998. From advances in technology, medicine, and communication to broader adoption of free enterprise practices and free trade agreements, today's world reflects unprecedented opportunity—and unique risks. Yet through all the changes, I believe the essential principles of successful investing endure.

Updated with new chapters, sections, and examples, this third edition of *Value Investing Today* seeks to demonstrate how the combination of *rational* fundamental analysis and *irrational* stock market prices can create opportunity for the diligent value investor.

Throughout this book, I frequently cite the philosophy and writings of Benjamin Graham. With David Dodd, Graham wrote the cornerstone book in the canon of investment publications, *Security Analysis*. Graham also wrote *The Intelligent Investor*, a book Warren Buffett called "the best book about investing ever written."[1] I had the privilege to meet and learn from Graham, a man many consider to be the father of security analysis and value investing. I am greatly indebted to Benjamin Graham, my mentor. His basic principles formed the solid foundations for my worldwide investment success.

For help in the preparation of this book, I share my deep appreciation with my colleagues at Brandes Investment Partners. With the dedication and hard work of the professionals with whom I work on a daily basis, we have built a respected investment management firm.

This book was written for investors who understand that the most precious things in life have to be earned, those who know that quick fixes often fail just as quickly. In the pages to follow, I'll discuss my definition of value investing, why it's important and why it works, how it can be applied on a company-by-company basis in markets worldwide, and why I believe it represents an approach best described as "intelligent investing."

Notes

1.   Warren E. Buffett, preface to *The Intelligent Investor: A Book of Practical Counsel,* 4th rev. ed., by Benjamin Graham, New York: Harper & Row, 1973, p. vii.

Introduction

You should focus on two ideas as you read this book. First, as an investor, you must accept that patience is necessary if large and enduring profits are to be made from purchasing stocks. Second, be aware that most investors' thinking is often misguided. The stock market is inherently misleading. Often, doing what everybody else is doing can be wrong. Benjamin Graham, widely considered the father of value investing, set down his central beliefs on how investors may achieve better-than-average results in the first chapter of his book *The Intelligent Investor*. He suggests investors follow policies that are "inherently sound and promising" and "not popular in Wall Street."[1] That's why *Value Investing Today* is important to you. Finding stocks that are "inherently sound and promising" is hard. Having the perseverance to buy and hold stocks that are "not popular in Wall Street" is harder still. In the chapters that follow, I'll try to provide guidance on both of these aspects of successful investing.

Graham himself realized that in-depth research and analysis were not enough. He believed investors must show courage to trust their convictions and take actions that are out of step with popular consensus. In essence, achieving better-than-average returns depends upon thinking and acting differently than the average market participant. Value investors believe that the low prices they pay for their investments are the result of a temporary disparity between the fair value of the business and its current market price. They believe that the gap between price and fair value will close, creating an opportunity for profit.

I also believe this book is important because investors today have many financial alternatives that were not around—or effectively available—during Graham's lifetime (1894–1976). It is important to

Achieving better-than-average returns depends upon thinking and acting differently than the average market participant.

address several of these issues within the context of Graham's principles.

There is one segment of readers who I especially believe could benefit from this book: individual investors with some experience in the market. In other words, *Value Investing Today* was not designed as a how-to book for total novices, nor as a textbook for highly skilled professionals. It should provide valuable assistance, however, to individual investors who have taken their first steps. I have spoken with many such investors and have noted that some have picked up all sorts of investment ideas and notions that could prove frustrating and expensive.

So, *Value Investing Today* addresses a philosophy and strategy that can help individual investors be more successful. As you read this book, you will discover sound methods of fact gathering and interpretation and begin to appreciate the need for discipline and patience.

Another point to consider: When I have talked with individual investors, the most striking aspect of our conversations has been their tendency to set sail on financial oceans without so much as a chart to guide them. In *Value Investing Today*, you will find a way to design and implement a conservative and effective investment philosophy. It is a philosophy, I emphasize, that has proved to be a successful means of building wealth and preserving capital.

WHAT TO EXPECT FROM THIS BOOK

This edition of *Value Investing Today* has been updated with lessons designed to protect long-term investors from severe losses and help them develop the discipline and patience to accumulate substantial wealth. The book includes fresh evidence reinforcing the benefits of value investing and draws on my more than 30 years in the investment industry.

Beyond mere facts and figures, this edition of *Value Investing Today* explores *why* the value approach to money management has been successful since first introduced by Benjamin Graham in the 1930s. I discuss how "intelligent" investors can apply an understanding of human behavior to the world's financial markets. Given Graham's assertion that "the investor's chief problem—and even his worst enemy—is likely to be himself,"[2] the book also provides practical advice on *how* investors can develop the patience and discipline they need to succeed through value investing. In addition, I share insights gleaned firsthand from Graham when I became his acquaintance.

My main purpose in writing this book is to help you take advantage of true investment opportunities by supplying you with the principles of the most successful means of investing over the past 70 years: value investing. I will admit to being a convert to this approach and, as with many converts, I am deeply committed to it. I have seen the results; I know it works; and I'm confident it can build wealth for those who apply its principles.

Notes

1. Benjamin Graham, *The Intelligent Investor: A Book of Practical Counsel,* 4th rev. ed. New York: Harper & Row, 1973, p. 13.

2. Ibid., p. xv.

VALUE
INVESTING
TODAY

What Is Value Investing and Why It Makes Dollars and Sense

The goal in Part 1 is to define value investing and establish clearly that the combination of rational fundamental analysis and irrational market prices creates opportunity for value investors. As such, Part 1 is designed to address value-investing principles, illustrate why the approach works, and deliver historical evidence supporting its merits.

1

WHAT IS "VALUE INVESTING"?

Which is a better value—a stock selling at $5 per share or a stock selling at $25 per share? If your answer hasn't already sprung to mind, be aware. The correct response is not the $5 stock. Nor is it the $25 stock.

The correct answer is that you can't tell. You *can* tell which is a *lower-priced* stock. But "lower price" isn't always synonymous with "better value." With the limited information I provided about these two stocks, you cannot make an informed decision about which is the better value. Share price is an important consideration when investing in stocks, but it's only one of two important factors to evaluate. The other vital factor is underlying business value.

If I went to the grocery store and purchased two items—one for $5 and one for $25—and asked you which was the better value, you would say, "Well, that depends. What did you buy?"

If I told you that I bought one onion for $5 and a 50-pound box of sirloin steaks for $25, you'd quickly recognize that I probably paid far too much for the onion, but got a great bargain on the steaks.

The price you pay for something—whether onions or steaks or stocks—is only relevant as it relates to its underlying value. This is the essence of value investing, that is, purchasing shares of a company at a *price* that is substantially lower than the company's underlying *value*.

Some people believe there is no difference between share price and business worth. They believe that if you buy shares of stock in a company for $30 a share, they must be worth $30 a share. I disagree. I believe price is what you pay; value is what you get. As cited earlier, it's the same concept when bargain hunting at the grocery store.

In practice, applying the value-investing philosophy is straightforward. Find companies with measurable worth. When their stock is selling at a price below that worth, buy it. In time, as others recognize these values, the stock's price likely will rise. When that happens, sell it and redeploy the proceeds to other undervalued companies.

Adherence to this approach has produced solid results for many long-term investors. I'll elaborate on and document the success of this strategy in greater detail in Chapter 3. Throughout this book, I'll also explore a number of concepts as they relate to the value-investing philosophy and process, building on the core principle contained in the previous paragraph. Let's start with a concept known as the "margin of safety."

THE MARGIN OF SAFETY

Benjamin Graham, often thought of as the man who pioneered value investing, challenged himself to "distill the secret of sound investment into three words"[1] when he wrote *The Intelligent Investor*, a book published in 1949. The three words Graham chose were "margin of safety." What does this three-word phrase mean?

For value investors, the margin of safety represents the difference between a company's stock price and the value of the underlying business of that company, often called its *intrinsic value*. Generally, value investors are not interested in stocks that trade at a *slight* discount to their underlying value. Rather, they seek a *substantial* discrepancy. Why? They are looking for solid companies whose stock prices are selling at "pennies on the dollar" compared with the intrinsic values of the businesses they represent. Value investors believe that a large margin of safety provides greater return potential as well as a greater degree of protection over the long term.

Graham believed that purchasing stocks at sizable discounts would protect investors against permanent loss and allow them to dispense with the need for making accurate estimates of the future. I'll discuss this in greater detail when I examine the differences between value and growth investing.

Before I do that, I want to illustrate the margin of safety concept using two charts. In Exhibit 1-1, a horizontal line represents a hypothetical company's intrinsic value—the underlying value of the business. Later in this book, I'll explain how this value is derived. For now, understand that a company's intrinsic value does not change that often and certainly not as frequently as its stock price, which may change from day to day and moment to moment.

In addition to the company's intrinsic value, I show in Exhibit 1-1 an example of a value investor's required *discount* to that intrinsic value. In other words, this is the gap between the intrinsic value and the price at which shares of the company would be purchased. Keep in mind that when purchasing shares, I seek a *significant* discount to intrinsic value, otherwise known as a large margin of safety.

In Exhibit 1-2, I add a line representing how the company's stock price fluctuates over time. You'll notice the stock price rises above and falls below the company's intrinsic value. These price fluctuations create opportunities for value investors. When the stock price of the company falls sufficiently below the intrinsic value, it creates a buying opportunity. The shaded area between the company's stock price and its discount to intrinsic value illustrates when value investors should consider purchasing the stock.

Value investors expect that over time, as others recognize the true value of the company, its share price will climb toward its intrinsic value. As this happens, the margin of safety shrinks. When the share price equals or exceeds the company's intrinsic value, the margin of safety has disappeared and the shares should be sold.

EXHIBIT 1-1   The Margin of Safety Concept

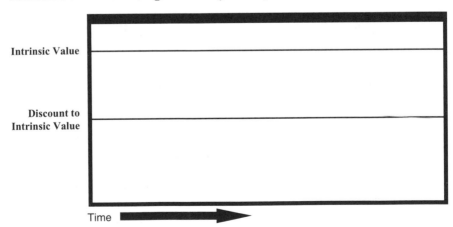

EXHIBIT 1-2   The Margin of Safety Concept

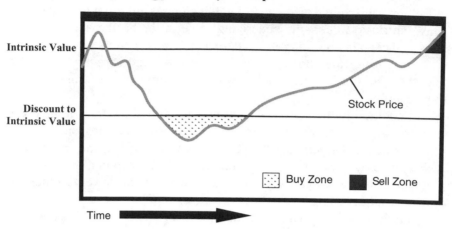

Hopefully, these exhibits provide a clear illustration of how the value-investment philosophy is applied. On paper, the logic of this approach may appear obvious: buy stocks at a bargain price and sell them after the price has gone up. However, investment decisions are not made in theory. They are made in an ever-changing environment where logic can be overshadowed by emotion. I'll address this point in greater detail throughout the book and offer guidance on how investors can help protect themselves by maintaining strict adherence to this value-investment principle.

Often, it takes a great deal of conviction to stick to value-investment disciplines, especially when a company's stock price declines after you purchase its shares. For those who focus only on price, share price declines can be devastating emotionally. Even worse, this can lead to bad decisions, such as selling just because the price is down. Some market participants only focus on how much a stock's price has declined in the short term. However, for long-term investors who evaluate share price in relation to business value, price declines can represent tremendous opportunity.

To me, investors are those who have the confidence and patience to back their judgment by buying stocks that they are prepared to hold for 5 years or more if needed. If you are looking for a quick way to turn a profit in the stock market, this book is not for you. Value investors do not focus on day-to-day oscillations in share price. They adopt and maintain a disciplined approach for evaluating business value. They are confident of their research and analysis and patient in implementing their strategy.

VALUE AND GROWTH INVESTING

In recent years, it's become more popular to classify investors' approaches as being either "value" or "growth." These have become accepted as being polar opposites, almost like taking sides in a sports event: do you support "value" or "growth"? You may not be surprised that I reject this popular approach to classifying investment styles. Value and growth are not enemies, nor are they based on incompatible beliefs. For investors

Company-specific fundamental research and analysis enable the value investor to assess intrinsic business value, independent of the volatility of short-term stock price movements. In my experience, a portfolio of securities, bought at a discount to intrinsic value, has provided superior long-term returns.

(in contrast with speculators, whom I'll address below), company fundamentals support either a value or a growth approach to selecting stocks. I believe that value investing is the more profitable discipline in the long term, but there are many successful, fundamental growth investors. However, most speculators consider themselves "growth investors," and it's among this group that I expect to see a high failure rate.

Even at the stock level, let's be clear. I do not believe in classifying stocks as value or growth. Often, such generalizations reflect guidelines imposed by index sponsors and have little or nothing to do with fundamental analysis at the individual company level. During my 30+ years of practical investment experience, I have investigated companies all over the world in every sector and industry. With the goal of uncovering investment opportunities that offer the greatest margin of safety, the search has led me to undervalued businesses in what many may perceive to be growth industries such as technology or pharmaceuticals.

I encourage you to discard any preconceptions you may have regarding value investing. It's not a purely defensive tactic that should be applied only in bear markets. It does not focus exclusively on backward-looking businesses in dying industries. And value investors do not buy stock only in companies that "make things that rust," as I once heard someone say. The diligent value investor searches for promising investments offering a large margin of safety—in whatever country or industry they may be.

Many times, I see promising businesses behind what many people call growth stocks: solid, well-established companies that offer quality products or services. But I will not consider them for purchase if their stock prices far exceed their underlying business worth—in other words, if they offer no margin of safety.

Near the peak of the Internet stock mania in early 2000, share prices for various dot-com or "New Economy" companies (many of which were not solid or established and offered unproven products or services) were leaping to successive record highs. At the same time, share prices languished for "Old Economy" companies in industries such as insurance, utilities, and manufacturing. At that point, some market participants mistakenly believed that New Economy growth stocks were stocks that went up, while Old Economy value stocks were those that went down.

Returns for value and growth stock indices appeared to support this notion. By the end of March 2000—even as technology stocks began their retreat—the Nasdaq 100, a measure of returns for the 100 largest companies in the technology-heavy Nasdaq Composite, had gained 108.7 percent in the prior 12 months versus only 13.3 percent for the venerable Dow Jones Industrial Average (DJIA). The DJIA measures returns for 30 major U.S. companies. Technology stocks, spurred by shares of start-up Internet firms, were soaring while it seemed the rest of the market was being left behind, some said "for good."

In fact, many of the best-performing stocks at the time were initial public offerings or IPOs—companies that had never issued stock before. Of the 486 IPOs in 1999, about half were Internet-related companies that gained, on average, 147 percent their first *day* of trading. Exhibit 1-3 illustrates the divergent paths of technology growth stocks, as measured by the Nasdaq 100, versus the broader market, as measured by the S&P 500 Index.

At that time, I believed this divergence between growth and value stocks represented the biggest two-tiered market bubble that I had seen since starting my career in 1968. I didn't believe the gains were sustainable because the prices for so many stocks climbed to ridiculous heights—levels that were well beyond the intrinsic values of the underlying companies. While I was scratching my head over the market's ridiculous excesses, my firm was taking advantage of that environment by adding to our portfolios solid businesses trading at extremely attractive prices. I was more excited about the opportunities available for value investors, especially in the United States, than I had been in nearly 20 years.

When the bubble burst in March 2000, the majority of dot-com stocks offered no margin of safety. In the wake of huge losses, market participants returned their attention to fundamental strengths and the "out-of-favor" stocks my firm had purchased during the Internet-stock run-up were once

EXHIBIT 1-3   Two-Tiered Market (Growth of $1 from March 1, 1999 to March 1, 2000)

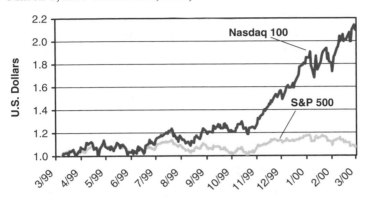

Note: All performance is historical and cannot guarantee future results. Indices are unmanaged and cannot be directly invested into. Reinvestment of dividend and capital gains assumed. Your actual results may vary.

Source: RIMES Technologies Corp. Data as of March 1, 2000.

again attracting attention. Their share prices generally rose while many of the highly touted New Economy stocks declined. I'll share more insights on the Internet stock bubble throughout Part 1 of this book.

The Internet bubble illustrated one important difference between growth stocks and value stocks: Growth stocks tend to be accompanied by expectations for future earnings that are far greater than the average shown in the past. Such stocks are often in exciting new industries, about which there is a great deal of promise and optimism. During the Internet-stock heyday, you may recall all the articles that claimed, "this time it's different"; a statement I'd rank for reliability right up there with "the check's in the mail."

However, when it comes to future earnings growth, it is extremely difficult to project it with a high degree of confidence. Additionally, the farther out the prediction, the more likely it's going to be off target. It is particularly questionable to build long-term forecasts of well-above-average growth in earnings for companies, as unforeseen competition will almost certainly arise to wrest away some of these hyperprofits, making such predictions very unreliable. Value investors believe that the best approach is to focus on the current state of the business: what it would be worth now to someone who wanted to buy the whole company. This is a more conservative approach, recognizing the limitations of trying to out-forecast other investors.

STRAW HATS IN WINTER

When comparing the value- and growth-investment styles, here's a down-to-earth example that simplifies the difference between these philosophies. Go to a department store on a winter day and walk through the clothing section. You'll see scores of shoppers looking at heavy coats, sweaters, and wool hats. Since these items are in season, demand for them—and, therefore, the prices—will be high. Think of these shoppers as growth investors.

Meanwhile, over in a corner of the store will be a clearance rack full of swimsuits, tank tops, and straw hats. It's winter, of course, and few people are interested in buying lightweight apparel. But every once in a while, someone will walk over and buy an item for pennies on the dollar. That shopper is a value investor.

The "buying straw hats in winter" analogy neatly captures two hallmarks of value investing: evaluating the true worth of an item (whether a hat or a stock) and purchasing it when it's out of favor and its price is below its true value. As mentioned earlier, the soul of value investing is to buy company shares at a discount. The heart of the concept is simple. At any given time there are excellent businesses that attract a good deal of attention. Meanwhile, other segments are overlooked by investors. These wallflower segments contain a wide variety of businesses in which investments could be made—if the price were right.

That is a commonplace observation. What is not so commonplace, however, is this: While many businesses are not worth what they sell for in the stock market, some businesses are almost given away. Like those straw hats in winter for the farsighted shopper, these are the types of companies, those with a significantly large margin of safety, that cause a glint in the eyes of value investors. Or they should. The way to find them is by looking *internally*, that is, at the performance of the underlying business and also at its resources. We'll address this in greater detail in Part 2 (starting with Chapter 4).

The value investor pays little heed to factors that have no impact on business value: market or interest-rate forecasts, or day-to-day stock price fluctuations. By maintaining a strict focus on the relationship between business value and stock price at the company-specific level and largely ignoring the broader market's fascination with short-term developments, value investors can exploit market behavior for long-term gains.

SHORT-TERM THINKING

I once heard a comedian say, "Instant gratification takes too long." No wonder there is no end to the parade of get-rich-quick investment schemes that surface on Wall Street.

Back in the 1960s, visions of boundless wealth floated before investors with the advent of a new magic formula: *synergy*. Synergy meant that combining companies enabled management to make more profits, as the combined companies would work together increasing revenue while cutting shared costs. It became the driving force behind the craze to create *conglomerates*—large companies composed of a variety of often-unrelated smaller companies. In theory, synergy meant that under astute corporate management, 2 plus 2 could indeed equal 5. It worked for a while, at least in terms of the stock price, and at least until it became apparent to investors that the eventual total might not have been 5, and might even be closer to 3!

Synergy was neither the first—nor the last—of such gimmicks. Indeed, as with most fashions, it comes back periodically. There were go-go stocks, the high-turnover performance game, market timing, and momentum investing. The popularity of momentum investing—the notion of buying stocks simply because they were going up—contributed to the Internet-stock craze previously cited. The epitome of this was the "day trader," hailed as a new profession in the late 1990s and, to my mind, the exact opposite of everything that investment means. What all of these schemes have in common are an obsession with short-term results, a complete disregard for fundamental business values, and the ability to cause major losses to speculators who jump on the bandwagon.

Sophisticated investors responsible for investing billions of dollars on behalf of others as well as individual investors managing their own portfolios have proved equally susceptible to these bandwagons. Both are prone to short-term thinking. Many pension funds, for example, hire professional money managers and measure their performance on a quarterly basis, leading to short-term "hire and fire" decisions. Inevitably, this encourages managers to chase what's hot and disregard sound investment principles. In fact, the IPO bubble of the late 1990s was as much a product of institutional excesses as of the mistakes of individual investors.

Some pension funds, insurance companies, and other institutional investors have abandoned the practice of making an in-depth analysis of the companies they buy. Almost uniformly, a variety of strategies have been adopted that may differ in some respects but have one horrendous defect in common: they all reject the need or feasibility of making company-by-company judgments about price and value or the need to examine time horizons or other factors that relate to the basic fundamentals necessary for long-term investing.

The combination of the age-old desire to get rich quick, plus the speed of today's TV and Internet communication, means we are increasingly preoccupied with short-term events and short-term results. To borrow a few words from Sir John Templeton, a global money manager, "There is too much emphasis now on everything yesterday." I think we are no longer as thrifty as we should be, and this is leading to more speculation, more danger, more risk. We are bombarded by data from an escalating number of sources, such as 24-hour-a-day financial news on cable television, Internet Web sites, radio, newspapers, and magazines. As our appetites for information and expectations have increased, our ability to wait and anticipate has decreased.

Most people recognize that stocks are a good long-term investment, yet most people don't hold them for long. Why? Part of the reason may lie in the mixed messages investors receive from professionals and the financial media. In one breath, investors are advised to stay the course and to hang on for the long haul. In the next breath, they are given a road map to short-term riches and reasonable-sounding guides to switch paths and chase the latest fad.

Evidence suggests that most are doing the latter, according to an updated version of Dalbar, Inc.'s "Quantitative Analysis of Investor Behavior" (QAIB) study.[2] Dalbar describes the study as an examination of the real returns from equity, fixed income, and money market mutual funds from January 1984 through December 2000. Originally conducted in 1994 and updated more recently, the QAIB investigates how mutual fund investors' behavior affects the returns they actually earn.

The study suggests that mutual fund investors do not have a long-term perspective, which adversely affects their results. First, the average fund retention—or how long someone stayed invested with a particular fund—was only 2.6 years in 2000 (down from 2.8 in 1999, but up from 1.7 after the stock market crash in 1987). Second, when compared to corresponding indices, the lack of adherence to a buy-and-hold strategy appears to have hurt returns:

- The average fixed-income investor[3] realized an annualized return of only 6.08 percent, compared to 11.83 percent for the long-term Government Bond Index.

- The average equity fund investor realized an annualized return of only 5.32 percent, compared to 16.29 percent for the S&P 500 Index.

If investors are to make money consistently, what is required is a return to farsighted, long-term investing. In my opinion, that is the kind of investing that promises rational investors the greatest potential for rewards over the long haul.

INVESTING VERSUS SPECULATION

What's the difference between investing and speculation? What do I mean when I use each term? Why is this important?

I refer to Benjamin Graham frequently in this book. I was privileged to become his acquaintance in the early 1970s and learned a great deal from this legendary investor. Graham, together with another Columbia University professor, David Dodd, introduced value-investing principles in their 778-page epic, *Security Analysis,* first published in 1934. I adopted the principles Graham developed for successful investing to help found and build an investment firm that managed more than $50 billion for institutional and individual investors worldwide at year-end 2002. I'll share more details about my encounters with Graham in Chapter 3.

On the question of investing and speculation, I turn to Graham because he addresses the differences between them on the very first page of his book, *The Intelligent Investor*. Graham writes, "An investment operation is one which, upon thorough analysis, promises safety of principal and an adequate return."[4] Based on this definition, there are three components to investing: thorough analysis, safety of principal, and adequate return. Graham adds, "Operations not meeting these requirements are speculative."[5]

To this, I would add: (1) Any contemplated holding period shorter than a normal business cycle (typically 3 to 5 years) is speculation, and (2) any purchase based on anticipated market movements or forecasting is also speculation. Given what I've already addressed regarding value investing in this chapter (its focus on individual company analysis to determine intrinsic value, the margin of safety concept, and its success over the long term), it certainly meets Graham's definition of investing.

The distinction between investing and speculation is important for a reason Graham cited in 1949 and remains true today: ". . . in the easy language of Wall Street, everyone who buys or sells a security has become an investor, regardless of what he buys, or for what purpose, or at what price. . . ."[6] The

> *" . . . in the easy language of Wall Street, everyone who buys or sells a security has become an investor, regardless of what he buys, or for what purpose, or at what price. . . ."*
>
> Benjamin Graham

financial media often refers to "investors" taking profits, bargain hunting, or driving prices higher or lower on a particular day. When I hear about such actions, I attribute them to speculators, not investors.

Investors and speculators approach their tasks differently. Investors want to know what a business is worth and imagine themselves as owning the business as a whole. Unlike speculators, investors maintain a long-term perspective—at least 3 to 5 years. They look at a company from the perspective of owners. This means they're interested in factors such as corporate governance, structure, and succession issues that may affect a company's future and its ability to create wealth for years to come. Investors may use their voting rights to assist in enhancing company value over the long term. Speculators, on the other hand, are less interested in what a business is actually worth and more concerned with what a third party will pay to own shares on a given day. They may be concerned only with short-term changes in a stock's price, not in the underlying value of the company itself.

The problem with speculation is simple: Who can predict what a third party will pay for your shares today, tomorrow, or any day? Stock market prices typically swing between extremes, stoked by the irrational emotions of fear and greed. These market swings became more pronounced in the late 1990s. In fact, there were 9 days in 1998 when prices for the S&P 500 Index advanced or fell more than 3 percent—after only 8 such days in the years 1990 through 1997 combined. Volatility tended to be even higher in subsequent years, with the number of up-or-down-3-percent days coming in at 17 in 2002.

Such dramatic price fluctuation on a day-to-day basis can test long-term investors' mettle in maintaining their focus on business value. Remember the chart in Exhibit 1-1 and the tendency for business values to remain relatively stable? Day-to-day price changes should hold little interest for the long-term investor, unless a price has fallen to the "buying level" that represents a sizable margin of safety. But that's often difficult to remember when newspaper headlines, TV news anchors, friends, and coworkers are lamenting or lauding the market's most recent lurch forward or back.

With a clearer understanding of *what* value investing means—what it is and how it works—let's turn our attention in Chapter 2 to *why* it works.

Notes

1. Benjamin Graham, *The Intelligent Investor: A Book of Practical Counsel*, 4th rev. ed., New York: Harper & Row, 1973, p. 277.

2. Dalbar issued a press release with the results of an update to its "Quantitative Analysis of Investor Behavior" Report on June 21, 2002. The press release is posted at the company's Web site, www.dalbarinc.com.

3. Although Dalbar publishes the results of its study at its Web site, it does not disclose its methodology for how it determines what constitutes an "average fixed-income investor" or "average equity fund investor." Details regarding the models it creates to calculate results must be purchased. For more information, contact Dalbar at 617-723-6400.

4. Graham, *The Intelligent Investor,* p. 1.

5. Ibid.

6. Ibid., p. 2.

2

BEHAVIORAL BIASES: WHY VALUE INVESTING WORKS

Here's a simple question: How good a driver are you?
Think of the other drivers you encounter on the road and estimate your driving ability on a scale of 1 to 10, with 10 being the
best. Feel free to use any reasonable set of criteria to evaluate yourself:
reaction time, years of experience, driving record, adherence to traffic
rules, courtesy, maneuvering skills, and so on. After weighing these factors,
what number did you assign yourself?

If you rated yourself a 7 or better, you are a typical respondent. If you
ranked your driving skill as greater than 5, you are in the overwhelming
majority. Regardless of your actual driving ability, it is highly unlikely that
your self-appraisal was 4 or less. When researchers pose this question to virtually any group, the average answer is generally around 8 or 9. Think about
that for a moment: On a scale of 1 to 10, the *average* answer is 8 or 9. In
other words, a majority of participants all believe they are substantially
above average—which, of course, is statistically impossible.

This example[1] illustrates one of many systematic errors of judgment that impede our daily decision making. Psychologists have studied these biases for decades to better understand human behavior.

So what does this have to do with value investing?

Despite theories that the markets are efficient (which I'll address later in this chapter), I believe that most people make investment decisions that include these psychological biases, generally without realizing they're doing so. Often, these biases influence a substantial proportion of market participants in the same direction, contributing to the short-term irrationality of stock prices that value investors see as an opportunity. But (and this is a key point), value investors can only profit from this if they are able to resist the same biases that are influencing everyone else. That means they must be aware of these influences, and they must set up their own investment disciplines to make sure they don't fall victim to them.

Let's take a look at what these behavioral biases actually are. The studies of investor psychology have led to the development of what is known as *behavioral finance*. The results of numerous studies reveal that a variety of biases, including flaws such as optimism, hindsight, extrapolation, anchoring, and faulty intuition, cause investors to become susceptible to surprise or disappointment. And when surprise or disappointment occurs, investors tend to overreact, resulting in poor decisions.[2] As I've said, to counter such biases, investors must follow a disciplined approach that stresses a pre-established rational process rather than personal preference or out-of-context judgments.

Investors can apply a rational approach in a market crowded with irrational participants, and expect much improved results.

Human nature is far more predictable over time than the day-to-day swings of the stock market. By understanding and applying the lessons of behavioral finance, investors can apply a rational approach in a market crowded with irrational participants, and expect much improved results.

Remember that value investing—essentially, buying and holding inexpensive, out-of-favor common stocks—seeks to combine company-specific fundamental research and an objective, unbiased approach that exploits innate human shortcomings. This approach has proved its merit for decades, long before behavioral finance became a topic of study. As you read on, you'll see that many aspects of this field of investor psychology always have been part of the value investor's discipline. All that's new is that now we're able to understand in more detail why these disciplines work. In my opinion, you're always better off understanding why something works, rather than just applying the process blindly. It improves both your confidence and your judgment within the framework of the discipline.

THE DANGERS OF FAULTY INTUITION, EXTRAPOLATION, AND OPTIMISM

In Chapter 3, I'll examine evidence showing just how well the value approach has done. But for now, let's start with exploring some of the reasons why value investing has delivered such solid results by briefly examining faulty intuition, extrapolation, and optimism. For all three, I'll share real-world examples and market-related applications. Hopefully, by better understanding these tendencies, you can guard yourself against their potentially adverse influences.

Faulty Intuition

Suppose we conducted two experiments. In the first, we flipped a coin nine times and recorded the outcomes of each flip. The results—heads (H) or tails (T)—were as follows:

T-T-H-T-H-H-T-H-T

In the second experiment, we took the same coin and flipped it again. This time, the results were as follows:

T-T-T-H-H-H-H-H-H

Which do you believe is a more probable outcome? If we do this experiment another 1000 times, which pattern would repeat itself more frequently—the first result or the second?

When most people see these two results, they believe the first pattern is more likely to occur. Is that the one you picked? To many, the first result *seems* more likely, even though they may have no definitive evidence to support their belief. It just feels right. The second pattern seems too contrived to recur with any frequency.

Well, actually, both outcomes are *equally* probable. The results in the first experiment are no more likely to occur than the results in the second experiment.

Now, if we extended the first experiment and said we were going to flip the coin a tenth time, most people would say it's virtually impossible to predict the result of the next flip. Yet, in the second experiment, many people would make a prediction. They might predict heads as a continuation of the trend or tails for a trend reversal. Either way, they believe they can see a pattern in these random outcomes and make an accurate prediction of the future. This misperception is the essence of faulty intuition.

This cognitive error—seeing a pattern or predictability in random, short-term events—is so common and so imbedded in stock market analysis that we practically take it for granted. In fact, there's an entire school of investment thought devoted to finding patterns in the short-term movement of stock prices. It's called *technical analysis.* Market participants (I refrain from calling them investors) who use this approach study patterns and trends in past stock prices in order to predict future price movements. They may look for patterns such as "head and shoulders" or "ascending triangles" or spend time on trend analysis. I don't recognize this as investing. To me, it is purely speculation and has about as much chance at *long-term* success as consistently predicting the results of coin flips.

Extrapolation

Attempting to establish patterns to explain random events with the hope of predicting the future can lead to yet another important behavioral bias—extrapolation.

For example, while sitting in a traffic jam, maybe you've thought, "It took me 30 minutes to go 1 mile. At this pace, I'll get home tomorrow afternoon." Or perhaps, while playing golf, you made a birdie putt on the thirteenth hole and thought, "If I keep that up, I'll shoot a 33 on the back nine!"

These are examples of extrapolation—basing a longer-term forecast on an emotional reaction to short-term developments. Over the years at my firm, my colleagues and I repeatedly have seen the dangerous effects of extrapolation. Market participants often look at negative short-term performance and think, "If this continues, I'll lose all my money in 3 weeks." Or if performance is good, they may say, "At this rate, I'll quadruple my money in 6 months!"

Much like the example of being stuck in traffic or playing golf, the results are rarely as good, or as bad, as we envision. We often set ourselves up for disappointment or surprises when reality differs from our expectations. It's a quirk of human nature—and one that consistently has surfaced in the investment industry.

For example, market analysts often project historical trends too far into the future. They project sales, earnings, stock prices, and many other statistics for years or decades despite evidence that these quantities are inherently difficult to predict. In forecasting the future growth of rapidly expanding com-

> *Many market participants look at the recent past, believe those patterns will continue, and then extend their predictions too far into the future.*

panies, their expectations are often tied to the recent past even though growth rates usually revert toward an average. Remember two things about market analysts' predictions. First, they are rewarded for doing a "thorough job," and extending a growth rate projection for a few more years in today's world of computerized spreadsheets is a very easy way of looking impressively thorough. Second, and even more important, be especially wary of any projection that extends beyond the time that the analyst expects to be in that job!

Near the peak of the technology stock boom in early 2000, an analyst at a major Wall Street firm predicted the price for shares of QUALCOMM, a telecommunications company based in the same city as my firm, would climb to $250 from its then-current price of around $125. (Both prices have been adjusted for a subsequent stock split.) The analyst based his prediction on the extrapolation of cell phone sales over 20 years. He failed to consider the possibility that the firm's technology would be replaced, or that cell phone usage might level off, or that other competitors would chip away at QUALCOMM's customers, or that the cost of cell phones would decline. Basing a long-term forecast of the company's prospects by extending what it's done in the recent past is dangerous, as evidenced by what happened to QUALCOMM's stock price. After climbing to $150 per share in early 2000, it fell below $30 in 2002.

Optimism

The QUALCOMM example also helps illustrate the dangers of optimism. We tend to think of optimism as a desirable trait and, in most cases, it can be. However, when investing, dispassionate analysis often proves more profitable. Decisions should be based on the relationship between business value and stock price. Period. All investors should be wary of becoming too optimistic as the desire to win on Wall Street may have quite the opposite effect. In addition to guarding against personal optimism, be wary of adopting *others'* optimistic views on particular companies even if those others are professional analysts.

Exhibit 2-1 illustrates the perennial overoptimism of Wall Street analysts and economists. Based on research by David Dreman, Standard & Poor's, and First Call, analysts have, on average, predicted an earnings growth rate roughly four times that of the average rate observed. Economists, far from being the pessimistic "dismal scientists" we might have expected, have predicted a growth rate nearly three times the actual rate.

A striking characteristic of this optimistic pattern is its persistence, even when the forecasters may have seen that their predictions were overshooting the mark year after year. Observing that their predictions bore little resemblance to reality, they might have reassessed the inherent predictability of earnings and adjusted their predictions downward, closer to the long-term historical average. Truly rational forecasters might have adopted a more regressive approach: the lower the inherent predictability, the closer the prediction should be to the long-term average. But there does not seem to be any evidence that the forecasters are recalibrating their estimates.

Why should analysts be systematically overly optimistic? A 2002 study shows Wall Street analysts get paid more if they are. Research by Harrison Hong, an associate professor at Stanford Business School, and Jeffrey Kubik of Syracuse University found that analysts who deliver optimistic earnings forecasts (not necessarily *accurate* forecasts) are more likely to be promoted.[3] This is yet another reason to be cautious when analyzing businesses and acting on information provided by "experts."

Faulty intuition, extrapolation, and optimism can set the stage for overconfidence and subsequent overreaction. While overconfidence in intuitive models can lead to losses, it also may cause investors to *miss* opportunities for gains. For example, an incorrect model might lead to the belief that a poorly performing business will never recover. In the late 1970s and early 1980s, expectations of continued "stagflation" led to a general negative overreaction by investors. The resulting low stock prices prompted *BusinessWeek* magazine to proclaim the "Death of Equities" in a cover story published on August 13, 1979. As it turned out, within a few years, stocks began what would become the greatest bull market in U.S. history.

EXHIBIT 2-1   Congenital Optimism: Earnings Growth for the S&P 500 Index 1982–2002

Year	Analysts' Estimate	Economists' Estimate	Actual Growth
1982	26.2%	5.3%	−17.8%
1983	32.2%	24.7%	11.4%
1984	34.2%	27.7%	18.4%
1985	10.8%	12.9%	−12.2%
1986	22.8%	22.9%	−0.9%
1987	32.6%	18.8%	20.9%
1988	29.8%	14.5%	35.8%
1989	10.5%	4.4%	−3.7%
1990	13.8%	12.0%	−6.7%
1991	1.9%	6.7%	−25.2%
1992	38.0%	48.7%	19.5%
1993	22.8%	36.4%	14.7%
1994	38.9%	28.6%	39.8%
1995	10.9%	4.8%	11.0%
1996	18.2%	11.7%	14.1%
1997	13.7%	5.8%	2.6%
1998	13.6%	6.7%	−5.1%
1999	14.6%	4.5%	27.7%
2000	16.0%	0.0%	3.8%
2001	16.0%	7.7%	−50.6%
2002	17.0%	10.1%	13.4%
Average	20.7%	15.0%	5.3%

Sources: David Dreman; Standard & Poor's; First Call.

Value investors recognize tendencies such as faulty intuition, extrapolation, and optimism and establish predetermined processes based on objective analysis rather than personal preference or out-of-context judgments to guide their investment decisions. I will explore the benefits of establishing and following investment processes in greater detail in Parts 2 and 4 of this book, when I more closely study how to identify value stocks and manage portfolios.

VALUE INVESTING: EXPLOITING MARKET BEHAVIOR

Investors who strictly adhere to value disciplines have earned favorable performance results with limited risk over the long term because they seize opportunities created by flaws that are inherent in human nature. These emotional biases often cause stock prices to fluctuate in the short term much more than the intrinsic value of businesses. It is precisely these exaggerated price movements that create opportunities for astute investors. Virtually by definition, value investors take a course of action that runs counter to popular trends. When many market participants are selling, value investors often are buying, and vice versa. Value investors realize that achieving better-than-average returns depends upon thinking and acting differently than the average investor.

BMW provides a good example of a solid company that was largely unappreciated by the market during the New Economy boom of the late 1990s. At a time when shares of New Economy companies commanded premiums in the market, many perceived BMW as a staid company lacking the tremendous growth potential of more glamorous firms.

The premium automobile manufacturer's Rover subsidiary had recorded losses for consecutive years, and by 1999 the company's CEO-equivalent was dismissed and the head of product development resigned. BMW's apparent commitment to the Rover division sparked concerns of ongoing losses and erosion of the entire company's value. The company's joint venture with Rolls Royce to manufacture aerospace engines also failed to show a profit. This venture was perceived by many as another area of cash-burn for an Old Economy company.

While investors extrapolated continued cash-burn in the Rover and aerospace divisions, BMW was still a premium global automobile manufacturer with a defendable competitive advantage, a prestigious brand image, and a highly profitable auto-financing unit. The company's conservative accounting practices, geared to minimize the tax burden in the German economy, presented a chance to find hidden value. For instance, the company applied accelerated depreciation to assets, understating the firm's profitability and assets. An astute investor could have invested in the company in 1999 when it traded in the $12 to $17 price range.

By 2002, the company's "staid" business attracted more attention as many of the New Economy stocks' aggressive accounting practices and growth projections were exposed. In addition, BMW had sold the Rover and aerospace engine divisions, recognizing better opportunities for capital investment. As a result, investors who purchased BMW shares in 1999 at prices between $12 and $17 saw the company's share price appreciate to $30 in 2002. BMW represents another example of the rewards available to investors who think and act differently than the crowds.

Value investment strategies tend to work because the majority of investors remain captive to judgmental errors or emotional biases that adversely influence their decisions. Even when objective facts contradict their biased views, investors often continue to overreact, sending market prices to extreme highs or lows. As illustrated, human behavior is not always dictated by rational thought. It is, however, often predictable. Remember the

Value investors realize that achieving better-than-average returns depends upon thinking and acting differently than the average investor.

simple question that opened this chapter: How good a driver are you? Ask members of your family, friends, or coworkers this question and note their responses. With the knowledge you have already acquired about human behavior, you will probably not be surprised by their answers.

The same principles, applied to investing in the stock market, can limit your vulnerability to overreact to short-term developments. The key is to adhere to investment policies and procedures that circumvent bias and reflect sustained objectivity. As a value investor, you don't want to fall victim to the very behaviors you seek to exploit.

I hope I haven't made this sound too easy, because it isn't. As Ben Graham wrote, "To achieve *satisfactory* investment results is easier than most people realize; to achieve *superior* results is harder than it looks."[4]

Merely accepting that these ideas make sense doesn't mean they are simple to apply in today's challenging financial markets. If you've ever been on a diet, you know how easy it is to decide that tomorrow you'll eat less. (It's usually easiest to decide that right after dinner today!) But the next time you're offered a piece of chocolate cake, there's usually some excuse to deviate from your dieting plans: You don't want to offend your host, or it's just *so* tempting. The temptations of human behavior are well ingrained in all of us. They are difficult to keep in check. In Chapter 13, I'll review some specific disciplines designed to keep you firmly on the value-investing path.

Put simply, the reason a value approach works is not because investors benefit from predicting fluctuations in interest rates or economic output. Success for value investing isn't predicated upon the strength of corporate earnings or which political party holds the upper hand in Washington. *Value*

Human behavior is not always dictated by rational thought. It is, however, often predictable.

investors first, last, and always, think of buying the business, not the stock. Value investing works for two reasons: It reflects a consistent focus on the relationship between value and price, *and* it takes advantage of innate human foibles.

EFFICIENT MARKET THEORY: DEBUNKING THE MYTH

Many academics, observers, and pundits argue that the stock market acts efficiently. That's portfolio-speak for the theory that stock prices always accurately reflect everything known about a company's prospects. According to this view, studying fundamentals such as earnings and book values is as useless and unreliable as reading tarot cards or tea leaves. The reason? Undervalued stocks—or so it is claimed—don't actually exist, because security analysts and other market participants already have harvested all available information and thereby ensured unfailingly appropriate prices.

Proponents of this notion have embellished their belief with jazzy computer printouts and a three-letter acronym, EMT (efficient market theory, or EMH, efficient market hypothesis). EMT is divided into three parts: weak, semi-strong, and strong.

Weak

The weak version of the efficient market theory holds that past prices have no bearing on future prices. In other words, what investors will pay to own shares of a company in the future is essentially independent of their past actions; price patterns over the long haul are completely random.

Generally, value investors have no quarrel with this weak form of the theory. Technical analysis of price behavior, the approach to forecasting future returns based on the study of past price movements, has not served adequately as a substitute for fundamental company-specific analysis, in my view. Studies have revealed that a weak link between past and future prices may exist, although certainly not enough of a link to generate trading profits after transaction costs.

Semi-Strong

The semi-strong form states that markets are efficient because of the rapid way that knowledge is dispersed in the Information Age. There is no denying that as information about companies, industries, and the economy arrives at the marketplace, prices reflect the quick assimilation of this new data.

Transmitting information quickly, however, doesn't guarantee that the conclusions drawn are accurate. Rapidly transmitted information may suggest one picture, but a significantly different picture may emerge as the ideas are interpreted over time.

Strong

This version of the efficient market theory holds that, at any given moment, security prices already accurately reflect *all knowable public and private information*. In other words, there can never be a difference between underlying business value and stock price. The margin of safety addressed in Chapter 1, or the gap between a company's intrinsic value and its share price that creates a bargain-priced stock, is an illusion. No amount of skilled interpretation of available public data would enable any investor to profit from discrepancies between business value and stock price. In this view, the efforts of security analysts to identify mispricings are entirely successful in creating market efficiency.

However, the theory is predicated on a world where every investor has all available knowledge, understands it, and is able to act logically on it. And as I have already reviewed, markets aren't orderly or logical. Regarding the flaws associated with EMT, Clifford F. Pratten of the University of Cambridge writes, "Irrational influences, hope, fear, and so on, do play a part: the oft-quoted statement that the market is driven by altering bouts of greed and fear sums up the position."[5]

The Internet stock bubble of the late 1990s provides ample examples of real-world opportunities created by market illogic. Excessive optimism and greed pushed prices for dot-com companies well beyond their underlying values. Many investors assumed the Internet would have a major impact on *every* business, and dot-com companies appeared to be best positioned to benefit. Accordingly, these investors clamored for Internet-related stocks and shunned much of the rest of the market.

In this environment, prices for Old Economy companies such as U.S. consumer-products-based firms Heinz and Sara Lee fell well below their intrinsic values, creating opportunities for value investors who sought high-quality businesses. In early 2000, a value investor could have purchased shares of Heinz and Sara Lee for $29 and $15, respectively. Two years later, Heinz had climbed to $37, and Sara Lee's stock price reached $21.

EMT—CLOSING ARGUMENTS

Additional evidence calls into serious doubt many basic assumptions of the efficient market theory. According to Pratten, "The 1987 Crash, when the Dow Jones index fell by 30.7% in six days, gave a new impetus and direction to tests of the EMT and added credibility to tests which contradicted the hypothesis: because such a *large* and *swift* fall was not compatible with changes in stock market prices being determined by new information concerning fundamentals alone."[6] Pratten concludes, "Important assumptions underpinning the EMH simply do not apply in practice."

Robert A. Haugen, a professor of finance at the University of California, Irvine, also has studied the EMT and found it lacking. "We now see a market that is highly inefficient and overreactive; a market literally turned upside down—where the highest-risk adjusted stocks can be expected to produce the lowest returns and the lowest-risk stocks, the highest returns!"[7]

Like Professor Pratten, Haugen found that emotions play an important role in stock prices. "Overwhelming evidence is piling up that investors overreact to the past performance of stocks, pricing growth stocks—stocks which are expected to grow faster than average—too high and value stocks—stocks which are expected to grow slower than average—too low. Subsequent to these overreactions, growth stocks produce low returns for the investors who buy them at high prices, and similarly, value stocks produce high returns for their investors."[8]

CONCLUSION

In the real world, where emotions such as fear and greed abound, logic is often a scarce commodity. This situation is rewarding for the value investor, provided, however, that the gap between price and value caused by such inefficiency can be successfully exploited. In the next chapter, I'll review empirical evidence that illustrates the merits of the value-investing approach.

Notes

1. Daniel Kahneman, "The Psychology of the Non-Professional Investor," article presented at Harvard seminar on Behavioral Finance, November 1998.

2. There are many other cognitive illusions and biases. For a more exhaustive list, see publications by David Dreman, Daniel Kahneman, and Amos Tversky.

3. Harrison Hong and Jeffrey Kubik, "Analyzing the Analysts: Career Concerns and Biased Earnings Forecasts," *The Financial Times,* February 2002.

4. Benjamin Graham, *The Intelligent Investor: A Book of Practical Counsel,* 4th rev. ed., New York: Harper & Row, 1973, p. 287.

5. Cliff Pratten, *The Stock Market,* Cambridge: University Press, 1993, p. 174.

6. Ibid., p. 25.

7. Robert A. Haugen, *The New Finance: The Case against Efficient Markets,* Englewood Cliffs, N.J.: Prentice Hall, 1995, p. 1.

8. Ibid.

3

THE VALUE PEDIGREE AND THE REWARDS OF VALUE INVESTING

C ertain investors are obtaining superior results, watching their portfolios grow, taking some profits, and encountering minimal risk
over the long term.

How? Not by listening to innumerable prophets, the ones that spring up
during bad times with "new" strategies and advice. Nor by employing complicated theories such as market timing, technical analysis, or efficient
market hypotheses—or any of the intricate tools of academics or market
technicians for that matter. And certainly not by happenstance or accident.
These investors' goals are being accomplished instead by doing it the old-
fashioned way—through fundamental, classic value investing.

The purpose of this chapter is to review the potential rewards of value
investing. Actual records of professional money managers, as well as
results from performance studies, are presented. Keep in mind that value

investing is not a get-rich-quick scheme or an investment panacea. By carefully following its principles, however, prudent, rational investors may obtain three significant advantages.

THREE BENEFITS OF VALUE INVESTING

The first benefit of value investing is that it can lower your risk, especially compared to pure growth or other strategies. And in this case, I mean the risk of losing your money over the long term. In this sense, value investing largely has been synonymous with capital preservation.

The second benefit is reduced trading costs. Since value proponents hold securities for extended periods, buying and selling costs are cut. The savings go to the patient investor. In addition, reduced trading costs can potentially lower capital gains taxes.

The third benefit is more pragmatic—the proverbial pot of gold. The bottom line is that value investing has paid off in dollars and cents.

Beyond these benefits, value investing can lower portfolio volatility. By volatility, I mean fluctuation in returns—the ups and downs from month to month or quarter to quarter. I understand that it can be difficult to tolerate swift, short-term changes in portfolio value, and value investing can help limit these fluctuations. At the same time, volatility is not necessarily bad; the chapters ahead will demonstrate why volatility should not concern most investors.

A MATTER OF STYLE

There are many variations of investment management, but two general styles predominate: value and growth. I have touched on these styles earlier. Here, I delve a bit deeper into the similarities and differences between them. The distinctions between both styles of investing can be confusing because both strategies seek *growth of principal* as a primary objective.

Growth-oriented managers tend to buy stocks of companies whose profits are expected to increase rapidly. Value-oriented managers typically own the stocks of companies that are inexpensive relative to fundamental gauges of value such as earnings, dividends, book value, or cash flow.

THE SENTIMENTAL JOURNEY

Historically, value investing has delivered better long-term returns than growth investing because sentiment can distort what investors are willing to pay to own a stock. The aggregate holdings of a growth-style manager typically have an above-average price-earnings ratio and a below-average dividend yield. Growth portfolios also tend to be expensive relative to aggregate book value and cash flow.

Why the hefty price tag on growth stocks? In effect, growth investors pay extra because of the expectation that a company will grow its earnings rapidly. But high expectations are difficult to meet. As Glenn Carlson, senior portfolio manager at my firm, said near the peak of the Internet-stock bubble, "Historically, stocks haven't held lofty P/E ratios for extended periods. One of two things tends to happen—earnings rise dramatically to justify the prices. Or the prices decline to come in line with earnings."

In December 1994, *The Journal of Finance* published a study by professors Josef Lakonishok, Andrei Shleifer, and Robert W. Vishny (a trio often referred to collectively as LSV) that stated, "Given their expectations, investors are disappointed in the performance of glamour [growth] stocks relative to out-of-favor [value] stocks." [1]

How overblown are those expectations? The study concluded that "the expected growth of glamour stocks relative to value stocks implicit in their relative multiples significantly overestimates actual future growth . . . contrary to the market's expectations . . . glamour stocks did not grow faster than value stocks. For example, while cash flow of glamour stocks was expected to grow 11.3% faster, it actually grew 0.4% slower." [2] When a company fails to match Wall Street's earnings estimates—a development known as a "negative surprise"—its stock can be hammered mercilessly.

LSV's study also noted that value stocks—those with low prices relative to factors such as earnings and book value—tended to outperform their higher-priced counterparts dramatically over the study period, which stretched from 1968 to 1994. Professionals at a division of my firm known as the Brandes Institute conducted a similar study extending the time period through 2003. The findings? Value-stock outperformance remained robust. For more information, visit the Brandes Institute Web site at www.brandes.com/institute.

Value stocks are priced differently. By definition, value stocks sell for below-average prices relative to their normalized fundamentals. That's why they are called value. Investors' expectations for these companies are low, and their stocks are priced to reflect their supposedly modest prospects. Not all such companies are good investments, of course, but skilled value investors can uncover overlooked gems. The value investor sells when the overlooked gem is no longer overlooked and the newfound attention drives its price to where it equals or overstates the company's true potential. The value investor exploits the "sentimental journey" from under- to overvalued.

The value investor doesn't try to forecast exactly *when* that transformation in sentiment will take place—that would be speculating. But the value investor believes that free markets will price businesses appropriately over time. And when it does, converts to the company's story will come looking for shares.

THE DOLLARS AND SENSE OF VALUE INVESTING

Seeing is believing. And what better way to appreciate what value investing can accomplish than to scrutinize historical results for value strategies, as measured by objective, third-party studies *and* the track records of some of value investing's most notable practitioners.

Let's start with data compiled by Ibbotson Associates that measures returns for value and growth stocks between 1927 and 2002. Ibbotson Associates provides historical market data, as well as education and investment materials. Exhibit 3-1 illustrates the long-term outperformance of value stocks versus growth stocks over a 75-year period. During that period, the annualized return for large-cap value stocks was 11.5 percent versus 9.1 percent for large-cap growth stocks. Annualized returns for smaller-cap value stocks were even better, up 14.1 percent compared to 8.7 percent for small-cap growth stocks.

Returns from proprietary indices compiled by the Frank Russell Company also reveal the long-term superiority of value stocks. A $100,000 investment in the Russell 3000 Value Index at the end of 1979 would have grown to roughly $1.9 million by year-end 2002, or about $800,000 *more* than an equal-sized investment in the Russell 3000 Growth Index. Both indices are subsets of the Russell 3000 Index, which comprises approximately 98 percent of the investable U.S. universe.

ACTUAL TRACK RECORDS

Data provided by Ibbotson help illustrate the benefits of adopting value-investment principles, as do returns for value and growth indices such as

EXHIBIT 3-1   Growth and Value Investing, 1927–2002

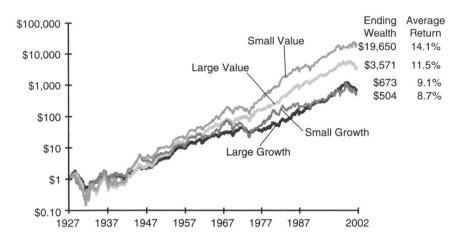

Note: Hypothetical value of $1 invested at year-end 1927. Assumes reinvestment of income and no transaction costs or taxes. Indices are unmanaged. Performance is historical. An investor's actual results will vary. This is for illustrative purposes only and not indicative of any investment. Past performance is no guarantee of future results.

Source: Copyright © 2003 by Ibbotson Associates, Inc., March 1, 2003.

those provided by the Frank Russell Company. Actual returns posted by many value-investing practitioners also underscore the benefits of the value approach.

Exhibit 3-2 compares the performance of shares of John Neff's Vanguard Windsor mutual fund, William Ruane's Sequoia mutual fund, and Warren Buffett's holding company Berkshire Hathaway with the S&P 500 over the 30-year period from 1973 through 2002. While I recognize that mutual funds and holding companies do not share the same structures, fees, or expenses, I believe a comparison of their respective returns does shed light on value investing's long-term potential for success. The bottom line is that Neff, Ruane, and Buffett are all widely recognized value investors, and, as the first row of Exhibit 3-2 indicates, each of their investment vehicles outperformed the S&P 500 substantially over the last 3 decades. (Neff managed Vanguard Windsor until 1995; the fund was subsequently managed by Wellington Management and then Sanford C. Bernstein & Co.)

Another valuable lesson emerges from the track records of these accomplished value practitioners: Investing is a marathon, not a sprint. Each of the three value investors posted negative returns in at least 5 of the

EXHIBIT 3-2   Select Value Investors versus the S&P 500

	Vanguard Windsor	Sequoia Fund	Berkshire Hathaway	S&P 500
Annualized return: 1973–2002	12.9%	16.9%	25.5%	10.6%
Number of negative years	5	5	6	8
Number of years of underperformance vs. S&P 500	13	10	8	—

Note: Past performance is no guarantee of future results. Reinvestment of dividends and capital gains assumed. Taxes and other expenses are not included. Indices are unmanaged and cannot be directly invested into.

Sources: Vanguard Windsor: www.vanguard.com; Sequoia Fund: www.sequoiafund.com; Berkshire Hathaway: Compustat; S&P 500; Bloomberg, as of December 31, 2002.

30 years under review—and each underperformed the market at least one-quarter of the time. But the fact that superior overall results were achieved despite an occasional short-term stumble highlights the importance of adopting and maintaining a long-term horizon.

SKILL—NOT LUCK

Critics might argue that the extraordinary track records compiled by these value investors are the result of simple chance. I disagree. In my opinion, what distinguishes the results achieved by each of these value-investing practitioners is that each set out with the preestablished objective of following an investment approach based on Graham's principles. To borrow an analogy from Warren Buffett, if you could get a million monkeys to sit in front of typewriters for a million years and bang on the keys, one result, through some quirk of chance, may produce something akin to Shakespeare's *Hamlet*. But none of those million monkeys would have set out to create a finished work comparable to Shakespeare's masterful tragedy. Instead, it might have happened by accident. I believe the results achieved by the investors cited above were no accident. Each followed Graham's approach and each delivered solid long-term results.

After reviewing Exhibit 3-2, you may wonder if these superior returns were the result of each manager's magical touch. Can the average value investor expect to do as well? Good questions. Certainly some portfolio managers are more skilled than others. Not all investors will achieve the same results, even if they apply the same selection criteria. As in any profession, skill levels vary.

But evidence also suggests that value investors have the benefit of a superior approach to portfolio management. In other words, given the same level of expertise, the value investor tends to win over the long haul. The LSV study noted earlier concluded that "[certain] value strategies outperform glamour strategies by 8% per year." The same researchers also found that "the value strategy clearly does better when the market falls. The value strategy performs most closely to the glamour strategy in the 122 positive months [of the study] other than the best 25. In the very best months, the value strategy significantly outperforms the glamour strategy and the [market] index, but not by as much as it does when the market falls sharply. Overall, the value strategy appears to do somewhat better than the glamour strategy in all [economic] states and significantly better in some states."

MORE RETURN, LESS "VOLATILITY"?

Earlier, I cited lower volatility as an additional advantage of value investing. The LSV study, as well as returns and volatility statistics for the Russell 3000 Index, suggests that value stocks have delivered exceptional returns—with less volatility. For example, as previously addressed, returns for the Russell 3000 Value Index outpaced gains for the Russell 3000 Growth Index between 1979 and 2002. In addition to delivering better performance, the Russell 3000 Value Index had a lower standard deviation of quarterly returns (7.6 percent versus 10.5 percent) over the same period, reflecting lower volatility.

High returns *and* low risk? Sounds too good to be true. First of all, it's vital to recognize that the terms *volatility* and *risk* often are used synonymously—yet they can have quite different connotations. In Chapter 11, I'll delve deeper into common misperceptions regarding volatility and risk. For now, I adopt the common vernacular for the purposes of this discussion.

We've all heard the investing maxim, "The only way to achieve higher returns is to take more risk." That statement is true if the assets you invest in are all priced efficiently (price = intrinsic value). But if our view that stocks get *mispriced* regularly is correct, then you indeed may be able to

EXHIBIT 3-3   40 Years of Growth and Value

	Annualized Return 1962–2002	Annualized Standard Deviation	1973–74 Return	Worst 12-Month Loss
Small growth	7.7%	24.4%	−62.6%	−50.6%
Large growth	9.8%	16.7%	−44.6%	−45.8%
Small value	17.4%	18.7%	−41.0%	−34.4%
Large value	13.7%	15.4%	−26.2%	−30.2%

Sources: Brandes Investment Partners; Kenneth French (http://mba.tuck.dartmouth.edu/pages/faculty/ken.french/), as of December 31, 2002.

achieve *higher* returns with *less* risk. In comparing value and growth strategies, the LSV study states, "We also look at the betas and standard deviations of value and glamour strategies. We find little, if any, support for the view that value strategies are fundamentally riskier."

On his Web site,[3] Dartmouth College finance professor Kenneth French compiles historical value-versus-growth stock returns. French uses price-to-book ratios to separate value from growth stocks. Analysis of data at his Web site for the 40-year period ended September 30, 2001, yields compelling results, as shown in Exhibit 3-3.

French and the University of Chicago's Eugene Fama have spent years studying the relative success of the value and growth strategies. The pair finds that, for both small- and large-cap stocks, value stocks—or those with lower price-to-book ratios—have returned substantially more than those with higher book-value multiples over the last 40 years. In addition, value stocks have outperformed growth stocks with less annual volatility (as measured by standard deviation), with a smaller bear market dip, and with a less painful "worst 12 months." In other words, the value style has enjoyed higher long-term returns and, at the same time, substantially less short-term volatility.

HIGHER RETURN WITHOUT HIGHER RISK—HOW CAN THAT BE?

Efficient market theory (EMT) contends that risk and reward go hand in hand. As such, EMT suggests that value stocks only have delivered greater long-term returns than growth stocks because they are inherently riskier investments. Using standard deviation as a measure of risk, the Fama and French data cited above show that value strategies have delivered the best of both worlds: high return *and* low risk. But how can that be? How can value stocks deliver better returns with *less* risk?

> *Value strategies have delivered the best of both worlds: high return and low risk. But how can that be?*

One plausible hypothesis is that value stocks are consistently underpriced compared to their actual risk-return characteristics. Most value investors probably would agree that their strategies produce favorable returns because they counter the often irrational strategies followed by other market participants. The latter strategies often contain one or more of a number of the inherent biases we addressed in Chapter 2. In essence, investors apparently get excessively excited about glamorous growth stocks and drive up their prices. Similarly, they often overreact and sell down stocks that are the subject of bad news, causing these stocks to become unpopular and underpriced.

By underpriced, we are referring to the difference or gap between a company's true worth and its stock price—also known as the *margin of safety*. Prices for growth stocks may be dependent upon the companies living up to lofty expectations. When actual performance fails to meet those expectations, the company's stock price can be especially vulnerable.

Value stocks, because of their margin of safety, usually are not as susceptible to sharp and painful downturns. Essentially, when growth companies stumble, their profit estimates often tumble along with their valuation multiples resulting in steep stock price declines. Not only does the price-to-earnings ratio come down sharply due to the market's disappointment, but the underlying earnings number is also reduced. (This is sometimes referred to by the highly technical name "the double whammy.") For value stocks, future profit expectations may decline, but typically not as drastically as the inflated ones associated with glamour stocks. And already low multiples for value stocks often tend to insulate them from significant, further stock price declines.

Given this evidence, why does a preference for growth or glamour stocks persist? According to Graham, "The chief losses to investors come from the purchase of *low-quality* securities at times of favorable business conditions. The purchasers . . . assume that prosperity is synonymous with safety."[4] Here, Graham's comments reflect his understanding of the important role that market behavior plays when investing—and that applies to both individual and professional investors alike.

First, glamour stocks, ironically, often may appear to be the more prudent investments. Because of growth stocks' popularity, investors may feel there is safety in numbers. By their nature, value stocks are not popular. But as Graham noted, "popular" doesn't necessarily mean "prudent." Professional portfolio managers, like individual investors, can be fooled into thinking they are making a conservative investment when, in fact, they are merely being conventional.

Further, even if they personally believe in value principles, portfolio managers may find it hard to face clients and superiors with unpopular stock holdings. Often, the value manager must be willing to look foolish to his or her clients, at least over the short term. For example, in a meeting with clients, it is often easier to point to a portfolio of popular blue-chip holdings than to explain why a portfolio resembles a kennel crammed with underperforming, out-of-favor "dogs."

Another possible reason a number of market participants continue to prefer growth stocks—and continue to underperform value strategies—is the short-term time horizon of many investors. This also can be true for professional investors. Anchoring on an index for comparison and framing their evaluation of performance within a narrow time interval, professional investors may simply lose patience before a value strategy can succeed. Value strategies may take a long time to pay off optimally, but professional portfolio managers often cannot afford to underperform an index, even for a short time. A true value investor would think a period as long as even 2 years is trivial, but some portfolio managers are measured on their performance every *3 months*.

Underperformance can have significant career consequences for investment professionals: An underperforming manager or analyst can miss a bonus payment, be passed over for promotion, or even lose his or her job. Thus, a value strategy that takes 3 to 5 years to show meaningful results might be too risky for portfolio managers from the standpoint of career security. LSV stated, ". . . the career concerns of money managers and employees of their institutional clients may cause money managers to tilt towards 'glamour' stocks." Even for those brave enough to defy the herd instinct personally, their employer or clients may lose patience and overrule (or fire) them, often making the switch back to the herd approach just as they approach the edge of the investment "cliff." To get the best long-term results, therefore, not only the portfolio manager but the investment management firm and client must all be committed to the approach.

Scientific evidence has shown that people under the influence of a bias are reluctant to give it up, even when they become fully aware of its existence. So, despite the availability of the data, it is not surprising that glamour strategies continue to draw investors' attention. Everyone wants to own a piece of a company whose future seems bright. This focus on business prospects, however, overshadows a crucial element of security analysis: price. The data support the view that value strategies produce higher returns, at least in part, because they avoid the high prices attached to stocks for which the market is intensely optimistic. On the contrary, value strategies typically invest in stocks for which the market is severely pessimistic. As David Dreman wrote, "If one had to speculate about the future, it probably would be safer to project a continuation of investors' psychological reactions than to predict the exact financial performance of companies themselves. "[5] As we have already addressed, the combination of *rational* fundamental analysis and *irrational* market prices creates opportunity for value investors.

MEETING BENJAMIN GRAHAM AND THE FOUNDING OF BRANDES INVESTMENT PARTNERS

Before founding the business that would evolve into Brandes Investment Partners, I met Benjamin Graham in the early 1970s while I was a stockbroker. The meeting changed my life. I became an acquaintance of Graham's and met with him periodically to enhance my understanding and appreciation of his investment principles.

In January 1973, U.S. stocks began an agonizing descent that drained 45.1 percent off the Dow Jones Industrial Average over a 23-month period. Because of the bear market, a lot of stocks were getting extremely inexpensive. Even though everyone was bearish, from a fundamental value investor's perspective, it was a great time to be buying stocks. In 1974, I founded my own firm and applied Graham and Dodd principles to global markets from day one. The firm has grown to provide investment management services for thousands of individual investors and a number of institutional clients. As of December 31, 2002, assets under management totaled more than $50 billion.

DOES VALUE STILL WORK?

The skeptic still might be unconvinced. The performance statistics appear impressive. But hasn't the investment world changed since Warren Buffett first started looking for values in the 1950s?

Yes, financial markets have changed, but in ways that can make value investing even more profitable. Two of the dominant trends of the last 30 years—the growing importance of professional investors and the shrinking of investment time frames—have increased stock price volatility and pushed share prices to even more irrational levels, playing into the hands of the patient value investor.

Also, keep in mind that while investment markets may have changed, I believe investor behavior has remained largely the same. As cited in Chapter 2, there are persistent human biases that impair rational decision making and create opportunities for disciplined value investors. These behavioral shortcomings can be exacerbated by what appears to be an escalating desire for short-term profits.

The LSV study contends that "[m]any individuals look for stocks that will earn them abnormally high returns for a few months. . . . Institutional money managers often have even shorter time horizons." LSV adds, "When both individuals and institutional money managers prefer glamour [growth] and avoid value strategies, value stocks will be cheap and earn a higher average return."[6] In other words, the trend toward instant financial gratification rewards the value investor by keeping a segment of stock prices cheap.

CAN VALUE STOCKS BE FOUND?

As to whether attractive value-investment candidates can be identified, efficient market theorists would probably answer resoundingly: "No. The market can't be beat. There are too many smart analysts who know too much about too many companies."

I disagree. Diligent value investors have been uncovering promising opportunities for decades. Here, I share insights on two companies, EDS and Nestle, which support my conviction for finding great values.

Electronic Data Systems

EDS, or Electronic Data Systems, helps businesses to manage their information technology (IT) needs, including data, technology infrastructure, and desktop personal computer support. Spun off from General Motors in 1996, EDS was somewhat inefficient but possessed strong technical talent and experience in managing large IT projects. A new management team assumed leadership in 1999 and contributed to improving the company's fundamentals. While the company's workforce was cut by 15 percent, revenue increased 20 percent, profit margins widened, and customer satisfaction improved. However, as the company grew and the stock price rose, EDS may have become overly optimistic while bidding for new contracts, incorporating excessive cost reductions or discretionary "add-on" revenue into its projections.

In 2002, amid widespread concerns over corporate accounting improprieties, market participants questioned the disparity between EDS's reported income and free cash flow. Additionally, the company announced that it would miss third-quarter earnings targets by 85 percent—largely because of a sluggish economy and reduced spending for add-on work for existing client contracts. Following this announcement, the shares fell 55 percent—then another 30 percent a couple of days later.

Upon a thorough investigation, a value investor may have recognized the broader market's potential overreaction to the company's accounting methodology and earnings shortfall. At that time, market participants largely avoided companies with a hint of accounting improprieties. However, it is precisely these types of default judgments upon which the value investor looks to capitalize. While it's probable that many of EDS's large projects were less profitable than the market (and management) expected, these could be worked through in time. More important, the market was offering EDS stock at a price that didn't require all of the firm's projects to be profitable.

An astute value investor seeks to invest in these types of companies on occasions when the profitability of some projects is questioned and problems arise. On those occasions, not only is there likely a stock price overreaction, but management then tends to focus intently on preventing those problems again.

In EDS's case, the firm had a solid history of creating value through a cycle, and therefore the stock's sharp pullback presented a buying opportunity. The shares fell to a little over $10 per share in October 2002, but then climbed to $17 within 3 months, a rebound of more than 70 percent. Such short-term price rebounds are not necessarily typical. Further, EDS's stock price may vary considerably. A turnaround situation such as this often progresses in fits and starts rather than smoothly, but this should be of little concern to the long-term value investor.

Nestle

Nestle is one of the world's largest food companies, with leading market shares in many of the categories in which it participates. Its main product categories are beverages, dairy products, pet foods, chocolate and confectionery, and pharmaceuticals. Additionally, Nestle owns 25 percent of L'Oreal, currently the largest cosmetics company in the world. It is a truly global company, generating revenues from virtually every continent. Two-thirds of its revenues are generated in the stable, mature markets of Western Europe and North America, while the balance comes from developing nations.

Nestle's operating margins tend to be lower than most of its peers due to its extremely high amount of spending on marketing, which in turn supports its most valuable asset, its brands. The company takes a very long-term view in terms of supporting the value of its brands and aims to have the number one or number two market share in every one of its product categories in every market in which it operates. Nestle's shares fell in late 1998 after it issued a profit warning due to poor performance in Asia, Russia, and Latin America. While Nestle had extremely high market share in a number of these regions, many of the countries were experiencing currency, economic, and/or political crises that weighed on consumer sentiment and stock prices.

Thorough investigation of the company's business might have revealed that, despite sluggish sales in various regions in 1998, Nestle was an attractive investment candidate for a number of reasons: its solid portfolio of branded products with leading market shares, its strong balance sheet, its history of consistently growing earnings, and its potential for margin enhancement. The share price decline in late 1998 proved a good opportunity to purchase shares: they climbed 60 percent between late 1998 and early 2002.

CONCLUSION

The charm of value investing—its mechanical simplicity—permits investors to use value strategies if they are willing to be patient, to dig, and to remain disciplined. In Part 1 of this book, you have gained insights into key elements of value investing, reviewed its impressive results, and learned why it has worked. In the following chapters, I will explain practical methods designed to help turn challenges and complexities among the world's financial markets into successful value-investing rewards. I'll share with you the primary approach for identifying value companies and building and monitoring a portfolio of value stocks.

Notes

1. Josef Lakonishok, Andrei Shleifer, and Robert W. Vishny, "Contrarian Investment, Extrapolation, and Risk," *The Journal of Finance,* vol. XLIX, no. 5, December 1994.
2. Ibid.
3. mba.tuck.dartmouth.edu/pages/faculty/ken.french/.
4. Benjamin Graham, *The Intelligent Investor: A Book of Practical Counsel,* 4th rev. ed., New York: Harper & Row, 1973, p. 280.
5. David Dreman, *Contrarian Investment Strategies: The Next Generation,* New York: Simon & Schuster, 1998, p. 257.
6. Lakonishok et al., "Contrarian Investment, Extrapolation, and Risk."

2

How to Find Value Companies

In this section I provide guidance on how to identify value companies: what to look for and what to avoid, when to purchase shares, and when to sell. To distinguish this book from other "how to" type investment books, in later chapters I will address the psychological pressures that accompany value investing and describe how to create an objective investment process designed to keep investors from succumbing to the very behaviors they seek to exploit in the broader market. I also will compare and contrast an individual's investment process with that of groups, such as investment clubs and professional money managers. I will address the dynamics of group decision making and reinforce the necessity of establishing and adhering to a dispassionate investment philosophy and process. I'll touch on all of these areas in Part 4, "Value Investing and You."

In the last part of the book, I will explore investor psychology at the individual level (versus the macro level addressed earlier) and challenge you to follow the lessons you will have learned. I will also discuss the influence of the Information Age and how the availability of financial data and the ease with which investors can make changes to their portfolios may clash with the goal of maintaining a long-term perspective.

But let's not get ahead of ourselves. Here, in Part 2, I'll show you how to identify value companies—what fundamental traits to analyze and where you might find promising opportunities. I'll also share 10 tips on identifying companies to avoid. In addition, I will comment on issues related to "corporate governance." Here, I share my views on how publicly traded businesses should be run. We've got a lot of ground to cover. Let's get started.

4

CHARACTERISTICS OF VALUE

I've reviewed the basic tenets of value investing. Now it's time for the big question: Which companies qualify as value companies, and how does a value investor know what to look for?

Even though value companies come in all sizes—and from a wide variety of different industries—they tend to have some key characteristics in common. This chapter begins with a discussion of these basic value traits. Next, you'll learn about assorted areas where attractive investment opportunities often congregate. Finally, the chapter turns the tables and examines company-level red flags that can help value investors recognize companies to *avoid*.

Don't worry if, at the beginning, the factors discussed seem overly general or vague. In subsequent chapters you'll find more in-depth tests of a company's investment fitness, as well as information on which research tools belong in a value investor's toolbox.

VALUE BASICS

In many respects, value companies are hard to pigeonhole. Value investors find opportunities in a variety of industries and among companies of all sizes. (As a result, the strategy's practitioners pay scant attention to the copious lists of companies by sales, market capitalization, and so on, published by *Fortune*, *Forbes*, and other financial magazines.) Similarly, location varies widely. Value opportunities may be found in San Diego, Sao Paulo, London, and elsewhere. It is possible, however, to list a few key traits that value companies tend to have in common. As noted earlier, value investors look for companies selling at substantial discounts to their intrinsic values. Therefore, the price of the business versus its long-term private business value is paramount. The companies most attractive to value investors typically also share the following characteristics:

1. **Understandable products and services.** Without solid understanding of a business's products and services—what it sells to earn money—how can its strengths and weaknesses be evaluated thoroughly? Moreover, how can its intrinsic value be determined? Value practitioners invest in companies whose products and services they can understand. Comprehension paves the way for in-depth analysis of investment opportunities as well as proper monitoring of existing holdings. Knowledge also provides an important measure of self-defense. Understanding a business diminishes the likelihood that you'll buckle to sensational (but perhaps false) stories in the media that could adversely influence your investment decisions over the short term.

2. **Consistent earnings generation.** Earnings records for value companies typically demonstrate lengthy, stable histories of income creation. That's not to say that intermittent losses rule out a potential investment opportunity; to the contrary, the negative sentiment that frequently accompanies temporary earnings downturns sometimes pushes a company's stock price down to attractive levels. Overall, value investors believe that—although past results do not guarantee future success—a consistent long-term earnings record can be a strong indicator of near-term future potential.

3. **Strong financial health.** By generally focusing on companies with low debt levels, value investors help ensure that their holdings will stay strong in the event of economic or company-specific hard times. The next chapter reviews specific measures useful for conducting financial health checkups.

What about growth? As a value investor, I very much would like to see a business growing. At the same time, I want to ensure that this growth creates value rather than destroys it. Value-destructive growth occurs when a company's investments generate returns below its cost of capital, which can occur in spite of sales or earnings per share growth. In other words, the opportunity costs of growing the business exceed the income that the business generates. This value-impairing growth can occur organically, such as when a company may become overly aggressive in its pricing to win new business, or externally, when a company overpays for acquisitions.

An example of shareholder impairment through acquisition can be seen in Service Corporation International (SRV), the nation's largest funeral and cemetery provider. This industry had been very fragmented, characterized primarily by small, local, independent funeral homes and cemeteries. As early as the 1960s, SRV recognized the benefits of consolidating these independent operators into regional and national "clusters," creating significant cost and revenue synergies. This resulted in attractive growth for the company, as it was able to generate these synergies at reasonable acquisition prices. SRV financed acquisitions with cash, by issuing debt, or by using its stock as currency.

However, in the middle to late 1990s, the acquisition environment turned decidedly less attractive. Other consolidators began bidding for possible target businesses, resulting in increasingly expensive acquisition prices. At the same time, the industry's growth caught the attention of Wall Street, which encouraged and rewarded additional growth. Eventually acquisition prices rose to a level where new deals became value destructive, and successfully integrating the volume of acquired businesses became difficult.

SRV was not alone. The entire industry's problems became evident in 1998 and 1999 amid a difficult operating environment. Earnings targets were missed, resulting in reduced stock prices, and therefore an inability to do additional deals with their "rich currency." SRV and others were left with excessive debt, and in some cases forced to divest previously acquired businesses at prices significantly lower than those at which they were purchased. The industry's four largest companies saw their stock prices fall an average of 70 percent in 1999, and the second-largest competitor filed for bankruptcy.

The bottom line is that a value company's attributes *can* include growth as long as that growth has a positive influence on the company's wealth creation potential. Overall, although there are no hard and fast definitions of what makes a value company, low debt, consistent earnings, and comprehensible business activities are key traits that tend to characterize the equities that value investors prefer. Given these traits, it's not surprising that true value investors did not purchase shares of dot-com companies during the Internet bubble of the late 1990s.

WHERE TO BEGIN

Generally, investors begin their search for attractive candidates in one of two ways: top-down or bottom-up.

Top-down investors start broadly and narrow the search for individual stocks based on a number of assumptions. For example, before looking at the company-specific traits cited above, top-down investors might start by trying to gauge the strength of a certain country or region. They may study forecasts of economic growth, business sentiment, or the recent performance of stocks in that area. If pleased with the prospects for a region or country, they may then seek what they believe are the most promising sectors or industries within that area, perhaps drawing on projections of sales or the profit potential of new products or services. In addition, top-down investors may factor in expectations for interest rate moves, changes in the political climate, or shifts in broad economic trends. After weighing all these factors and targeting a specific niche, top-down investors will then try to pinpoint specific stocks within that niche.

Bottom-up investors *start* at the company-specific level. They evaluate thousands of individual businesses simultaneously, researching and analyzing companies in diverse industries, sectors, and countries. They seek the most attractive candidates they can find, regardless of where they are located. They pay less attention to macroeconomic factors such as interest rates or unemployment or gross domestic product. They do not have to forecast which sectors or industries will be the top performers in the short term. They focus principally on the prospects for individual companies.

My investment firm is a bottom-up manager. Using the latest investment technology tools, a team of research professionals dedicated to evaluating businesses all over the world analyzes opportunities every day. My firm invests a great deal of time and effort in its focus on individual companies. I realize that individual investors may not have the time and resources to conduct such extensive, company-specific evaluations. With that in mind, next I'll offer a few short cuts to searching for value companies.

Before I do, I want to make an important point. Some individual investors may believe they do not have the time or talent to invest successfully. That's not necessarily true. With dedication, commitment, and patience, I'm confident you can achieve solid long-term results. In my opinion, your success largely depends on two things: stock selection and adherence to value principles.

Professional money managers may have more extensive resources than individuals. Despite these resources, they still may fall victim to the very behaviors addressed in previous chapters that value investors seek to exploit, such as overconfidence and extrapolation. Strict adherence to a value investment approach is as important as selecting appropriate stocks. I address how to stick to your value game plan in Part 4. For now, let's examine a few specific areas where opportunities for investment might be found.

Out-of-Favor Industries   Value investors frequently search for bargains among companies or sectors relegated to the scrap heap by the public. For example, stresses on the financial system in the aftermath of the 1990–1991 recession resulted in tremendous bargains in the banking sector. Many banks sold for below book value. As the economy recovered, regional and money-center banks staged a powerful rally.

Geographic Hard Times   The value strategy's practitioners can also look for troubles unique to a particular geographic region. In the 1980s, the collapse of energy prices temporarily depressed economies in the oil patch of Texas and Oklahoma. Similarly, budget cuts in the defense sector hurt the California economy in the early 1990s. Economic woes and the threat of currency devaluation in Southeast Asia in 1997 weighed on sentiment and dragged down share prices for a number of solid businesses. Remember, the goal is to profit from the investing public's overly emotional reaction to a temporary situation.

New Lows   Another source of potential bargains is the daily stock tables, which contain information on companies whose stock prices have fallen to new lows. Major business publications like *Investor's Business Daily* or *The Wall Street Journal* regularly list companies that fell to new 12-month lows the previous day. Such companies certainly qualify as out of favor and could warrant further investigation. You may be surprised at how often companies that pop up in these three categories (out-of-favor industries and regions or in the new-low stock tables) also pass the tests of financial health, earnings generation, and understandable businesses.

"Falling Knives"   In addition to companies that have fallen to new lows, value investors may find opportunities among companies whose share prices have fallen sharply in a short period. The Brandes Institute—a division of my firm dedicated to research and education—published a study exploring the validity of the Wall Street adage "never catch a falling knife." This long-standing maxim advises investors to avoid purchasing stocks that have declined sharply in a short period of time. When it comes to bankruptcy risk, Wall Street's warning may be on to something. While the annual bankruptcy rate for publicly traded companies is under 1 percent, a full 13 percent of the "falling knives" identified in the study went bankrupt within 3 years. However, investors who "never catch a falling knife" might be missing an opportunity to earn significant returns. On average, the falling knives in the study, including those that went bankrupt, outperformed the S&P 500 Index by an annualized 17.7 percent in the 3 years following their identification. This means that a diversified portfolio of falling knives might enhance overall returns significantly. For more information on Brandes Institute research results, visit the Web site at www.brandes.com/institute.

Value Portfolios You also might study the portfolios of value investors who have put together lengthy and outstanding track records. For example, a review of the equity offerings of value-based fund groups such as Longleaf Partners, Third Avenue Funds, or Tweedy, Browne could point to potential investment opportunities. A fund's shareholder report, which lists its recent holdings, can usually be requested over the Internet, or in writing. *Warning:* Don't buy a stock only because a highly touted professional investor has done so. You should understand and have confidence in the logic of the decision to avoid buying or selling at the wrong time or for the wrong reason.

Media Good value-based ideas can be found in such publications as *Barron's, The Wall Street Journal, The New York Times, Investor's Business Daily,* or *The Financial Times.* These publications each print rosy developments—and some not so rosy—about companies that Wall Street already loves. Occasionally, however, they also feature information about companies that meet value criteria such as having undervalued assets.

As you review these publications, try not to pay too much attention to one of their favorite topics: short-term movements in the price level of the overall market. Remember, true value investors focus on a bottom-up, company-by-company search for large discrepancies between a stock's price and its fair value. Accordingly, the broad market's day-to-day fluctuations are of little significance.

IPOs Typically, initial public offerings (IPOs) are not recommended for the average value investor. Consider the conflict of interest associated with these shares. Private owners seek to sell shares at the *highest* price possible while value investors seek the *lowest* possible price. Be especially wary of IPOs when the stock market is surging to successive record highs. The hype that usually accompanies IPOs during a bull market tends to push their valuations beyond the range that would interest a value investor. Price-earnings ratios for IPOs, for example, can reach double or triple that of the overall market; some of the hotter new offerings sell on nothing more than a wing and a prayer. With expectations set so high, the odds of disappointment are often too great. A value approach to stock selection requires that investors pay only for what is seen, not for what is hoped.

One example of the perils of IPO investing is eToys, which was a darling of the investment world in the late 1990s. The online retailer went public in May 1999 and soon boasted a market capitalization of $5 billion—despite recording only $100 million in annual sales. By comparison, Toys "R" Us, an Old Economy company with $12 billion in sales, was valued at only $1 billion by the market.

Many experts rationalized the eToys premium with overly optimistic projections for the company's success. In November 1999, an analyst at Thomas Weisel Partners offered the following analysis: "We believe that eToys is exploiting a $75 billion market opportunity and that the company itself has the potential to grow to at least $10 billion in sales. In this context, the current valuation (at $50) is extremely attractive in our view . . . we rate [eToys] 'strong buy' with an $85 price target. Our long-term growth assumption is 75%."

eToys filed for bankruptcy 16 months later. In October 2002, eToys completed its Chapter 11 liquidation plan. "All equity interests in former eToys will be cancelled and shareholders will receive nothing under the plan," CBSMarketWatch.com reported. In contrast, by the end of 2002, the market cap for Toys "R" Us had doubled to $2 billion, and the company's toys were sold through a joint venture with online retailer Amazon.com.

Despite horror stories like eToys, young public companies shouldn't be dismissed out of hand. There is a time to look at them, but in most cases it's after the stock has traded for a period and the initial fanfare has faded. Problems may have arisen in the young company's fortunes: either management can't handle growth, fails at diversification, and expands too rapidly or competition becomes more intense.

Two scenarios might occur: The stock is richly priced in the offering, rises for a while, then falls back as earnings difficulties arise. Or, the company's stock is overpriced to begin with and immediately falls below the initial offering price.

Bargains are there for the asking in the post-IPO market if you have the patience to look and wait. You should determine, however, whether any problems with a young company are only temporary and will be rectified in a reasonable time.

Keep in mind that the absence of a lengthy operating history means many IPO opportunities don't deserve a value investor's time. Sometimes, however, companies with stable operating histories spin off divisions as IPOs. In other cases, a private company with a long-term track record may raise capital through an IPO. These special cases may present opportunities for value investors. Again, always evaluate the value of the underlying business against its stock price.

BUSINESSES TO AVOID

No matter where value investors search for opportunity, they'll undoubtedly encounter dozens of potential investments that can be ruled out after a cursory review. How can undesirable businesses be spotted quickly? The following guidelines explore several easy-to-recognize warning signs. (Keep in mind that these guidelines are not necessarily universal. Experienced value investors might recognize opportunity in a company priced well below its true value, even if it falls short in one or more of the following categories.)

1. Avoid businesses loaded with debt. A good rule is "Businesses should have no more debt than equity." (Of course, that's not true in all cases. For example, the rule doesn't apply to financial companies, whose lines of business often require high levels of debt relative to equity.)

2. Run from corporate managers who seem concerned with perks, golden parachutes, bonuses, and excessively high salaries in relation to the return to shareholders. How does the value investor get answers to these concerns? Simply thumb through a company's SEC-required filings, such as the 10-K report or notice of shareholders' meeting and proxy statement. Also take a quick glance at industry reports, which provide benchmarks for executive compensation in a particular type of business.

3. Don't invest in businesses that generate money through accounting cleverness rather than real cash. Such businesses require more investment as sales grow, resulting in a lack of working capital. Look at cash flow figures; a healthy cash flow indicates that a company can pay all of its bills with enough left over to buy shares, pay out a larger dividend, or invest. I address more aspects of what we call "corporate governance," including accounting practices and executive salaries, in Chapter 7.

4.   Detour around companies that change character every time a hot idea appears on the horizon. Many defense contractors, for example, promote sweeping and risky new programs just to stay in business. Other managers assume so much risk it is literally a "bet your company" circumstance.

5.   Stay away from companies committed to providing services or commodities at fixed prices for a long time in the future. Rising inflation could wreak havoc here.

6.   Bypass capital-intensive companies. Often the cash flow of such companies is insufficient to provide a satisfactory return while still maintaining a plant at competitive levels. These companies must regularly borrow or issue stock to stay in business.

7.   Be particularly cautious about businesses subject to government regulation. These firms generally don't make good long-term investments since their rates of return are limited by law.

8.   Watch out for companies with different classes of stock. Shareholders may be disenfranchised through limited or nonvoting stock. Also be careful to avoid foreign companies issuing different classes of stock for nondomestic shareholders. These shares may trade at substantially different levels from those of stocks owned by domestic investors.

9.   Pass by companies with managements that only occasionally initiate cost-reduction programs. Cost reduction should be an ongoing way of doing business.

10.   Avoid companies that continually issue additional shares. Each subsequent equity offering dilutes the ownership value of existing shareholders. The dilution also lowers a company's earnings per share, an important factor in determining a stock's fair value. Be especially cautious if the proceeds from a secondary stock offering are used to invest in businesses with lower rates of return or those for which management seems ill prepared. Remember, a bigger pie is not always a better pie.

A GOOD COMPANY VERSUS A GOOD INVESTMENT

One more general idea that value investors keep in mind is that a good *company* is not necessarily the same as a good *investment*. An established firm with high revenue levels and a stable, strong earnings record, for instance, certainly sounds like a good company. But like any company, that

EXHIBIT 4-1   Cisco Systems in April 2000: A Good Investment?

Company	Market Cap: 4/00	1999 Revenues	1999 Earnings
Cisco Systems	**$468.0**	**$15.0**	**$2.5**
Ford	$65.8	$162.6	$7.2
Texaco	$27.8	$35.1	$1.2
Merrill Lynch	$37.6	$34.9	$2.6
DuPont	$56.3	$26.9	$7.7
International Paper	$16.4	$24.6	$0.2
Sara Lee	$14.9	$20.2	$1.2
FedEx	$11.0	$17.4	$0.6
McDonald's	$44.0	$13.3	$2.0
Goodyear Tire & Rubber	$4.5	$12.9	$0.2
J.P. Morgan	$20.8	$11.8	$2.0
Anheuser Busch	$30.6	$11.7	$1.4
Eli Lilly	$82.6	$9.9	$2.7
Fox Entertainment	$17.8	$7.9	$0.2
Consolidated Edison	$6.8	$7.5	$0.7
Apple Computer	$20.6	$6.8	$0.6
Dow Jones	$5.9	$2.0	$0.3
Total	**$463.4**	**$405.5**	**$30.8**

Note: All numbers in US$ billions.
Source: Worldscope, April 30, 2000.

A good company is not necessarily the same as a good investment.

firm only represents a good investment if it can be purchased at a favorable price.

Take Cisco Systems as an example. In April 2000, Cisco qualified as a good company by almost any investor's standards. As a supplier of data networking products for the Internet, the firm was logging strong sales and demonstrating real earnings power, as well. In 1999, Cisco posted $15 billion in revenue and $2.5 billion in net income. Even as many technology companies were fading fast, Cisco's dominant market share in an important industry meant the firm's future prospects were bright.

Despite its strengths as a company, however, most value investors stopped short of calling Cisco a good investment. The firm's stock price translated into an astronomical market capitalization of more than $465 billion—nearly half a *trillion* dollars! This figure dwarfed Cisco's revenue and earnings numbers, an indication that shareholders were counting on tremendous long-term growth from the company in the years ahead. If this growth failed to materialize, Cisco's market value faced the risk of substantial declines.

As a result, most value investors avoided Cisco and looked for stocks with prices that were less dependent on extremely high expectations. Luckily, these opportunities were widely available in April 2000. Exhibit 4-1 lists 16 established companies with a *combined* market capitalization of less than $465 billion. These firms—which include established businesses such as Ford, Texaco, and Merrill Lynch—had combined 1999 sales of $405 billion and earnings of $30.7 billion.

Effectively, investors could purchase slices of all 16 firms for the same price as an equivalent slice of Cisco and receive much more in terms of underlying sales and earnings in the process. Accordingly, most value investors passed on Cisco shares. The firm qualified as a good company but not as a good investment.

CONCLUSION

In this chapter, we've discussed some typical traits of value companies, as well as broad characteristics of companies that value investors tend to avoid. We also explored the idea that a good company is not necessarily the same as a good investment.

Up next, we'll turn these generalizations into quantifiable rules that can be applied in company-by-company analysis of investment opportunities.

5

NARROWING
YOUR FOCUS

In Chapter 4, I noted that, while they can come in all sizes and be found in all industries, defensive value stocks that are priced right tend to be characterized by traits such as strong financial health and consistent earnings generation. I also talked about types of companies that adherents to the value investing philosophy would probably avoid.

This chapter sharpens the general ideas from Chapter 4 into usable guidelines designed to pinpoint value stocks and to screen out their less desirable counterparts. First, I examine quantitative screens that Ben Graham used to uncover compelling investment opportunities. In this review, you'll see how the father of security analysis translated his fondness for attractively priced, high-quality companies into formulas which could be used to evaluate most stocks in just minutes.

Next, I'll share four of my own guidelines, each aimed at helping you narrow a list of potential investments down to low-risk stocks offering significant return potential. I'll also discuss the concept of intrinsic value, the cornerstone upon which solid value portfolios are built. Finally, I'll review a simple but important gauge of a stock's relative value: the price-to-earnings (P/E) ratio.

As you read this chapter, you'll notice that it refers to company-level data such as shareholders' equity and total debt. Don't be alarmed if you're not sure where to find these numbers; all of them are published in a company's financial statements, which I'll review in Chapter 6.

GRAHAM'S NET-NET METHOD

Graham's most famous screen for value focused on "net-net" current assets. He calculated this value by subtracting all of a company's liabilities—the total amount of money owed to various creditors—from its current assets, which essentially equal the company's cash or near cash (such as receivables) on hand. In other words, a company with positive net-net current assets theoretically could pay off all of its debtholders' claims using its cash on hand and still have cash left over.

Graham believed that if a stock's price was less than two-thirds of net-net current assets per share—and if the company was currently profitable—investors needed no other yardstick: The stock was a buy. The reasoning behind this rule is straightforward. When share price is less than two-thirds of net-net current assets, investors can effectively buy this excess cash for less than 67 cents on the dollar and get a full claim on the company's permanent assets for free. In Graham's eyes, this was an extremely attractive investment as long as the company in question was currently generating profits.

"What about companies that qualified except for recent profitability?" I asked Graham. Those companies, he told me, were dangerously situated. He believed losses could rapidly burn up corporate assets and subsequently endanger the potential payoff of an investment.

Admittedly, during Graham's lifetime, few companies met the stringent criteria of the net-net method—except at the bottom of major market declines. And today, elevated valuations and increased investor vigilance make it nearly impossible to find a profitable company selling at a one-third discount to its net-net current assets.

GRAHAM'S SECOND BEST-KNOWN METHOD

While the net-net approach used net-net current assets and profitability to evaluate a stock's potential, Ben Graham's second best-known method focused on a trio of metrics: earnings yield, dividend yield, and balance sheet debt. A stock that was attractive in all three areas, he believed, qualified as a true bargain.

Earnings Yield

Earnings yield is calculated by dividing a company's earnings per share (EPS) by its stock price. If XYZ Co., for example, has recently reported $3 in EPS and has a stock price of $20, its earnings yield is 0.15, or 15 percent. (An alternative way to calculate earnings yield is to take the inverse of a company's price-to-earnings ratio; that is, to divide 1 by the company's P/E. I'll talk more about P/Es later in this chapter.)

Graham believed that by comparing earnings yield to the long-term (20-year) yield on AAA bonds, investors could begin to gauge a stock's investment potential. Specifically, he thought a bargain stock's earnings yield needed to be at least double the average long-term AAA bond yield to qualify as attractive.

To continue our example, suppose that at the time XYZ Co. had an earnings yield of 15 percent, long-term AAA bonds were yielding 6 percent. Because XYZ's yield is more than twice the long-term AAA bond yield, the stock would pass muster in this segment of Graham's evaluation.

Dividend Yield

Dividend yield came next on Graham's three-part list. Similar to earnings yield, dividend yield is calculated by dividing all dividends paid per share in the last year by the current stock price. If XYZ Co. paid $1 in dividends and traded at $20, for example, the stock's dividend yield would equal 0.05, or 5 percent.

Like earnings yield, Graham sized up dividend yield by comparing it to the yield on long-term AAA bonds. In his opinion, a bargain stock's dividend yield must be no less than two-thirds of the long-term AAA bond yield. With long-term AAA bonds yielding 6 percent, XYZ Co. would meet this threshold: The company's dividend yield of 5 percent exceeds 4 percent, which is two-thirds of the AAA rate.

Balance Sheet Debt

The final leg of Graham's three-tiered review was balance sheet debt. Graham considered high debt levels to be troubling because they typically lead to heavy, asset-draining interest expense. As a result, investing in debt-burdened companies means gambling that future earnings will be high enough to meet debt service. To Graham, investors were better off scouting for companies with low debt.

So how much debt is too much? Graham's general rule was that companies should owe no more than they are worth. More formally stated, a company's total debt should not exceed its shareholder's equity. This means a bargain stock's debt-to-equity ratio should be less than 1.0.

It's important to note that the evaluation of a company's debt level depends on the nature of the company and its business. Banks, for example, depend on funds borrowed via savings and checking accounts to make profit-generating loans. As a result, banking companies with debt-to-equity ratios much higher than 1.0 are often well financed and may represent sound investments.

In general, however, high debt is dangerous, and Graham considered an aversion to firms with debt-to-equity ratios greater than 1.0 to be a sensible rule of thumb. He believed the combination of this debt-to-equity rule with the requirement for earnings yield and dividend yield formed a solid foundation for the analysis of most investment opportunities. In the next section, I'll share one more of Graham's bargain-hunting techniques.

A THIRD EVALUATION TECHNIQUE

An additional method Graham offered to identify attractive opportunities combined five tests for value with five tests for safety. The value tests focus on income and income-generating assets, while the safety tests put the spotlight on risk factors such as debt levels and earnings stability. If a stock satisfied at least one of the criteria on each list, he believed, it probably qualified as a good bargain.

Five Tests for Value

1. Earnings yield is at least twice the yield on long-term AAA bonds.
2. The P/E ratio falls among the lowest 10 percent of P/Es in the universe.
3. Dividend yield is at least two-thirds the yield on long-term AAA bonds.
4. Stock price is less than two-thirds of tangible book value (total book value minus goodwill) per share.
5. Stock price is less than two-thirds of net current assets (current assets minus current liabilities).

Five Tests for Safety

1. Debt-to-equity ratio is less than 1.0.
2. Current assets are at least twice current liabilities.
3. Total debt is less than twice net current assets.
4. Annual earnings growth is at least 7 percent over the previous decade.
5. No more than two year-to-year earnings declines of more than 5 percent during the previous decade.

MY FOUR-STEP TEST FOR VALUE

Drawing on Graham's teachings and my experience, I've condensed the most significant precepts of the value philosophy into a four-step test you can quickly apply to any company that interests you. A stock that measures up to each of the four criteria below likely qualifies as a true value stock. If the issue falls short in one or more areas, I recommend proceeding with caution.

1. No losses were sustained within the past 5 years.
2. Total debt is less than 100 percent of total tangible equity.
3. Share price is less than book value per share.
4. Earnings yield is at least twice the yield on long-term (20-year) AAA bonds.

Admittedly, these guidelines are strict. Is there any wiggle room? Yes, but be careful not to rationalize yourself into taking on too much risk. The *experienced* value investor might possibly ignore one or more of the criteria, but only if compelling and well-researched reasons exist for doing so. For example, the second criterion might be overlooked if a company's debt has a low interest rate, or if a company's earnings are especially strong and stable. Or, number three could be ignored, provided the company has sustained high rates of return on book value. If that analysis proves too tricky, however, it may be safer to follow the precise guidelines.

A COMPLEMENTARY APPROACH: INTRINSIC VALUE

You may have noticed some common themes spanning Graham's various methods as well as my four-step test for value. Each approach places strong emphasis on three factors that value investors consider critical. First is earnings strength, a quality measured by a variety of criteria including consistency of annual earnings per share and freedom from periods of net losses. Second is financial strength, which is typically evaluated using metrics like debt-to-equity ratios. Third is low price, a factor accounted for in ratios such as price-to-book and earnings yield.

All three of these factors are also integral to another key value-investing approach: purchasing companies at substantial discounts to their intrinsic values. But what is intrinsic value, exactly? And how is it calculated in practice?

To answer the first question, I'll share a definition provided by Warren Buffett in a 1996 publication to shareholders of his company, Berkshire Hathaway.[1] "Intrinsic value can be defined simply," Buffett wrote. "It is the discounted value of the cash that can be taken out of a business during its remaining life." In other words, a company's intrinsic value is equal to the value today of all of the money it will deliver in the future.

So how is intrinsic value calculated? Unfortunately, the answer to this question is not as simple. As our definition above suggests, one path to estimating a company's intrinsic value involves projections regarding its future cash generation. Of course, for even the most stable companies, the future is filled with uncertainty.

Accordingly, the value strategy's adherents tend to place significant emphasis on insights gained from a thorough analysis of a company's past and present. This is where the three factors mentioned above come into play. To calculate intrinsic value, value investors rigorously examine qualities such as financial strength and earnings strength in the context of the company's past results, its current operations, and its future prospects. Once calculated, this value is divided by the number of shares outstanding to arrive at an estimate of intrinsic value per share. Then, this per-share intrinsic value is compared with the company's stock price. If the stock price is low enough to offer a significant discount to intrinsic value, the stock is purchased.

To calculate intrinsic value, value investors rigorously examine qualities such as financial strength and earnings strength in the context of the company's past results, its current operations, and its future prospects.

It's important to note that an estimated intrinsic value *range* is often just as useful as a precise number when evaluating the suitability of a potential investment. As Ben Graham points out in *Security Analysis*, a book he coauthored with David Dodd in 1934, "It is quite possible to decide by inspection that a woman is old enough to vote without knowing her age, or that a man is heavier than he should be without knowing his exact weight."[2] Similarly, a ballpark estimate of intrinsic value sometimes can be enough to discern an investment opportunity if a stock is trading at a much lower price.

Another essential point is that value investors don't expect to be able to come up with intrinsic value estimates for every stock in the market. Firms operating in nascent industries with rapidly changing dynamics, for example, are often surrounded by levels of uncertainty that make any estimates of underlying worth dubious. In cases like these, value investors recognize the limits of their abilities and move on to evaluate other companies.

Overall, the process of calculating intrinsic value may involve as much art as science. At the same time, the familiar factors of earnings strength, financial strength, and low price stand out as key themes. A focus on these qualities—applied within the realm of one's expertise—is critical to the value investor's approach.

THE P/E RATIO, A SIMPLE BUT IMPORTANT METRIC

The price-to-earnings or P/E ratio is an oft-mentioned metric that, despite its simplicity, can help greatly in the evaluation of investment opportunities. In its most basic form, the P/E ratio is calculated by dividing a company's share price by its earnings per share (EPS) over the most recent four quarters. Remember our XYZ Co. example above when I addressed earnings yield? We imagined that firm was trading at $20 and had recently reported $3 in EPS. The company's P/E would then equal 20 divided by 3, or about 6.7.

So what does that 6.7 mean? A useful way to think of P/E ratios is to view them as a price tag on $1 of earnings. XYZ's P/E of 6.7 means a buyer of the stock is paying $6.70 for every $1 the company earns. From this perspective, you can begin to harness the power of the P/E as an evaluation metric.

By comparing XYZ's P/E to the P/E ratio of the overall market, for example, you can get a quick idea of the company's relative cost. An S&P 500 P/E of 15, for instance, means the going rate on $1 of earnings from the average company in the index is $15. XYZ would seem inexpensive by comparison and might warrant further investigation. The current P/E ratio for major market indices can frequently be found on the index providers'

Web sites. (For a recent calculation of the unmanaged S&P 500's P/E, see the Standard & Poor's Web site, www.standardandpoors.com.) Over the last 40 years, the P/E ratio of the S&P 500 has ranged from a low of roughly 8 times earnings to a high of close to 45 times earnings. See Exhibit 5-1.

P/E ratios are also useful for stock-by-stock comparisons. Imagine a firm called QRS, with a current price of $24 and EPS of $2. The P/E ratio for QRS would come in at 12; in other words, with QRS, investors must pay $12 for $1 of earnings. By comparison, XYZ's P/E of 6.7 strikes me as a better deal—probably.

Wait a minute—probably? With a P/E of 6.7, how could QRS be anything but a better deal? The answer is that not all P/Es are created equal. Let's look at some examples of how P/E-to-P/E comparisons can drift into "apples and oranges" territory—and how you can make sure your analysis stays strictly apples to apples.

The main limitation on the power of the P/E is the fact that the "E" in the equation equals EPS from just 1 year. What if QRS, our company with a P/E of 12, was coming off an unusually difficult period that saw its EPS take a one-time dip? Perhaps in a normal year, QRS would have delivered EPS closer to $4. With that in mind, does XYZ still look as compelling in comparison? Maybe not.

A good way to account for the year-to-year fluctuations in EPS is to look at "sustainable EPS." A nonscientific but useful way to calculate sustainable EPS is to simply average a company's EPS figures over the last several years. I recommend reaching back 3 to 5 years in your calculation. Usually that's enough history to smooth out any unusual events

EXHIBIT 5-1   Monthly S&P 500 P/E Ratio: 1962–2002

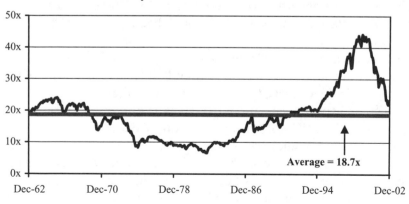

Source: Robert Shiller (www.econ.yale.edu/~shiller/), as of December 31, 2002.

and variations in the company's business cycle. Of course, any analysis based on estimates of sustainable earnings estimates must incorporate any doubts as to the true sustainability of the company's earnings power in the future.

Another P/E option involves "estimated EPS." Many publicly traded firms are monitored by Wall Street analysts, who frequently publish estimates of the company's EPS for the current year as well as the year ahead. These earnings estimates often ignore unusual items, so P/E ratios with estimated EPS in the denominator might help keep company-to-company comparisons legitimate. Earnings estimates must be used with extreme care, however; reality frequently diverges from Wall Street's projections! (Consensus earnings estimates are calculated and published by sources such as FirstCall and IBES.)

CONCLUSION

In this chapter, I examined three techniques Benjamin Graham used to separate value stocks from the rest of the pack. I also presented a short list of criteria that I believe distinguish true bargain opportunities, and I discussed the concept of intrinsic value—another key approach to identifying value stocks. The chapter concluded with a discussion of the P/E ratio, a straightforward measure of company value that I believe is of benefit to every investor.

From current assets to earnings per share, this chapter repeatedly mentioned company-specific data items and how they can be used to evaluate investment opportunities. In Chapter 6 I'll take a look at company financial statements and where these numbers are gathered and published for the benefit of all investors. In addition, I'll list sources of additional important data.

Notes

1.   Warren E. Buffett, "An Owner's Manual." Distributed to Berkshire Hathaway Class A and Class B shareholders at the firm's annual shareholders' meeting in June 1996. A copy of this booklet is available online at www.berkshirehathaway.com/2001ar/ownersmanual.html.

2.   Benjamin Graham and David L. Dodd, *Security Analysis,* 5th ed., New York: McGraw-Hill, 1976, p. 19.

6

GATHERING
COMPANY
INFORMATION

The last two chapters identified typical characteristics of value stocks and set out some quantitative rules for pinpointing promising investment opportunities. So, how can an investor apply these criteria to a company that has caught his or her eye? What sources yield clues to a company's strengths and weaknesses, and where can numbers like shareholders' equity and earnings per share be found?

I'll answer these questions by exploring key sources of the information critical to company-by-company analysis. I'll start with a quick review of some useful Web sites loaded with general company data. Then I'll take an in-depth look at the investor's most important source of company facts and figures: the financial statements.

GETTING STARTED

Value practitioners frame company analysis with a pair of simple questions: Would a rational investor want to own this business? And, if so,

Value practitioners frame company analysis with a pair of simple questions: Would a rational investor want to own this business? And, if so, at what price? at what price? To answer these questions, of course, you need lots of facts, including all available information about a company's history, its type of business, and its potential for cyclical highs and lows. The information-gathering process can be time-consuming, but the cold, hard facts it gener-

ates often make the difference between a successful investment and one that goes bust.

Before I grab my calculator and dive into a company's numbers, I like to have a general understanding of the firm's history, its current lines of business, and any significant recent events that may have affected its stock price. Thanks to the power of the Internet, much of this data is just a few mouse clicks away.

One site that may prove useful to an investor aiming to evaluate an investment opportunity is Hoover's Company Capsules (www.hoovers.com). Hoover's offers free company profiles on hundreds of publicly traded firms. With content ranging from timelines of company history to consensus estimates of future earnings, the profiles are structured to help you quickly get up to speed with a given firm. Additional in-depth research is available with registration.

Another Internet tool worth adding to your toolbox is ValueLine Investment Survey (www.valueline.com). This site's free features include a comprehensive, company-by-company archive of recent news as well as interactive price charts, where investors can compare a stock's price performance with other equities and even market indices. Subscribers gain access to ValueLine's company reports, which contain buckets of important financial data in a compact, easy-to-read format.

Web technology lends itself nicely to screening, and many sites offer tools that quickly sift through reams of data to spotlight stocks meeting user-specified qualifications. Kiplinger (www.kiplinger.com), for example, features an easy-to-use Stock Finder page that screens thousands of stocks based on customizable criteria such as market capitalization, annual revenue, P/E ratios, and debt-to-equity levels. Lead generators like Stock Finder can be quite useful to value investors in the early stages of a hunt for investment ideas.

While Hoover's, ValueLine, and Kiplinger tend to focus on U.S.-based firms, J.P. Morgan's adr.com (www.adr.com) offers similar content with an international emphasis. ADRs, or American Depositary Receipts, essentially are securities created to allow larger non-U.S. firms to be traded in the United States. At adr.com, J.P. Morgan provides a wide range of firm-by-firm information for hundreds of non-U.S. companies with ADRs in circulation. (I'll take a closer look at international equities in Chapters 8 through 10.)

It's helpful to read widely, of course, but always read critically. Keeping a wary eye on the information coming your way helps develop your own particular viewpoint. Although sources such as those above can be of great assistance, they're not necessarily free from bias—a fact that value investors need to keep in mind.

One more Internet resource in the quest for company information is, of course, the site managed by the company itself. Virtually all publicly traded firms have sites these days, and they often contain insights into the firm's business activities in the firm's own words. In addition, most corporate sites have pages dedicated to communicating with investors. On these pages, you'll typically find e-mail addresses and phone numbers of investor relations staff you can contact with questions or information requests. Usually, the sites also offer direct links leading to the real goods: annual reports and SEC forms containing the company's financial statements. (SEC filings and forms can also be accessed and downloaded freely via EDGAR at www.sec.gov/edgar.shtml.)

THE BIG THREE

Once you've gained a broad familiarity with a company's history and its current operations, it's time to move on to the all-important triumvirate of investment information: the balance sheet, the income statement, and the statement of cash flows.

In this section, I'll examine the fundamental contents of the three major financial statements. This examination is by no means a complete review: Thick textbooks and in-depth college courses are dedicated to understanding and analyzing financial statements, and the following discussion is not intended to serve as a substitute. At the same time, a broad familiarity with the financial statements should help you begin to make sense of the vast amount of data they contain.

The Balance Sheet

Also called a statement of financial position, the balance sheet reports on the levels of three distinct items at a specific point in time:

- Assets, which are resources owned or controlled by the firm

- Liabilities, or external claims on those assets

- Shareholders' equity, which is the capital contributed by owners or generated internally

The interrelationship of these three items is governed by a simple equation: assets = liabilities + shareholders' equity. Rearranging this equation leads to an alternative definition of shareholders' equity: It's equal to assets less liabilities, or the amount of assets that would remain if all creditors' claims were settled.

Shareholders' equity—also known as book value—is one of the most important data items listed on the balance sheet. Investors can't take the number at face value, however. The listed value of assets like property, equipment, and inventory, for example, must be reviewed for appropriateness. If any of these values are overstated or understated, shareholders' equity must be reduced or increased accordingly.

Other important balance sheet categories include current assets—the portion of assets the company could convert to cash in a hurry—as well as both short-term debt and long-term debt. Many of these items can be used in combination to begin evaluating the health of the company. Total debt, for instance, is calculated by adding short-term debt and long-term debt. Dividing the resulting value by shareholders' equity leads to the firm's debt-to-equity ratio, a central indicator of financial fitness.

Flexibility in accounting rules means firms have leeway in calculating some of the balance sheet's items. Inventory is a good example, as generally accepted accounting principles (GAAP) allow for more than one approach to inventory valuation. If one widget manufacturer uses the LIFO ("last in, first out") technique and a second uses an alternative called FIFO ("first in, first out"), the two companies could report dramatically different inventory values—*even if they have an identical number of widgets in their respective warehouses.* Investors must be cognizant of such subtleties and make adjustments accordingly.

Hidden or undervalued assets can be one of the value investor's best friends. Corporate assets are sometimes not reflected on balance sheets. Real estate, for instance, frequently falls into the undervalued asset category, since land is carried at cost and buildings at depreciated cost. Suppose land prices go up? When that happens, real estate's actual market value can be considerably above its value on the books.

Additional balance sheet items of note include goodwill and other intangible assets. Goodwill is the difference between the amount paid for an acquired firm and the fair market value of its net assets. In essence, this difference represents a premium paid for the acquired firm's profitability. Other intangibles are identifiable, nonmonetary resources such as licenses, leasehold rights, copyrights, patents, and brand names.

While goodwill and other intangible assets lack physical substance, they sometimes generate significant revenues and can represent an important portion of the value of a firm. In addition, some investments which accounting rules consider expenses—such as those associated with research and development—might be more accurately classified as assets for analytical purposes. As a result, investors should keep an eye on each of these items and fine-tune their analysis as necessary.

The Income Statement

Whereas the balance sheet reflects company information *as of* a particular *date*, the income statement reports the firm's performance *over* a particular *period*, such as a quarter or a year. Similar to the balance sheet, the income statement has three primary components:

- Revenues, also known as sales

- Expenses, the costs of producing goods and rendering services

- Net income, which equals revenues less expenses

These items are calculated based on the accrual accounting principle, which holds that revenues should be recognized when a firm delivers goods, rather than when it collects cash. Similarly, expenses should be recorded as the firm incurs costs, not necessarily when it makes payment for the services. By matching a period's proper revenues with its related expenses, the income statement measures the period's appropriate net income.

Typical expenses include cost of goods sold, depreciation, interest, and taxes. These cost-of-doing-business indicators are useful in comparing a company with its competition. For example, if a company is paying taxes at a rate that is considerably lower than the corporate tax rate, an investor needs to understand why. The answer may reveal that the company will face a tax-rate boost in the future, which could negatively affect earnings over the long term.

Net income is synonymous with earnings, the data item which, on a per share basis, forms the denominator of the P/E ratio. When working with this figure, investors must watch out for "managed" earnings. Some companies might try to give earnings a one-time boost through maneuvers such as property sales or the disposal of investments in subsidiaries. Profits from such activity should be excluded from the calculation of true earnings.

Because net income tends to fluctuate from year to year, it's also important to avoid placing too much emphasis on a company's earnings during any one period. As I mentioned in Chapter 5, calculating "sustainable" or "normalized" earnings can shed light on true earnings power by smoothing income swings. Again, this calculation involves averaging net income numbers over the last several years.

The Statement of Cash Flows

The income statement's focus on accrual accounting means it doesn't tell investors about a crucial detail: how much cold, hard cash came into and flowed out of the company during the period under review. This information is found in the statement of cash flows, where the company classifies all of its cash receipts and payments into one of three categories:

- Operating cash flows

- Investing cash flows

- Financing cash flows

Operating cash flows involve cash generated or used by the firm as a result of its production and sales of goods and services. Funds generated internally can be used to pay dividends, repay loans, replace existing capacity, or invest for future growth. For most firms, positive operating cash flows are essential for long-term survival, although negative cash flows from operations are expected in some circumstances, such as rapid expansion.

Investing cash flows involve purchases of property and equipment, as well as subsidiaries or business segments and investments in other firms. These purchases allow a company to maintain its current operating capacity and to create new capacity for growth. Cash flows from investing also include receipts from disposal of business segments or assets.

Financing cash flows relate to the debt and equity the firm uses to raise capital. The issuance or retirement of debt, as well as outflows for interest payments, are reported in this section. Similarly, cash flows from financing include issuance or repurchase of shares of stock and dividend payments to shareholders.

Broadly speaking, the statement of cash flows is designed to shed light on a company's ability to sustain and increase cash from current operations. When professionals read these documents, the items they focus on include the strength of cash generation from operations and the cash consequences of investing and financing decisions. In general, a strong, positive cash flow usually bodes well for a company's long-term health. Temporarily losing money—in an accounting sense, at least—is acceptable. Even so, beware of chronic negative cash flow.

CONCLUSION

Information provided in the financial statements is typically accompanied by footnotes and other disclosures. These sections contain data on subjects such as off-balance-sheet obligations, business segments, and the company's retirement plans. A careful review of all supplementary materials is critical to evaluation of the firm.

Even after reading every inch of fine print, the investor must realize that the financial statements can't provide a complete picture of 100 percent of a company's situation. Unfortunately, there is no way for the average investor to learn a corporation's innermost secrets or to look into a crystal ball and see the company's future. Despite their limitations, however, the financial statements are a key resource in the quest for information, and their contents help answer many of the questions a value investor should ask.

Recent accounting scandals have some investors asking if company financial data can be trusted at all. In my opinion, these concerns are overstated. While the potential for fraud is always a reality, I believe the accounting statements for the vast majority of publicly traded companies reflect integrity and accuracy.

One way to protect yourself is to pay close attention to the auditors' letter, found at the end of audited financial statements. Such letters can be "clean," that is, presented without qualification. If, however, the letters are "subject to" certain conditions, the investor should view the preceding data with special scrutiny.

A final thought: Take a look at a company's proxy statement disclosures for clues regarding management's propensity for self-indulgence. In these pages, investors can examine executive compensation, read up on insider borrowing, and look for any other sweetheart transactions between management and the shareholders it serves.

In the next chapter, I'll address in further detail the relationship between management and shareholders as well as other matters of corporate governance.

7

CORPORATE GOVERNANCE AND THE VALUE INVESTOR

C orporate governance, and the related topic of shareholder activism, attracted increased attention recently. Given that these phrases (along with other exciting ones like "long-term pension funding" or "modern portfolio theory") usually put audiences to sleep fast, something is clearly going on.

What is corporate governance, and why does it matter? Basically, it comes down to control over power and money (two strong human motivators). Multi-billion-dollar corporations are owned by shareholders (that's you and me), but they are run by a board of directors and management team (the "managers"). At least in theory, these managers are appointed by us, the shareholders, so they presumably are looking after our financial interests. In practice, it doesn't always work out like that, as several examples have illustrated over the years, including companies such as Enron, World-Com, Tyco, and Vivendi Universal.

Corporate governance essentially focuses on whether the managers are looking after the interests of the shareholders, and whether there are appropriate rules, processes, and safeguards to make sure that is indeed the case. Shareholder activism is what happens (or at least should happen) if these corporate governance rules aren't working. I enjoyed a recent cartoon that showed an aggrieved management team asserting to a new controlling shareholder, "Just because you bought all our shares, it doesn't mean you can walk in and act as if you own the place!" Unfortunately, that kind of attitude is too common in today's world.

Why does corporate governance matter to a value investor in particular? When value investors buy shares in a company, they've done their homework and are expecting that over time, the intrinsic value of that company will be recognized in its market price. If the company's own management is acting in a way that stops that from happening (and I'll show you later how that can occur), then they are obstructing the rationale for why the investment was made. Put simply, they are stopping investors from obtaining a good return on investment. Sometimes this obstruction reflects a difference of opinion between the management and investors. Increasingly, however, there are conflicts of interest between management and shareholders, or even cases of outright dishonesty.

So what should an investor do? I believe that the right approach, ethically and financially, is to open discussions with the management team or, in other words, to initiate "shareholder activism."

In the balance of this chapter, I address corporate governance and shareholder activism in more detail, including how active shareholders may attempt to improve governance at the companies in their portfolio. As the founder of Brandes Investment Partners, I have more than 25 years of business management experience. When investing, I look for companies that are managed in the same way my firm manages its business. For example, I seek companies run by executives who are committed to building shareholder value not personal empires.

The personal empire is in fact at the root of many manager-shareholder conflicts. In the early days of American capitalism, there were many personal empires, but the people who ran them also owned them, and in many cases had also built them from scratch. Think of Rockefeller, Hearst, Carnegie, Mellon, and Vanderbilt. No conflict there!

Nowadays, though, you are much more likely to come across companies where the management team derives its compensation (including money, power, and perks) from sources *other* than the return on the value of the shares. Even management stock options, which were originally intended to align the interests of managers and shareholders, have unintended side effects (unintended for shareholders, that is). This is where today's conflicts of interest are most visible and need attention.

As shareholders, we should be aware that running a business is not easy. Management executives must constantly balance the sometimes competing, sometimes complementary, interests of a variety of constituencies, including:

- Short-term shareholders

- Long-term shareholders

- Employees

- Strategic partners

- Customers and/or clients

- Politicians

- Vendors and/or suppliers

- Community interest groups

Nevertheless, sound corporate governance can make the job of managing a corporation easier for executives by creating a framework for the execution and review of important management decisions, and providing a way for shareholders to make their views known where appropriate.

CORPORATE GOVERNANCE IN PRACTICE

As I outlined, corporate governance is the relationship between a company and its shareholders. At the core of corporate governance lie two important issues: control and ownership. Senior managers, such as the chief executive officer at a corporation, represent "control." They manage the corporation and make day-to-day decisions affecting every aspect of the firm—from the products and/or services the business provides, to interaction with customers and prospects and, ultimately, profits and losses.

Shareholders represent "ownership." Everyone who purchases shares of common stock in a business is a stockholder and, as stockholders, they own a portion of the business. While stockholders are the legal owners of the corporation, their liability is limited. For example, if the corporation is sued, the shareholders are not named in the suit and are not held responsible for any judgments against the corporation. If the corporation goes bankrupt, the most shareholders can lose is the money they invested. Their credit histories are not tarnished. No one will place a lien against their assets. This limited liability is one reason corporations are able to attract investors and raise money to start or fund their operations.

Along with limited liability, shareholders also have limited control. Publicly traded companies around the world are, with some differences in terminology, managed by executive officers under the supervision of a board of directors. Again, in most cases, the owners of a publicly listed company (the shareholders) are not involved directly in management of the company. Instead, they rely upon a board of directors (elected by shareholders) and officers (who are appointed by the directors) to make virtually all key decisions that affect the day-to-day management of the business. Herein lies the potential for problems: The shareholders who own the business are not necessarily controlling how the business is run.

Andrei Shleifer and Robert Vishny, who helped research and write the study on undervalued stocks that was cited earlier in this book, wrote that corporate governance "deals with the ways in which suppliers of finance to corporations assure themselves of getting a return on their investment."[1]

In this sense, the term *suppliers of finance* refers to shareholders. When corporations issue shares of stock, they use the money people pay for those shares to finance the business: to build production plants, for example, or research a new product or service, pay salaries to employees, or advertise products to potential customers. As suppliers of finance, shareholders expect senior management to use their money wisely and maximize profitability. Shareholders expect the value of their shares to rise in the future as the company grows, attracts new customers, and increases its revenues. Ideally, corporate governance gives shareholders a better opportunity for achieving the appreciation that they seek in the value of their shares.

IS GOOD CORPORATE GOVERNANCE IMPORTANT?

Is there a relationship between good corporate governance and shareholder value? I believe the answer is "yes." If corporate governance is designed to provide a blueprint for success, then *good* governance should result in a *good* business and attractive shareholder value.

Statistically, this has been harder to prove, especially in more developed markets where standards are meant to be higher. For example, in a working paper, Stanford law professor Bernard Black notes that in the

United States, ". . . efforts to find a correlation between a firm's governance attributes and its value mostly show weak or no results."[2] I think it is important to note that, despite this broad conclusion, Black *did* find that in certain "governance-challenged" markets, such as Russia, there was a direct relationship between good governance characteristics and shareholder value.

While Black's study casts doubt on the merit of good governance, a report by McKinsey & Company[3] yielded a number of interesting findings among institutional investors:

- More than 70 percent said they would pay more for the shares of a well-governed company than for those of a poorly governed company with comparable financial performance.

- More than half said corporate governance is equally or more important than financial issues, such as profit performance and growth potential, when evaluating companies in which they might invest.

- As shown in Exhibit 7-1, the actual premium investors said they would be willing to pay for a well-governed company differed by country. For example, investors said they would pay 12 percent more for the shares of a well-governed U.K. company. They would be willing to pay a 21 percent premium for one in Japan and a 38 percent premium for one in Russia.

As Exhibit 7-1 suggests, the report also indicated that corporate governance is, understandably, a greater concern in regions characterized by less stringent accounting standards. "The size of the premium that institutional investors say they are willing to pay for good governance seems to reflect

EXHIBIT 7-1   Average Premium Investors Willing to Pay for Well-Governed Company

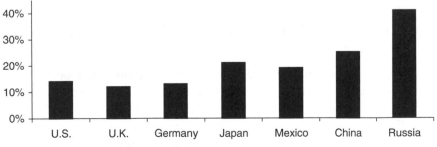

Source: McKinsey Global Investor Opinion Survey on Corporate Governance, 2002.

the extent to which they believe there is room for improvement." To me, that makes sense and is similar to the basic principle of insurance: You pay more in premiums to insure against adverse events that are more likely to happen, or more costly if they do.

Even without a clear statistical connection, there is mounting circumstantial evidence that "good governance pays." Paul Coombes, Director at McKinsey & Company's London office, pointed to the majority of investors who take corporate governance issues into consideration when making investment decisions as a "powerful argument in favor of corporate governance reform." In McKinsey & Company's 2000 survey, Coombes wrote, "If companies could capture but a small proportion of the governance premium that is apparently available, they would create significant shareholder value."

If one does believe that sound governance can enhance shareholder value, what should investors look for?

The first warning signals are conflicts between the interests of shareholders (who seek the best return on their investment) and of managers (who may be more concerned with retaining their jobs or increasing their control, regardless of the financial impact on the company). Here are five principles that help avoid such conflicts:

1. The board of directors should have a majority of truly independent, nonexecutive directors.

2. The board should have a nomination committee, responsible for proposing director nominees.

3. The board should have a compensation committee, responsible for establishing fair and transparent compensation of executive directors.

4. The board should have an audit committee, responsible for interacting with outside accountants and ensuring integrity of the company's financial information.

5. A company should have effective, transparent, and fair procedures for conducting shareholder meetings and for allowing shareholders to exercise their votes.

With respect to having independent, nonexecutive members on the board of directors, the United States leads other key developed nations (measured as a percentage of total directors). See Exhibit 7-2. However, U.S. corporations tend to have a *non*independent member as the *head* of the board of directors by often combining the roles of chairperson of the board

EXHIBIT 7-2   Independent Nonexecutive Board Members (as a Percentage of Total Directors)

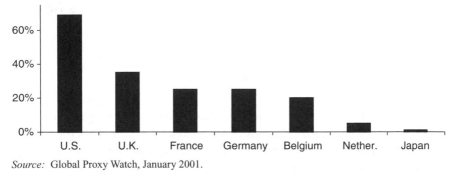

Source: Global Proxy Watch, January 2001.

with chief executive officer. More than 80 percent of S&P 500 companies feature combined chairperson-CEOs, placing the United States out of step with most other major markets.[4]

An "independent" board member refers to someone who serves on the board of directors for a company but is not employed by the company in any other capacity. In an article published in *The Wall Street Journal* in 2002, David Gale cited the collapse of Enron Corporation as an example of "shoddy oversight" on behalf of the company's board of directors. He added that it was typical of board practices in the United States: "Enron was a splendid example of a blue-ribbon group of directors who see their main role as one of monitoring a CEO's plan, not challenging it as independent and demanding representatives of the shareholders."[5]

Gale offered three suggestions (all of which I support) on how to create truly independent boards of directors:

1.   Make sure the selection process is taken away from corporate management.

2.   Mandate more candidates than vacancies so as to give a real choice.

3.   Allow any significant group of shareholders to make a nomination to the board in a reasonably simple way.

As I outlined a little earlier, I believe an independent board of directors is one of five key corporate governance elements to

While there is always the potential for fraud, I believe the accounting statements for the vast majority of businesses reflect integrity and accuracy.

avoid potential conflicts of interest. The others address such issues as compensation for executives, creating accessible avenues for shareholders to exercise their voting rights, and auditing the company's financial statements to limit fraud.

A FEW THOUGHTS ON CORPORATE ACCOUNTING STATEMENTS

The regulatory structure of the world's stock markets is designed to eliminate, or at least minimize, instances of accounting fraud. Human nature being what it is, the best regulations in the world have never been enough to stamp out thievery (and that's what accounting fraud is). When markets are in "bubbles" and stocks are climbing to successive record highs, investors tend to relax their standards and the rewards for such thievery become even more tempting to those in a position to steal.

After the technology-stock bubble of the late 1990s, accounting-related improprieties surfaced at a number of U.S. companies including Enron and WorldCom. The gamut ranged from overstating earnings (WorldCom, for example, managed to overstate by $7 billion), to insider trading, to siphoning cash out of the company. It had been rare for corporate executives to be indicted or convicted in fraud cases, but the authorities around the world gained increased regulatory powers and used them. In the case of World-Com, the Securities and Exchange Commission (SEC), the federal agency responsible for protecting investors and maintaining the integrity of the U.S. securities markets, charged the company with fraud and arrested senior executives at the firm.

Such examples of fraud attracted significant attention in the media and prompted the creation of new laws designed to bolster investor confidence in the validity of corporate accounting. While there is always the potential for fraud, I believe the accounting statements for the vast majority of businesses reflect integrity and accuracy.

At my firm, when we research companies, we delve deeply into accounting statements and scour footnotes. We seek to answer such deceptively simple questions as "What does this company do?" and "How does this company make money?" In cases where, after a thorough investigation, we cannot answer these questions with a high degree of confidence, we will generally avoid these businesses—as we did in the case of Enron and WorldCom. We have had, and continue to have, a bias in favor of companies with proven business models and relatively strong balance sheets.

Keep in mind that, despite such a focus on business specifics, there is no immunity against the risk that any company in which anyone invests may engage in deceptive accounting or go bankrupt. While my firm did not purchase shares of Enron, for example, there is no guarantee that we won't purchase shares of a company like Enron in the future—especially given the "against the grain" approach that is the hallmark of value investors.

Simply put, there is always company-specific risk associated with investing in stocks. The old adage about not "putting all your eggs in one basket" remains sound advice to reduce this risk. Based on my experience, I believe a focus on creating portfolios comprised of a number of securities that offer a reasonable margin of safety mitigates some risks and creates a good opportunity for favorable results over the long term.

OPTIONS ACCOUNTING

Evidence of recent accounting improprieties and fraud rekindled the debate regarding options, particularly how they should be classified on a company's accounting statements when they are given to employees. Typically, options give investors the right to purchase or sell shares of stock at a predetermined price within a specified period of time. People often purchase options because buying the *right* to purchase shares of stock is often cheaper than actually purchasing the shares themselves. Because options often are issued as short-term contracts (usually covering a few months), they are highly speculative instruments. I do not advocate the purchase or sale of options as an investment strategy because I don't perceive options as investments. They are for speculators.

When issued to employees, options can be a great motivating tool as they can spread ownership of a company among its workforce. As described, options represent the *right* to purchase or sell shares at a predetermined price within a predetermined period. For example, management at XYZ Corp. may reward employees by giving them the right to buy shares of XYZ stock for $35—even though the company's stock is trading at $70. This can be a great way to give employees an ownership stake in the business if employees choose to exercise their options and hold on to the company's shares.

However, because employees in this example could double their money by "exercising" this option (purchasing shares at $35 and then selling them at $70), there may be little incentive to *hold* the shares—and a greater incentive to make a short-term profit.

Alternatively, what would happen if the stock price fell from $70 to $20? In this case, the employees simply would not exercise their right to buy and would allow the option contracts to expire. (They wouldn't use their option to pay a *higher* price for shares when they could purchase them in the open market at a *lower* price if they really wanted them.) In cases where the stock price declines, companies sometimes "re-price" the options, in effect lowering the price at which employees can purchase shares. Unfortunately, the shareholders who are not employees do not share in such benefits.

By giving options, management often creates great potential for gains with virtually no risk for loss for its employees. To me, this does *not* encourage employees to establish an ownership stake in the company and remain long-term shareholders. As Warren Buffett said in countering the notion that granting employees options aligns their interests with the company, "In our book, alignment means being a partner in both directions, not just on the upside. Many 'alignment' plans flunk this basic test, being artful forms of 'heads I win, tails you lose.' "[6]

In the wake of corporate accounting scandals, options came under fire because of how companies issued them to employees and accounted for them on their books. I am not necessarily arguing against giving options to employees, although I think giving stock would promote broader ownership and encourage more long-term thinking. I *am* encouraging astute value investors to pay close attention to options accounting, particularly the rate of options issuance, as it can have a significant effect on a company's valuation. When investigating companies, you can find this information in the footnotes to the firm's financial statements.

Options Accounting: An Example

Many companies do not account for options as an expense, particularly technology firms. Executives at these companies contend that because no money actually is paid out (unlike a salary, for example), options aren't really a cost. Even if they *were* viewed as an expense, they argue that there is no accurate or commonly accepted way to value them. Thus, attempting to price them as an expense would unnecessarily distort the company's earnings. They also argue that giving options to all employees helps align shareholder and employee interests and supports the entrepreneurial environment they have worked to cultivate. I disagree. I believe there are costs associated with options issuance that need to be recognized and you *can* ascribe a value to them. Something that is *given* to employees reflects something taken away from equity holders.

Generally, there are two basic methods companies use when accounting for options. The first is to account for their cost as compensation expense on an after-tax basis. The second is not to account for them at all. If companies choose the second route, they are required to disclose the amount of net income and earnings per share that would have been reported had they used the first method.

Let's look at an example of how options accounting can influence how a company is evaluated. Taiwan Semiconductor is a large semiconductor manufacturer based in Taiwan and involved in a great deal of outsourcing business. In other words, it manufactures semiconductors for other companies.

Software engineers at Taiwan Semiconductor may command a total compensation package of $150,000 to $170,000. However, the base salary may be only $30,000 with the rest paid in stock bonuses. Stock bonuses are similar to options in that stock is essentially "given" to employees. If these bonuses are treated as expenses, it significantly raises the costs associated with salaries and diminishes the firm's earnings. In some cases, expensing options may reduce a company's earnings up to 50 percent. Thus, a business that at first appears to be attractively valued may turn out to be quite expensive after a closer investigation.

Thus far in this chapter, I have touched on various aspects of corporate governance—from options accounting to boardroom practices. I now turn my attention to courses of action for shareholders when they perceive injustices and seek to address them.

SHAREHOLDER ACTIVISM

When executives at a corporation achieve the objectives of building a highly profitable business and the value of its shares rises, management and shareholders tend to be happy. But what happens when executives do not achieve their objectives? What happens when shareholders believe that their interests are not being considered or are not properly aligned with management? What do you do when you believe a management team does not have all the skills and/or vision necessary to maximize the value of the shares you own?

Generally, when shareholders disagree with company management on important issues, they have three options:

1.   **"Hold and hope."**   They can hold on to their shares and hope management's decisions prove to be the best.
2.   **"Sell and shrug."**   They can sell their shares. This is also referred to as the "Wall Street Walk" or "voting with your feet."
3.   **"Push and prod."**   They can attempt to change the situation.

Broadly speaking, the first two options are docile approaches, while the third—an attempt to bring about a change—is loosely referred to as "shareholder activism."

Keep in mind that the topic of shareholder activism is quite broad and can refer to activities relating to what some refer to as "socially responsible" investing. These activities might include efforts aimed at altering a company's labor policies, environmental impact, or operations in certain countries. As the founder of a firm primarily dedicated to managing assets for individual and institutional investors, I confine the scope of my comments to activities aimed at improving corporate policies and practices with respect to shareholders' *economic* interests in the company.

For starters, I believe activism is more likely to succeed when it is focused on high-level corporate governance values, such as accountability, transparency, and the establishment of proper shareholder democracy, rather than on detailed operating issues. This is not to say that shareholders should not have opinions on "micro" issues. Rather, the point is simply that activism is more likely to garner support among the board, officers, and other shareholders if it is directed at key governance values, rather than social issues or matters clearly involving business judgment.

I also believe that activist efforts tend to have a greater chance of success when carried out by institutional investors rather than individuals. Institutional investors, many of whom manage money on behalf of thousands of individuals, may have more money, more extensive resources, and greater leverage than individuals.

In general, if shareholders believe that something needs to be done to realign management interests with their own, there is a broad array of tactics possible within an "active" investment strategy. These range from thoughtful proxy voting at one end of the spectrum to aggressive legal challenges, such as a proxy battle or lawsuit, at the other end. In my opinion, the most extreme measures are rarely necessary, as it is often possible for institutional investors to effect some change through private discussions with management. At the same time, as Paul Myners, chairman of Gartmore Investment Management, wrote in an extensive report addressing various aspects of institutional investment in the United Kingdom (including share-holder activism): ". . . merely meeting with senior management and expressing polite reservations about strategy is not sufficient. . . ." Instead, as he notes, successful activism often requires persistence and the willingness to raise "issues repeatedly over a period of time with firmness until concerns are addressed."[7]

John Bogle, founder of the Vanguard Group, an investment management firm, said institutional fund managers have "dropped the ball on governance for two reasons. First, most fund managers are short-term speculators, not long-term owners, so they don't have the patience or incentive to exercise oversight."[8] I agree. As addressed in Chapter 1, value investors are *not* speculators. Value investors have conviction in their research and, by nature of their long-term perspective, are generally more interested in various governance topics, especially as they relate to unlocking a company's underlying worth.

The second reason that fund managers have been lax in pushing for better governance, according to Bogle, is the potential conflict of interest between pursuing the best interests of existing shareholders and attracting potential clients.

Most publicly traded companies have pension plan committees that oversee the firm's pension plan assets. The committees also make decisions on which investment firms to hire—and which to fire—for the management of those pension plan assets. Upon learning of activist efforts targeted at their firm, these committee members may be reluctant to hire the activist manager. In most cases, any firm targeted for activism by an investment manager represents a potential client that likely can be crossed off the manager's prospecting list. But I believe the top priority for institutional money managers should be serving the best interests of their *existing* clients. This is exactly the way I have managed my firm since its inception in 1974.

In addition to losing potential clients, there are other reasons why institutional investors may be dissuaded from pursuing activist strategies, including expenses, legal issues, and the possibility of adverse publicity. Engaging in activism is often expensive. It may demand outside legal and accounting advice, proxy solicitation assistance, and public-media relations consulting. Further, the cost of hiring these external experts does not offset the costs associated with the diversion of time and talent for the firm's *internal* resources.

In addition, institutional investors may face a variety of legal and regulatory impediments demanding a significant investment of time and resources to overcome. Among the factors to consider are the potential for a manager to become an "insider" and face trading restrictions, complex rules governing communication with other shareholders, and complications related to potential appointments to the board of directors.

Further, managers must evaluate the potential that existing clients could be sensitive to the diversion of time and talent that activism entails, or may even view activism as an expensive rationalization for poor stock selection. Further, there is the potential for negative media coverage if managers embark upon activism—even if the managers are successful in effecting the changes they seek. Often, the tone and content of media messages are difficult to manage and publicity may have adverse effects on how the managers are perceived.

SO WHY ENGAGE IN SHAREHOLDER ACTIVISM?

In his book, *The Memoirs of the Dean of Wall Street,* Benjamin Graham shares an account of his first experience as a shareholder activist. In 1925, as a result of his careful research, he believed that shares of Northern Pipeline were trading at a significant discount to the company's underlying value. Northern Pipeline was one of 31 companies created following the U.S. Supreme Court's decision in 1911 to break up the Standard Oil monopoly. Graham discovered that Northern Pipeline owned large amounts of high-quality bonds, was operating with a large profit margin, carried no inventory, and "therefore had no need whatever for these bond investments."[9] Enthused by the results of his research, Graham wrote: "Here was Northern Pipeline, selling at only $65 a share, paying a $6 dividend—while holding some $95 in cash assets for each share, nearly all of which it could distribute to its stockholders without the slightest inconvenience to its operations. Talk about a bargain security!"

When Graham acquired about a 5 percent stake in the company, he attempted to "persuade Northern Pipeline management to do the right and obvious thing: to return a good part of the unneeded capital to the owners, the stockholders. Naively, I thought this should be rather easy to accomplish."[10]

Later Graham would write, "When, in all innocence, I made my first effort as a stockholder in 1926 to persuade a management to do something other than what it was doing, old Wall Street hands regarded me as a crack-brained Don Quixote tilting at a giant windmill. 'If you don't like the management or what it's doing, sell your stock'—that had long been the beginning and end of Wall Street's wisdom in this domain, and it is still the predominant doctrine."[11]

Through research and persistence, Graham described how he eventually became one of the first people not directly affiliated with the Standard Oil system to be elected to the board of directors for one of its affiliate companies. Eventually, Northern Pipeline followed Graham's advice and distributed unneeded capital and

> *Shareholder activism remains an option for institutional money managers and pension plans to consider on a case-by-case basis in seeking to foster long-term wealth creation.*

newly created shares to existing shareholders. Graham wrote that the value "of the new Northern Pipeline stock plus the cash returned ultimately reached an aggregate of more than $110 per old share." Keep in mind that when Graham began his research, shares were selling at $65 per share.

I share Graham's story because I believe it reflects the value of pursuing an activist strategy in certain cases. In light of the premium investors are willing to pay for sound corporate governance and what I believe to be the potential for unlocking additional shareholder value at select firms, I think shareholder activism remains an option for institutional money managers and pension plans to consider on a case-by-case basis in seeking to foster long-term wealth creation.

Like Graham, my firm has engaged selectively in activism. We have held discussions with senior management, traveled to shareholder meetings to present ideas, and challenged mergers and acquisitions—all with the intent of better unlocking shareholder value for existing clients. Our success in these pursuits has varied. Regardless of whether we achieve our objectives, if we believe we can make a positive contribution to generating shareholder value through activism, we will consider it.

CONCLUSION

Given the variety of constraints institutional money managers face when considering activism—from regulatory impediments to execution issues to profitability factors—I still believe that it is worthwhile for institutional investors and pension plans to devote some time and resources to evaluating whether activism is in the long-term interests of their beneficiaries. Assuming that this is the case, some effort should also be devoted to considering how institutional money managers can be encouraged, like Benjamin Graham, to periodically "tilt at windmills."

Notes

1. From www.encycogov.com/ *The Journal of Finance,* Shleifer and Vishny, 1997, p. 737.

2. Bernard Black, "The Corporate Governance Behavior and Market Value of Russian Firms," *Emerging Markets Review,* vol. 2, 2001.

3. McKinsey & Company's Global Investor Opinion Survey was undertaken between April and May 2002, in cooperation with the Global Corporate Governance Forum. The survey was based on responses from more than 200 institutional investors, who together are responsible for approximately US$2 trillion in assets.

4. Stephen Davis, ed., *Global Proxywatch: The Newsletter of International Corporate Governance and Shareowner Value,* vol. 6, no. 32, September 13, 2002.

5. David Gale, "How to Create Truly Independent Boards," *The Wall Street Journal,* August 12, 2002.

6. Lawrence A. Cunningham, ed., *The Essays of Warren Buffett: Lessons for Corporate America,* The Cunningham Group: New York, 2000, p. 60.

7. Paul Myners, "Institutional Investment in the United Kingdom: A Review," March 6, 2001, p. 92, www.hm-treasury.gov.uk/media//843F0/31.pdf.

8. Marc Gunther, "Investors of the World Unite!" *Fortune,* June 24, 2002, p. 86.

9. Benjamin Graham, *The Memoirs of the Dean of Wall Street,* New York: McGraw-Hill, 1996, p. 200.

10. Ibid., p. 201.

11. Ibid., p. 204.

3

Learning to Think Globally

Investors who limit their search for value stocks to their domestic market are missing out on a world of opportunities. In this section, I make the case for thinking globally and extending the application of value-investing principles to markets outside of your own. Value-investing principles can deliver solid long-term results, regardless of the country in which they're applied. I also explore the logistics of investing abroad, with a focus on the types of securities and funds a value investor with a global perspective needs to understand. Finally, I discuss the wide range of issues that accompany international investment, from currency fluctuations to political risks to country-by-country differences in accounting standards.

8

WHY GO OVERSEAS?

It's understandable that investors, regardless of where they live, may limit themselves to opportunities within their own country. Human nature drives us to keep within known boundaries. We're sometimes reluctant to place our trust and dreams in the markets of countries that might seem better suited to wild-eyed speculators than prudent investors.

Based on my experience, investors, and not just in the United States, put very limited amounts of their assets abroad—typically no more than 10 to 15 percent, if any. In today's world of global information, that seems a little odd, but there are two factors acting to narrow investors' horizons, no matter what their nationality.

First, investors may simply not know about the opportunities abroad: their local media coverage is focused largely on companies in their own country. Although they can certainly find out about overseas opportunities, generally no one is bringing them to their attention.

Second, even if they do know about opportunities around the world, they don't believe they know *enough* about them to make overseas investment worthwhile. In my view, that's a big mistake. Let me explain.

Back in 1974, when I started my firm, my first client wanted a global portfolio—one that included companies from all over the world, including the United States. As I built my experience and capabilities running this portfolio, it became clear to me that not only could I find more opportunities when looking around the world, but many times they were better opportunities than in the home market. The key for a global value investor is to maintain the value discipline, while using its flexibility to apply it potentially in all areas of the world. Remember that to succeed, you don't need to know everything about every company and every country. You just have to know *enough* to find the opportunities, evaluate them, and then move in with a patient value approach.

What makes me think that anyone can know *enough* about an investment abroad to profit from it, when the local investors may have a great deal more information on the company and on local market conditions? I've found over the years that while the "locals" may have more information, they tend to use it with a short-term time horizon and without a sense of global perspective. In other words, they know the trees in great detail, but they rarely look at the forest.

In Chapter 10, "Unique Aspects of Global Investing," I'll review some of the important considerations investors need to be aware of when purchasing shares in various markets around the world. Right now, I will focus on *why* investing abroad—including investing in emerging markets—can be advantageous.

There are two overriding reasons for diversifying your holdings to include a significant percentage of overseas stocks. First, as I've already said, markets outside one's home country can provide tremendous opportunity. No matter what country you live in, most of the world's businesses are located outside your market. And second, investing around the world can deliver diversification benefits, namely, the reduction of overall portfolio risk, as measured by volatility or fluctuation in short-term returns.

As I described briefly in Chapter 3, it's vital to recognize that the terms *risk* and *volatility* are often used interchangeably—yet they can have quite different connotations. Short-term volatility should not be of much concern to long-term value investors, unless they lack the temperament to adhere to a value-investing philosophy. In Chapter 11, I'll examine misperceptions regarding volatility and risk, and in Chapter 13, I'll share suggestions on how to stick to the principles described in this book.

In *this* chapter, I'll provide examples illustrating the benefits of investing abroad. I'll also address the concept of "correlation" among returns, how active management can be especially beneficial when investing in global markets, and the opportunities and risks of investing in developing countries.

A WORLD WITHOUT BOUNDARIES

Every few years, the cyclical nature of the world's markets leads to pronouncements from market "experts," such as *Things have changed*, or *It's different this time*. This sentiment seems to surface periodically in markets around the globe. During the 1980s, the boom years for the Japanese stock market, Japanese investors scoffed at the idea of investing in Europe or the United States. Then, during the late 1990s as the Nasdaq boomed, many U.S. investors began to question the wisdom of investing in Europe or Asia.

As an illustration, let's look at returns for the Morgan Stanley Capital International (MSCI) EAFE Index. MSCI is a leading provider of global indices for investors worldwide. "EAFE" stands for Europe, Australasia, and Far East. The term "Australasia" refers to Australia and New Zealand. Thus, the MSCI EAFE Index is a measure of non-U.S. stocks in developed countries.

From 1980 to 1989, the MSCI EAFE Index gained an annualized 22.0 percent per year, handily outpacing the S&P 500's 17.5 percent annualized gain. However, during the 1990–1999 era, the tables were turned, with the S&P 500 gaining an annualized 18.2 percent, well ahead of the MSCI EAFE's 7.0 percent annualized advance. (From the beginning of 2000 through 2002, both indices suffered substantial declines: The MSCI EAFE shed a total of 43.3 percent, while the S&P 500 fell a cumulative 37.6 percent.)

What lessons should we learn from the past performance of global markets? Did the benefits of international investing (defined from a U.S. viewpoint as investing outside the United States) indeed disappear in the 1990s?

First, you should expect that there likely will be regions where stocks outperform your home market over any specified time period. Exhibit 8-1 illustrates that, for U.S. investors, their home market was never the top performer during the 10-year period between 1993 and 2002. Even if your home market has been at the top of the rankings for a while, you'll find opportunities elsewhere. In fact, a period at the top may well be followed by a significant decline. Many investors make the mistake of trying to put their money in *after* a market has moved to the top, not before. That leads to a second point: If you're looking at a region of the world that has lagged recently, that suggests there may be more opportunities to be checked out, not fewer.

So the answer to my earlier question is: No, the benefits of international investing have not disappeared. There are *always* good reasons for diversifying your holdings among nonlocal markets, and these reasons

EXHIBIT 8-1   Best-Performing Equity Market, 1993–2002

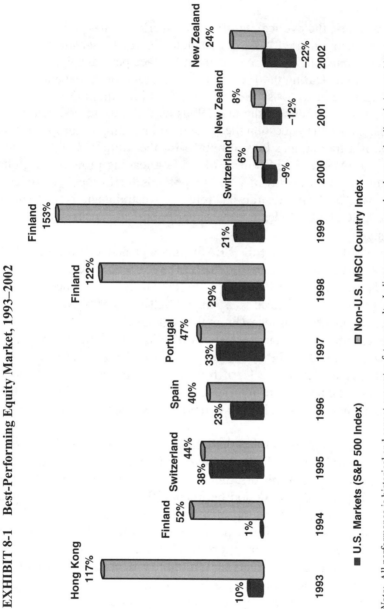

Note: All performance is historical and cannot guarantee future results. Indices are unmanaged and cannot be directly invested into.

Source: RIMES Technologies Corp. and Bloomberg (data as of December 31, 2002).

apply to both U.S. and non-U.S. investors. I'll now look in more detail at those opportunities and diversification benefits of international investing.

Opportunity

There are always good reasons for diversifying your holdings among nonlocal markets, and these reasons apply to both U.S. and non-U.S. investors.

Fear and greed, two driving factors behind irrational stock prices, are not limited to geopolitical borders. At any given time, investors can identify speculative markets where bargains are hard to find and depressed markets where bargains abound. Value investors who search outside their local stock market may find attractive opportunities in markets that have reacted adversely for a year or more, suffering the impact of short-term traders.

Markets worldwide have expanded over recent decades, more so in Europe and Asia than in North America. This is due to a combination of stock price moves and the substantial amount of new capital raised by existing and new companies. Non-U.S. markets represented 46 percent of the global total in 2002.[1] This compares to only 34 percent in 1970. It also represents $6 trillion in stocks based outside the United States. Anyone who claims that it's not worthwhile investing outside the United States is basically claiming that none of that $6 trillion in stocks represents the availability of a good investment opportunity. I find that hard to believe.

Although they are quite accessible, many overseas stocks remain less visible to institutional and individual investors. Let's use investors in the United States as an example. If they confine themselves to the North American markets, they limit themselves to less than one-half of the world's opportunities. An investor who researches only the U.S. and Canadian markets may find nearly 3200 stocks with a market capitalization of at least $100 million for consideration. The same investor who decides to look globally can select the best prospects from nearly 6700 stocks, a much greater universe to explore.[2]

McDonald's, for example, attracts much attention in the U.S. financial press. Morningstar, a global investment research firm, reported in early 2003 that 16 brokerage analysts in the United States review reports, data, and management decisions on the company, and every analyst offered estimates for annual earnings. Many widely read financial newspapers and magazines and popular financial television programs report constantly on developments for the company's outlook. It's also one of the best known of all U.S. companies worldwide, both to consumers and investors.

McDonald's may be a good investment for a value investor. However, it's widely recognized and well covered by analysts and based in a market with plenty of bargain-hunting value investors. This means that the decision to own the stock is generally going to be based on the investor's interpretation of the known information and analysis.

Contrast this with Telefónica, the telecom giant in Spain, a company whose market cap of roughly $50 billion exceeds that of McDonald's by roughly $36 billion. Yet, for most U.S. investors, Telefónica is off the radar screen: There's almost no media coverage or analysts following the company in North America. Morningstar reported just two U.S. analysts who cover the company, and only one offered an estimate of earnings. Of course, several analysts in Europe follow the company, but value investors are less common in Europe, so those analysts, and the investors they advise, don't necessarily look at Telefónica from our value-based perspective. Thus, despite analysis that's widely distributed to European investors, a U.S.-based value investor's decision to own the stock still may make sense as there may be few others looking at the company's "value attributes." That's an environment where bargains abound for a value investor with a global perspective. Keep in mind that when a limited number of investors are looking at the same information or at the company with the same perspective as you are, it can take years, not weeks, before its virtues are discovered.

Diversification Benefits

Putting all your money into the stocks of one *country* is a limiting strategy. Sensible investors diversify, and cross-border investing is an important part of that approach. Ironically, some investors equate the phrase "foreign stock" with risk. The reality is that just the opposite is true. Often, the inverse, or noncorrelating, relationship between stock markets can help *reduce* volatility in a balanced portfolio.

In addition, risk (defined here as the potential for losing money when investing) can be reduced through long-term investments in companies whose stock is undervalued in relation to the real value of the business, and the world's various stock markets offer tremendous opportunities to find such businesses. (Remember the basic principle from earlier chapters? No single factor tends to lower risk more than buying a company at a favorable price.) Looking forward, investors might be well served to pay heed to findings from a 2002 study by Dimson, Marsh, and Staunton:

Investors in most countries . . . would have been better off investing worldwide, but there were exceptions. These were countries that performed very well while enjoying low volatility. Unfortunately, we can spot these markets only with hindsight. If they could be identified in advance, they would be instantly re-rated, thus lowering their expected returns. So looking ahead, and while there are no guarantees, our best guess is that international investment will offer a higher reward for risk due to the risk reduction from international diversification.[3]

Small- and Mid-Cap Stocks

When looking overseas, do not restrict your search only to familiar, larger-cap companies. Attractive bargains and compelling opportunities can be found within the small- and mid-cap segments of international markets. Smaller caps may offer enhanced return and diversification benefits, particularly for U.S. investors. In 1996, the *Financial Analysts Journal* published an article that asserted that international value stocks and smaller-cap international stocks provided greater diversification benefits for U.S.-based investors than the constituents typically found in the EAFE Index. "In fact, a sensible reason to diversify internationally is to 'load up' on value stocks and small stocks without concentrating in one geographic region."[4]

Smaller-cap stocks, because they tend to attract less analyst coverage, can be ideal targets for diligent value investors. The lack of attention devoted to these smaller companies around the world can create opportunities for value investors to identify and capitalize on pricing inefficiencies. Keep in mind that investing in smaller caps often includes certain risks that may not be as prevalent among larger caps. For instance, small companies tend to have lower trading volumes and fewer shares outstanding. Thus, their stock prices can fluctuate more significantly in the short term.

Smaller caps also may be less liquid. In addition, the businesses may be more susceptible to macroeconomic factors. For example, recessions or rising interest rates may affect smaller businesses more acutely than well-established, larger-cap firms. Having shared these aspects associated with investing in smaller caps, I want to add that while these factors can influence stock prices in the short term, I think they're largely irrelevant for long-term investors. Over time, I believe investors in markets worldwide eventually come to recognize an undervalued business, regardless of the firm's size or where it is headquartered.

I urge you not to allow fears about global investing to keep you from participating in these potentially rewarding markets. Overall, I think we've learned to accept without question the international brand names with which we regularly come in contact: Airbus, Nokia, Nestle, and Sony, for example. Products and services from businesses around the world are an integral part of our lives. Yet what we have not learned to do with any consistency is to think beyond our borders—to think globally—when it comes to investment opportunities.

CORRELATION OF RETURNS

Some investors focus on "zigs and zags." They are overly concerned with short-term price volatility and the notion of *correlation*.

But what *is* correlation? The co-movement, or "correlation coefficient," is an impressive-sounding term for a statistical measure of the extent to which one market's movement can be explained by the movement of another market. Simply put, correlation refers to how closely returns in one market parallel returns in another. When one market zigs, another market often zags. And at any given time, the world's stock markets may well be out of sync with one another.

For example, while the S&P 500 Index returned a mere 5 percent in 1989, the Japanese stock market enjoyed a 43 percent gain. The Hong Kong stock market topped all performers for three different years between 1979 and 1988, but in 1982, it tumbled 42 percent while the S&P 500 advanced 21 percent. When the S&P 500 gained 1 percent in 1994, Finland's market rose by 52 percent. And when the S&P 500 lost 12 percent in 2001, New Zealand gained 8 percent. Thus, the addition of nondomestic stocks to a portfolio that contains only domestic stocks can reduce overall volatility by bringing together assets with low correlations.

Technically speaking, the correlation coefficient is measured on a scale ranging from −1.0 to +1.0. At one extreme, a +1.0 correlation between two markets means that they are moving in lock step. If market A moves up 1 percent, so does market B. Conversely, a −1.0 correlation between two markets means that they are moving in totally opposite directions, but by equal amounts. Thus, if market A moves up 1 percent, market B moves *down* 1 percent. A zero correlation signifies no relationship whatsoever—an independent relationship, not an inverse one. (Perhaps we would all like to have a zero correlation with that nosy neighbor who drops by too often.)

The purpose of tracking a market's correlation coefficient is to maximize the risk-reduction benefits of diversification. If half of an investor's assets are in U.S. stocks and the remaining portion is concentrated in markets with a high correlation to the United States, what little diversification is achieved will probably not translate into the meaningful reduction of volatility. Minimizing volatility requires diversifying into markets with *low* correlation coefficients. Put simply, *high* correlation means *low* diversification benefits. *Low* correlation means *high* benefits.

Overall, I believe correlation is only important if you're worried about short-term price fluctuations. For long-term value investors, it should not be an area of emphasis. I'll show you why.

CORRELATION CYCLES

Low correlations between various equity markets result from any of a number of factors. The most common reason is nonsynchronous economic cycles. For example, one country's economy could be falling into recession while another nation's economy may just be gathering steam. Politics, fiscal policy, and popular sentiment also may come into play to create different economic landscapes from one market to another.

The correlation between U.S. and non-U.S. stocks increased between 1997 and 2002.[5] In fact, in 2002, the correlation had climbed to its highest level in decades. As of year-end 2002, the 5-year rolling correlation was 0.89. (Remember that a correlation close to 1.0 suggests limited benefits.) See Exhibit 8-2. However, when the second edition of this book was published early in 1998, the correlation between these asset classes was near its *lowest* point in the last 20 years. The 5-year correlation was 0.25 in December 1997.

In 2002, many U.S. investors who were concerned with short-term volatility pointed to high correlations between U.S. and non-U.S. stocks and believed international diversification provided few benefits. I believe these concerns reflected too great an emphasis on a short-term time frame. As Exhibit 8-2 shows, the average 5-year correlation between U.S. stocks and non-U.S. stocks over the 25-year period ending December 31, 2002, was far lower: 0.63, suggesting meaningful benefits. I believe the short-term fluctuations in correlations underscore the need for *greater* diversification, not less.

In 2001, professors at Yale University published a report that highlighted the cyclical nature of diversification benefits. The professors argued that at some times, international stocks provide greater diversifica-

EXHIBIT 8-2   MSCI EAFE Index versus S&P 500 Index 5-Year Rolling Correlation

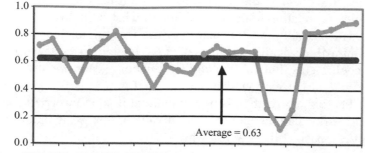

Note: All performance is historical and cannot guarantee future results. Indices are unmanaged and cannot be directly invested into.
Source: RIMES Technologies Corp. (data as of December 31, 2002).

tion benefits than at other times: ". . . the diversification benefits to global investing are not constant, and that they are currently low compared to the rest of capital market history."

At the time their report was published, correlations were high and thus, international stocks had not helped substantially diversify a portfolio in recent years. Some may have viewed the professors' findings as a reason to *eliminate* international exposure. Contrarians, believing correlations might revert toward their historical average, might have viewed the findings as a clue to *increase* international holdings. I did not endorse either approach.

In my opinion, such practices are speculative and similar to market timing. Instead, I encourage investors to consistently maintain adequate exposure to international equities in order to fully participate in the long-term appreciation potential that markets around the world provide. And for investors worried about short-term price fluctuations, I remind them that such volatility is inherent when investing. Diversifying assets across various markets can help to limit volatility—not necessarily over a 2- or 3-year period—but generally over the long term.

U.S. MULTINATIONALS

Some U.S. investors mistakenly believe that U.S.-based multinationals provide diversification benefits. By "multinationals," I refer to U.S-based

companies such as Pfizer and General Electric that derive a substantial portion of their business from
outside the United States. Based on
historical evidence, shares of U.S.

*U.S. multinationals are
poor substitutes for
non-U.S. stocks.*

multinationals, despite their overseas exposure, generally move in tandem
with the U.S. stock market. In essence, their overseas exposure does not
translate into a significant diversification benefit for U.S.-based investors.

Between January 1985 and March 1998, returns for an equal-weighted
portfolio of a group of U.S. multinationals showed a 0.89 correlation with
the S&P 500 Index. Over the same period, returns for the MSCI EAFE
Index were just 0.48 correlated with the S&P 500. (Remember, the MSCI
EAFE Index is a measure of returns in developed markets outside the
United States.) This study suggests U.S. multinationals (as measured by
companies deriving more than 50 percent of revenue from outside the
United States) are poor substitutes for non-U.S. stocks as they provide far
less diversification than the non-U.S. stocks contained in the MSCI EAFE
Index. "Just as each country's capital markets reflect its economy, individual companies tend to track their home markets, no matter how ubiquitous
their international presence," according to the study. "Buying companies
based abroad is required for true global diversification."[6]

CURRENCY FLUCTUATIONS

"How many euros can I get for 100 yen?"

Similar to correlations of returns between markets, global currency
values have fluctuated significantly and thus have had varying degrees of
influence for global investors at different times. I'll address currency movements in greater detail in Chapter 10, "Unique Aspects of Global Investing." For now, I'll note that all currencies—U.S. dollars, euros, Japanese
yen, Mexican pesos, and so on—can fluctuate in relative value. If you have
ever traveled to another country, you likely have first-hand experience with
differences in currency values. Residents of France, for example, may say
it's a good time to visit Japan because the euro (the currency in France) is
"strong relative to the yen." What does that mean? Put simply, when they
exchange euros for yen, French visitors will get far more yen to spend during their stay in Japan than they might have received months or years earlier. They will have greater purchasing power, and thus Japanese goods are
"cheaper" than they may have been in the past.

Just as currency fluctuations affect how much travelers can purchase when visiting overseas countries, currency moves influence returns for global investors.

However, as we saw with correlations, currency values have oscillated over time. Exhibit 8-3 shows the cost in U.S. dollars of 1 pound, 1 euro, and 10,000 yen over the 25-year period ending December 31, 2002. (The deutsche mark is used as a proxy for the euro prior to the latter currency's initial circulation at the beginning of 1999.)

As with country exposure, I advocate maintaining adequate exposure to various currencies to provide appreciation potential and diversification benefits.

INTERNATIONAL BARGAIN HUNTING

From a historical perspective, value investors who broadened their investment horizons to include stocks in various countries may have been able to take advantage of (or avoid) a number of irrational price anomalies in markets around the world. For example, valuations in Japan in the early 1990s (P/E ratios of 40 to 50 and earnings yields around 2 percent) made no sense. For that matter, Japan trading at three times earnings in 1963 made no sense either. Similarly, the U.S. market in 1981 offered a number of attractively priced stocks, while a number of stocks were extremely overvalued in 2000.

Why do markets swing to such extremes? Jeremy Grantham, a renowned investor, shared his thoughts: ". . . the market[s are] gloriously

EXHIBIT 8-3   25 Years of Currency Fluctuations (Change in Value of Pound Sterling, Euro, and Yen: 1977–2002)

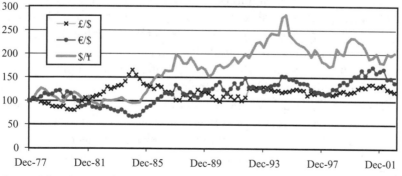

Source: Bloomberg, as of December 31, 2002.

inefficient . . . the manifestations of the inefficiency are that they horribly emphasize comfort and discomfort . . . they extrapolate today's conditions forever so if inflation is low, they assume inflation will be low forever . . . the real world is mean reverting. . . ."[7] Value investors who recognize market swings as opportunities often can uncover attractive investments in markets around the world.

CHOOSE THE COMPANY, NOT THE COUNTRY OR SECTOR

As a proponent of a bottom-up investment style, I have no use for the strategy that allocates worldwide stock purchases according to country. Bottom-up investors choose the stock first. Where the company happens to be domiciled plays a role in the decision-making process only to the extent that prudent managers should be cautious about becoming overly concentrated in securities based in any single country and the extent to which uncertainties demand a higher margin of safety.

Top-down investors take a different approach. Top-down strategies are based on country allocations as a first step. This approach has been a prevalent one among global managers for decades, especially those based in Europe and Asia. "Top-downers" begin by trying to identify the most attractive countries or local economies in which to invest; then they pick stocks in those regions. They also may attempt to build portfolios with country weightings that mirror a particular index.

At my firm, we are more interested in hunting down individual companies with promising fundamentals and attractive prices than we are in assessing general economic trends. Our assumption is that individual companies can be welcome additions to the portfolio, regardless of where the business is based. Limiting your investment scope only to the United States, for example, limits your opportunities. Here's an example.

POSCO is South Korea's largest integrated producer of various steel products. In 2002, its stock represented a reasonable valuation accompanied by world-class assets that afforded the company a cost position few global producers could match. In addition, the firm was operating with a consistently conservative debt-to-equity ratio that I believe often is prudent for cyclical businesses. With the stock selling at US$24 per ADR, the valuation represented a compelling 85 percent of book value, 12 times depressed 2001 earnings, and 4 times depressed 2001 cash flow.

By comparison, Nucor was the second-largest steel company in the United States at the time with a cost position that rivaled that of POSCO. Nucor was considered an entrepreneurial organization that used its debt-free balance sheet to make acquisitions at opportune moments. It sounded like a great business, if its shares could be purchased at the right price. Between 1997 and 2002, its stock price dropped to a level near the company's book value only once and only for a brief period. Most often, it traded at much higher multiples of book, earnings, and cash flows. With the stock at $45 per share in 2002, it traded at 1.6 times book, more than 30 times depressed 2001 earnings and 9 times depressed 2001 cash flow. Given these valuations, I believed POSCO represented a far more attractive investment candidate at the time.

This example offers a glimpse of the tremendous investment opportunities available overseas, and not only in developed markets but also in emerging countries. The world's emerging markets, countries such as South Korea, Brazil, Argentina, Turkey, and India, offer many compelling opportunities.

EMERGING MARKETS

As I stated earlier, there are advantages to applying a value approach where information is less well distributed, or less well analyzed, or where there are few other value investors looking at stocks in the same way. This describes the environment in emerging markets. Before reviewing the advantages of investing there, let's look at what comprises this segment of the world's markets.

The difference between developed and emerging markets is largely a function of the size of each country's underlying economy. The World Bank classifies 170 nations as "low income" or "middle income," with per capita gross national income (GNI) of $9205 or lower. In comparison, per capita GNI in the United States is over $25,000.

Not all of these 170 countries, however, have securities worth researching, and many don't have a stock market at all. I also take issue with calling a market emerging just because it's less developed. Many of these emerging markets can be described better as "submerging," at least from time to time. The emerging markets you should consider are those with sufficient infrastructure (both for the economy and their stock market), reasonably substantial companies, and potential for economic growth in the longer term.

As of December 31, 2002, the Morgan Stanley Capital International (MSCI) Emerging Markets Free (EMF) Index consisted of 26 emerging countries indices. As described earlier, MSCI is a leading provider of global indices. MSCI includes the following countries in the EMF Index: Argentina, Brazil, Chile, China, Colombia, Czech Republic, Egypt, Hungary, India, Indonesia, Israel, Jordan, Korea, Malaysia, Mexico, Morocco, Pakistan, Peru, the Philippines, Poland, Russia, South Africa, Taiwan, Thailand, Turkey, and Venezuela. Both MSCI and Citigroup* track regional emerging market indices for Latin America, Asia, Europe, the Middle East, and Africa.

The conventional arguments for investing in emerging market stocks can be summarized in the seven items below:

1. **Size.** Emerging markets include some very substantial economies, either by population measure (Brazil) or by GNI (South Korea). The nearly six billion people living in emerging nations account for more than 85 percent of the world's population.[8]

2. **Undercapitalized markets.** Output from developing economies represents roughly 18 percent of global GDP, yet emerging markets are capitalized at just 4 percent of the aggregate value of the world's equity markets.[9] Simply put, those figures suggest there is considerable room for share-price appreciation, even without above-average economic growth.

3. **Rapid growth.** Many of the fastest-growing countries in the world are home to emerging markets. According to the World Bank, the economies of low- and middle-income nations grew at a 3.5 percent annual rate between 1990 and 1999—substantially more than the 2.5 percent rate posted by high-income nations such as the United States.[10]

4. **Improving liquidity.** In the past, emerging markets were generally illiquid and often restricted investment from investors outside their regions. As developing economies become more dependent on capital to fund improvements in infrastructure, emerging markets likely will continue to be more open to foreign investment.

5. **Flexibility.** Another benefit of investing in emerging countries is their ability to adjust to periods of expansion and contraction. This is a direct result of minimal wage and employment restrictions. If the economy of an emerging country is slowing, companies are better able to adapt by adjusting production capacity than are companies in large industrialized countries, which often have strict minimum wage legislation and employment protection laws.

*Effective April 7, 2003, the names of Salomon Smith Barney indices were changed to Citigroup indices. For example, the name of the Salomon Smith Barney Global Equity Index was changed to the Citigroup Global Equity Index.

6.   **Market inefficiencies.** Since emerging markets are generally the
      least-researched segment of the equity universe, they can be a great
      source for undiscovered values. As a result, the astute international
      investor may be able to get in on the ground floor of many solid
      businesses and profit from emerging nations' typically above-
      average growth rates.

7.   **Diversification.** Investments in emerging markets usually
      diversify a portfolio to a greater extent than investing in only
      developed countries, or those in the MSCI EAFE Index, particu-
      larly for U.S. investors. That's because the equity markets in
      emerging countries have substantially lower correlations with the
      United States than do those of developed countries. For investors
      concerned with price fluctuation, including emerging markets in
      an international portfolio can decrease volatility while offering
      great growth prospects.

Those are the conventional arguments. Combined with the lack of competition from other well-informed, disciplined value investors, these are
compelling indeed. But there's one more aspect of emerging market
investing that to me is very appealing, but to others may be somewhat
controversial.

These markets can swing from euphoria to despondency in relatively
short periods. As a result, emerging market performance (as measured by
the MSCI EMF Index) has been as spectacular as 74.8 percent (1993) or as
awful as –30.6 percent (2000). Over longer periods, gains have been substantial: The annualized increase between 1987 and 2002 was about 10 percent, reinforcing the potential opportunity. The end result is that periodically
most investors will not go near emerging markets, and those value investors
who do pursue bargains at those times may be ridiculed by peers (or even
worse, by clients!). But this is exactly when the patience and discipline of
the true value investor may pay off spectacularly.

LESS COMPETITION

In most businesses, including the business of investing, lack of competition
often leads to higher profits. Whether investing in a developed country like
the United States, developed non-U.S. markets, or emerging markets, it's easier to find bargains when there are fewer bargain hunters around.

I believe that the majority of investors in non-U.S. markets still favor growth-investing strategies. In checking the InvestWorks database of investment managers at year-end 2002, I looked at the number of large-cap investment funds with a pronounced tilt (over 60 percent) to a growth or value style. For international funds, the number of growth funds offered outnumbered value funds by a ratio of more than 5 to 1. In contrast, among U.S. funds, there were about 30 percent more value funds offered than growth. That means it's a different story in North America, where there's considerably more elbowing than there used to be for undervalued domestic stocks. Value investing attracted many converts in the early 2000s, particularly after returns for growth stocks slumped. Outside North America, however, institutional or individual investors do not generally follow the disciplined value-investing philosophy. The combination of less empirical research and fewer investors seeking underpriced securities around the world provides opportunity for the disciplined value investor.

International accounting standards and worldwide electronic trading may eventually diminish many of these market inefficiencies. At the same time, I believe rationality will never fully determine market values—in *any* market. The gamut of human emotions—from greed and enthusiasm to fear and pessimism—can alter perceived or short-term values and send prices spinning up or down, creating opportunities for the perceptive investor with a global scope.

ACTIVE MANAGEMENT VERSUS INDEXING

Broadly speaking, the terms *passive management, investing in index funds,* and *indexing* refer to an approach that seeks to replicate the performance of a particular index such as the MSCI EAFE, the MSCI EMF, or the S&P 500. Thus, managers overseeing these portfolios tend to purchase only those companies in a certain index or enough of them to mimic the index's performance. Such strategies are called "passive" because the decisions regarding which stocks to purchase or sell are dictated by the composition of the index. If several companies are removed from the index and new ones are added, for example, passive managers likely will seek to replicate these changes in the portfolios they oversee.

Thus, instead of making reasoned choices by evaluating the value of an individual business in relation to its stock price, index fund managers buy

Index funds have been around for decades and come into increasing favor with each bull market.

and sell a basket of stocks to match the performance of some broad-based index that mirrors the market as a whole.

Index fund portfolio managers generally have no need to conduct extensive, company-specific fundamental analysis. They simply buy whatever stocks are in the index they are tracking. One advantage to such an approach is that the costs to run such funds are often less than actively managed funds where portfolio managers rely on their own research and stock-selection skills in creating and managing a portfolio.

Index funds have been around for decades and come into increasing favor with each bull market. In the late 1990s, for example, index funds delivered solid gains and raised questions about the usefulness of hiring active managers. However, there are important considerations investors need to recognize when investing in index funds, namely, their contribution toward irrational pricing. Think about what I've addressed throughout this book: the importance of evaluating the difference between business value and stock price for *every* holding in your portfolio. Managers of index funds don't adhere to this process. They simply buy what is held in a certain index.

Many index funds, like the indices they try to mirror, are capitalization weighted. That means that money invested in an index fund is not equally distributed among all the fund's holdings. Using a simple example, if you invested $100 in an index fund that held 100 stocks, it is unlikely that the fund would hold $1 worth of 100 stocks. Looking at a portion of your fund holdings, you might have $5 invested in one company and only 50 cents invested in 10 others. Thus, the stocks with the greatest weight in the portfolio have the greatest influence on returns. If their price climbs, they constitute a larger percentage of the portfolio and have a greater effect on overall results.

Further, if you *add* money to an index fund that's appreciating, your contributions will be distributed disproportionately among the holdings, that is, the companies with the greatest weighting receive the biggest allocation. This aspect of how index funds are structured reflects what I believe to be a built-in, irrational approach to investing. In essence, investors buy more of the stocks that have experienced significant price increases. Not surprisingly, this approach works magnificently during bull markets when escalating share prices create a short-term, self-fulfilling prophecy. But when the market turns and stock prices begin to fall, it exacerbates losses.

My philosophy, which is also central to that of my firm, is based on the premise that through fundamental research and application of value-investing principles, it is possible to achieve superior long-term performance. Indexing is a direct contradiction of that philosophy. Thus, rather than "following the crowd" or selecting stocks for a portfolio simply because they're part of an index, I urge you to conduct your own research—or hire an active portfolio manager—and invest only in those companies that are fundamentally sound and offer a margin of safety.

ACTIVE MANAGEMENT CAN ADD VALUE—ESPECIALLY OVERSEAS

Indexing has become a very popular way to manage assets. There was $1.4 trillion in index-based mutual funds in 2002, many of which are designed to mimic returns for the S&P 500.[11] To further illustrate the widespread influence of index investors, when Reebok was added to the S&P 500, its value rose in one day by more than $70 million because so many fund managers were obligated to buy it.

Many international fund managers base their investments on the market capitalization weighting of the world's stock market indices, such as the MSCI EAFE Index. For example, if Japanese stocks represent 30 percent of the EAFE Index, some managers will make sure their portfolios have a 30 percent weighting in Japan. When you think about it, allocation by country or sector is just another name for indexing, although you may be doing it on a worldwide basis. And indexing, I believe, is an approach unworthy of a talented investor, whether institutional or individual. This style of investing ignores the value of individual businesses within the chosen countries. Additionally, it ignores the possibility that markets with the most compelling values may be underrepresented due to recent losses in equity value.

As I noted earlier, the EAFE Index outperformed the S&P 500 substantially throughout the 1980s. At the end of that decade, fund managers with top-down styles willingly "bought" the EAFE Index, which included a large exposure to Japan even though it meant buying Japanese stocks at high valuations, roughly 60 times earnings. By 1992, the Tokyo market fell to a mere 50 percent of its former value, and Japan represented roughly 43 percent of the capitalization-weighted EAFE. (At year-end 2002, Japan comprised 21 percent of the EAFE Index.) In this case, adherence to an indexing philosophy resulted in significant losses and revealed indexing for what it was: a failed attempt at macroeconomic forecasting. That it failed was hardly surprising; neither countries nor companies are perpetual growth machines.

One consequence of the inefficient nature of global markets is that an even greater premium is put on active management. In an article published in the international newspaper *Pension Management*, authors Christopher Carabell and Elizabeth DeLalla describe the benefits active management can deliver when applied in global markets:

> Of the major asset classes, international equity affords the broadest potential for active managers. None of the criteria used in assessing the relative merits of active vs. passive—viable indices, available information, management fees, and transaction costs—strongly favor indexation when investing abroad. Active international management has the additional advantage of multidimensional investment opportunities, including country and stock selection. . . . Taken together, these factors clearly demonstrate why international equity should contain the most active approaches in the management structure.[12]

Indexing implies a macroeconomic forecast, and value investors do not forecast. As Warren Buffett once observed, "We've long felt that the only value of stock forecasters is to make fortune-tellers look good."[13] Value investors try to buy what they can measure today at a discount from its current worth. The only thing riskier than predicting the near-term economic outlook for a company is predicting the near-term economic outlook for an entire country, region, or sector.

CONCLUSION

Why limit yourself to investing in only one country?

There isn't any one market that consistently holds the most attractive investment values. Returns for one country's stock market have not outpaced all others year after year. This chapter has demonstrated the unique opportunities available when investing outside one's home country. There is a tremendous universe of companies that may fly under the radar of many investors. Less competition from other value investors in researching these companies may lead to potentially better relative values.

In closing, I reiterate my conviction for the benefits of maintaining exposure to equities around the world, including emerging markets. I caution investors about making long-term changes in their asset allocation strategies based on short-term developments.

In Chapter 9, I'll address different ways for value investors to access the opportunities available in international markets.

Notes

1. These figures are according to RIMES Technology Corp., as of December 31, 2002, and reflect the estimated market capitalization of all countries in the MSCI World Index in 1970 and the estimated market capitalization of the countries in the MSCI All Country World Index. All performance data is historical and cannot guarantee future results. Indices are unmanaged and cannot be directly invested into.

2. Salomon Smith Barney, as of December 31, 2002.

3. E. Dimson, P. Marsh, and M. Staunton, *Triumph of the Optimists,* Princeton, N.J.: Princeton University Press, 2002.

4. Rex A. Sinquefield, "Where Are the Gains from International Diversification?" *Financial Analysts Journal*, January/February 1996.

5. As measured by rolling 5-year returns for the S&P 500 and MSCI EAFE indices.

6. Results of this study, published by Bernstein Investment Research & Management, were based on an equal-weighted portfolio of the following U.S. multinationals: Avon, Coca-Cola, Colgate-Palmolive, Digital Equipment, Dole Foods, Exxon, Gillette, IBM, Johnson & Johnson, and Motorola. In addition to Bernstein, data sources for the study included Compustat and MSCI. The study, "Top 10 Reasons *Not* to Invest Abroad," is available at the Bernstein Web site, www.bernstein.com/research/stocks/stocks_topten.htm.

7. Dave Kovaleski, "Bear's Eye View," *Pensions & Investments,* December 23, 2002, p. 34.

8. World Bank, *2001 World Development Indicators,* World Bank, 2001, p. 14.

9. Ibid.

10. Ibid., p. 196.

11. Rich Blake, "Is Time Running Out for the S&P 500?" *Institutional Investor*, May 2002, p. 52.

12. Christopher C. Carabell and Elizabeth L. DeLalla, "Index vs. Active Investment," *Pension Management,* April 1995, pp. 11 and 38.

13. James P. Miller and Robert L. Rose, "Buffett Turns Wary on Rise of Stock Prices," *The Wall Street Journal,* March 17, 1997, p. C1.

9

HOW TO INVEST IN COMPANIES WORLDWIDE

W hen value investors go shopping overseas, they generally have three methods for purchasing stocks: "ordinary" foreign shares, depositary receipts, and prepackaged investments such as closed- and open-end mutual funds. In this chapter, I will discuss each of these means to gain access to international markets.

ORDINARY SHARES

"Ordinary" shares or "ORDs" (rhymes with "boards") represent the traditional way of buying shares around the world, locally or overseas. ORDs refer to the shares of a company trading on an exchange in a market outside of one's home country.

For example, if you're a U.S. investor buying stock in the United States, it's simple. You buy the actual shares of a U.S. company issued by that company. If you're a U.S. investor buying in Japan, it gets more complicated. Do you have a yen-based checking account so you can write a check to a Japanese broker? ORDs must be purchased with Japanese yen, not U.S. dollars. The securities pay dividends in yen, as well. To show you how complicated it can get, let's go through the steps.

When a U.S. investor seeks to invest in Nippon Telephone & Telegraph (NTT), a telecommunications company based in Japan, by purchasing NTT ORDs, here is what likely would happen:

1. The investor contacts a U.S. stockbroker.
2. The local broker finds a major institutional brokerage firm that can trade non-U.S. shares.
3. The institutional brokerage firm places the order in the stock's country of origin and buys the shares in the currency of that country. In this case, the trade would be executed in yen and might take place on the Tokyo Stock Exchange.
4. The institutional brokerage firm exchanges the yen for U.S. dollars, marks up the investment, and sells it to the local broker. From the client's perspective there is one trade reported in U.S. dollars, but in reality there is an equity trade and a currency trade involved in the transaction.
5. The local broker may act as the custodian for those shares if it has a Japanese subcustodian. Or, the broker may contract with another firm or bank to hold the securities for them as the shares cannot leave the country of origin.

In another scenario, the U.S. investor might be able to purchase NTT ORDs in the U.S. "Over the Counter" (OTC) market. Generally, securities traded in the OTC market are not listed or traded at a physical exchange such as the New York Stock Exchange, but are traded instead over computer exchanges such as the Nasdaq National Market System. There is a growing market for ORD shares that trade OTC in the United States. At year-end 2002, shares of 1500 non-U.S. companies were traded OTC.[1] The ability to hold ORD shares would depend on the client's stockbroker and the particular style of account. Some can custody ORDs; some can't.

Investors do not necessarily have to shoulder currency and custodial responsibilities on their own. For an additional fee, a number of U.S. brokerage firms will handle currency conversions and price ORDs in U.S. dollars. In addition, ORDs can be held at overseas branches of U.S. custodians, such as brokerage firms.

Many U.S.-based investors are often surprised to learn that their local brokerage house can hold foreign, ordinary shares. And in this custodian role, U.S. brokers are responsible for paying dividends in U.S. dollars.

Typically, the domestic brokerage would have a subcustodial relationship with a non-U.S. bank. If, for example, you were to buy Dutch ordinaries, the international broker would deliver those shares to a Dutch bank that has a custodial relationship with your U.S. broker. Thereafter, the shares would show up on your regular monthly statement, along with your U.S. shares.

ORDs and Transaction Costs

As described above, institutional brokerage firms mark up the cost for purchasing ORDs before selling them to local brokers. The markup typically ranges from 25 to 50 basis points (0.25 to 0.50 percent). That is a negligible number over time, assuming you are willing to be a long-term owner of international stocks. And if you are a value investor, by definition, you are an owner, not a trader. It is a different (and more expensive) story, however, if you are a trader who constantly buys and sells stocks in search of quick profits. Those with short time horizons find that transaction costs add up quickly overseas, and most traders are better off dealing with a broker who has offices in the company's home country.

DEPOSITARY RECEIPTS

Many investors don't like the hassle of going through the process of purchasing foreign ORDs, especially if it's only a small part of their portfolio. Ever alert to the possibility of doing more business, banks came up with the idea of making overseas share ownership as transparent and easy as owning local shares—for a fee, of course. They developed a security based on the "duck principle." If it quacks like a duck, looks like a duck, and walks like a duck, it must be a duck. These securities are known as depositary receipts and are designed to allow U.S. shareholders, for example, to own the equivalent of overseas ORDs, but without the hassle. As we'll see, like ducks, they come in different varieties.

So what *is* a depositary receipt?

In short, it's a security designed to make investing outside of one's home country easier. There are two primary types: American Depositary Receipts (ADRs) and Global Depositary Receipts (GDRs). As the names suggest, ADRs (pronounced by saying each letter, A-D-Rs) are designed for U.S.-based investors seeking to purchase shares of *non*-U.S. companies.

GDRs are typically designed for investors outside the United States who seek to purchase shares outside their "home" country. Although I'll spend much of this chapter focusing on ADRs, the concepts and logistics generally apply to GDRs also.

Let's revisit our example of a U.S. investor interested in NTT Corporation. As cited, purchasing NTT ORDs is one possibility. Buying NTT ADRs is another. Like any U.S. stock, an ADR is purchased with U.S. dollars, pays dividends in U.S. dollars, and is often listed on U.S. exchanges. NTT ADRs could be purchased on the New York Stock Exchange (NYSE). One additional note: There are some non-U.S., multinational firms that list their shares directly on the New York Stock Exchange. This bypasses the need for an ADR, as a U.S. investor is actually buying the underlying stock on the NYSE, the same way he or she could for any domestic stock. These companies have to abide by SEC standards and the NYSE rules as well as their own domestic regulations, so it's an expensive and time-consuming exercise for them. Typically, the few companies that go this route are large multinationals that regularly seek access to the U.S. capital markets or global companies with a significant U.S. business presence (for example, Unilever or Daimler-Chrysler).

History of Depositary Receipts

The first ADRs were introduced in the United States in 1927 when J.P. Morgan Bank issued receipts for the British retailer Selfridge Stores. Prior to the 1980s, ADRs were primarily used by non-U.S. companies to create stock-purchase plans for their U.S.-based employees. However, since the early 1980s, an increasing number of non-U.S. companies have issued ADRs to raise capital. At year-end 2002, there were more than 2100 depositary receipt programs in existence representing companies in more than 78 countries. According to Gavin Anderson & Company, 40 percent of U.S. foreign equity investment was held in ADRs in 2002, accounting for about 10 percent of all equity trading in the United States. As shown in Exhibit 9-1, share volume for depositary receipts (including ADRs and GDRs) grew every year since 1997, reaching 32.1 billion in 2002. While the dollar volume of those trades declined in 2001 and 2002 (as illustrated in Exhibit 9-2), paralleling the pullback in equity prices around the world, depositary receipt trading activity still represents a significant portion of global equity transactions.

EXHIBIT 9-1   Annual Share Volume of Listed Depositary Receipts (Trading Volume in Billions of Shares)

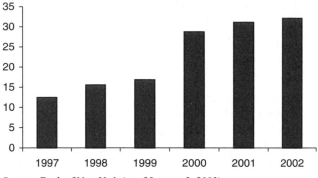

Source: Bank of New York (as of January 2, 2003).

EXHIBIT 9-2   Annual Dollar Volume of Listed Depositary Receipts (Trading Volume in Billions of U.S. Dollars)

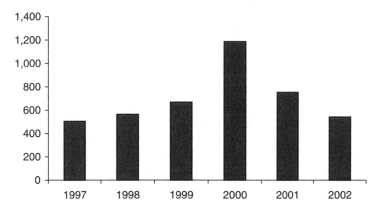

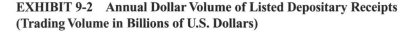

How Do ADRs Work?

Issued by a U.S. bank, an ADR is technically a receipt for an American Depositary Share (ADS). An ADS represents a specific number of shares (or a specific fraction of a share) of a non-U.S.-based company. While an ADS is the security actually used when trading, the term ADR generally refers to both the receipt and the security.

Non-U.S. companies may deposit shares of their stock at their local branch of a U.S. bank's subcustodian. The bank does not sell the actual shares on deposit. Instead the bank sells certificates, or receipts, that represent the shares of the non-U.S. company. The U.S. bank handles a number of responsibilities including holding the securities, collecting dividend payments, making currency conversions, and distributing dividend income to investors, who are recorded on the bank's books.

Types of ADRs

Generally, there are three types of ADRs.

Unsponsored ADRs   These ADRs are created without the consent of the underlying company by banks seeing a profitable market for the company's shares. They may be handled by more than one bank. At one time, unsponsored ADRs commanded a large share of the overall ADR market. However, they are becoming less popular with investors because company information and performance reports can be relatively difficult to obtain.

Sponsored ADRs   Today, nearly all ADRs are sponsored. This is the easiest method for non-U.S. companies to issue tradable securities in the United States. Most sponsored ADRs are not listed on U.S. exchanges. Instead, they are traded in the OTC market. Although these ADRs are not subject to the strict reporting requirements covering exchange-listed ADRs, the underlying companies generally supply fundamental information about the businesses. Thus, individual investors can acquire information needed to make a prudent buying decision.

Exchange-Listed ADRs   Exchange-Listed ADRs (a special type of sponsored ADR) provide more and better information to the holder than either unsponsored or nonexchange, sponsored ADRs. To qualify for a listing, international companies must complete extensive filings with U.S. governing bodies and generally provide financial reporting similar to that of U.S. companies. This helps U.S. holders weigh performance results and fundamentals against domestic investment alternatives.

The ADR Market

Non-U.S. companies issuing ADRs include well-known names such as Sony and British Airways as well as smaller, lesser-known companies such as Kuala Lumpur Kepong, a Malaysian plantation group. Privatization programs in the world's developing nations are spawning large companies hungry for international capital and recognition. For rapidly growing companies, ADRs are an effective means of capital raising and can help lift a company's profile

For rapidly growing companies, ADRs are an effective means of raising capital.

among investors worldwide. They can be used to establish a trading record, gain a following among investors and securities analysts, and pave the way for raising U.S. capital in the future. Exhibit 9-3 illustrates the growth in capital raised by depositary receipt offerings.

As a publicly traded security in the United States, an ADR may be used for cross-border mergers and acquisitions. For example, 13 non-U.S. companies used their ADRs to purchase U.S. and Canadian companies in 2000.

Although some countries, including Japan, prohibit companies from using ADRs to finance cross-border mergers and acquisitions and allow only cash transactions, J.P. Morgan reported that stock swaps accounted for more than half of all takeovers of public U.S. companies in 2000, up from 7 percent in 1988. Among the larger deals in the past several years involving ADRs were Deutsche Telekom's acquisition of VoiceStream Wireless and British Petroleum's purchase of Amoco. The *Financial Times* reported that Spain's Telefonica launched an ADR program to spin out its Terra Networks affiliate, which then used the ADRs to acquire Lycos, the U.S.-based Internet company.[2]

The need for companies outside the United States to gain access to international capital markets will likely increase the liquidity of ADRs and make more companies available for investing in ADR form. The greater the liquidity, the greater the opportunities for investors searching for opportunities around the world—including, of course, value investors.

EXHIBIT 9-3   Capital Raised through Depositary Receipt Programs (in Billions of U.S. Dollars)

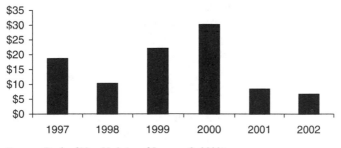

Source: Bank of New York (as of January 2, 2003).

An ADR Success Story

In the early 1980s, China began a major restructuring of its petroleum industry. One of the results of this effort led to the creation of three separate companies, all of which now trade in public equity markets. One of these companies, CNOOC, focuses on the exploration and development of China's offshore oil and gas reserves. Historically, the company made special arrangements to joint venture with other major oil companies to develop offshore reserves without the upfront exploration costs. As the company matured, it began to independently explore for and develop its own oil and gas reserves. Due to the risks associated with exploration and the need for large capital outlays to independently develop reserves, CNOOC, and more specifically, its shareholder, the Chinese government, needed to raise capital. The company had a 3-year development plan that called for $4.5 billion of capital expenditures, or $1.5 billion beyond expected cash flow from operating activities over the period of 2001 to 2003.

Companies in China typically gain access to capital through state-run banks. Some have issued shares through the exchange in Hong Kong, which, in 2001, had roughly only $500 billion of total market capitalization and an average daily trading volume of only $1 billion. The regional markets in Shanghai and Shenzhen are smaller still. CNOOC certainly had access to capital through these market exchanges, but was looking for lower-cost funds available in global markets. Further, China was undergoing rapid growth at the time and in order to sustain that pace, it sought access to global capital markets. Together with its entry into the World Trade Organization (WTO), China attempted to strengthen ties to Western economies and capital.

Early in 2001, CNOOC completed its initial public offering of American Depositary Shares to global investors with 1.6 billion shares and net proceeds exceeding $1 billion. The distribution of investors demonstrates the global reach of the offering. Roughly one-quarter of the offering went to investors in the United States, Europe, and the rest of Asia, while the balance went to a strategic investor and investors in Hong Kong.

ADRs versus ORDs

Often, you have a choice between buying a company's ADR or GDR and its ordinary shares. Assuming the company meets the value criteria we have discussed, what is the best way to invest? Before I address this question, I want to share two related points regarding ADRs and ORDs: The first has to do with the ratios between the two, and the second deals with the effects of currency fluctuations on ADRs.

Ratio of Ordinaries to ADRs   Some ADRs represent underlying shares or ordinaries on a one-for-one basis. For example, one ordinary share in the Italian Benetton Group equals one ADR. Other ADRs may represent more or less than one underlying share. Ten ordinaries of British Telecom, for example, equal one ADR. On the other hand, it takes a mere 0.01 underlying share of Swiss-based Nestle to equal one ADR.

The number of ordinaries represented by a single ADR reflects the overall pricing of shares on a national stock market. In Hong Kong, where quoted prices for blue-chip companies are often under $1 per share, an ADR usually represents multiple shares. Conversely, in Switzerland, the quoted price is often more than $1000 per blue-chip-company share. While the Hong Kong market welcomes small-investor participation, the Swiss market almost exclusively targets large-scale or institutional buyers. Generally, the issuing bank establishes the ratio with the hope of pricing the ADR within a generally accepted range designed to help U.S. investors feel comfortable—typically $5 to $100.

From the standpoint of investment value, these pricing policies are meaningless. As we saw in the example at the beginning of Chapter 1, comparing a Hong Kong share that sells for $1 with a Swiss share that sells for $1000 tells you nothing about the underlying worth of the companies in question. For the value investor, stock price is important only as it relates to underlying value.

Currency Fluctuations and ADRs   While ADRs are traded like domestic securities, they still represent the underlying foreign shares and are affected by currency fluctuations. For example, the price of a Nintendo ADR trading on the New York Stock Exchange will track the price of Nintendo stock on the Tokyo exchange *after adjusting for changes in the dollar-yen relationship*. The impact of currency fluctuations on ADR prices is a financial fact of life that is often overlooked, even by experienced market watchers. The key point to remember is that an ADR's price movement combines the movement of the underlying stock and the underlying currency. We will explain currency fluctuations and their effects on international investments in Chapter 10. Now, let's get back to the original question regarding the benefits and drawbacks of investing in ADRs and ORDs.

ADRs versus ORDs: Comparing and Contrasting

Often, investors have a choice between buying a company's ADR and its ordinary shares. Assuming the company meets the value criteria previously addressed, what is the better way to invest? In evaluating the relative merits of ADRs with the direct purchase of ordinary shares, investors should consider a variety of factors.

Pricing   Additional costs may be incurred in creating or canceling ADRs, and these costs could be passed on to the investor. For example, the bank issuing an ADR may keep a portion of any dividend as payment for services. (This is a disadvantage, of course, but keep in mind that the bank is also performing a major currency exchange transaction that converts the dividend payment from the company's local currency to U.S. dollars. The bank transaction can reduce exchange costs significantly for the individual investor.)

In theory, ADRs are slightly more expensive than underlying ordinaries because ADR prices include holding charges, processing costs, and the market maker's spread (the difference between the prices at which securities can be bought and sold).

It's important to know that *large* price differences between ADRs and underlying shares usually are eliminated quickly by arbitrageurs. Sometimes, the use of a single domestic broker in ADR trading actually winds up costing less than purchasing ordinaries with a non-U.S. brokerage firm. And non-U.S. investors sometimes buy ADRs to obtain lower commissions and avoid "stamp" taxes, a duty that may be imposed on the issue and transfer of stocks and bonds.

Arbitrageurs are professional investors who buy a security in one market and sell it in another to exploit momentary pricing differentials. Typically, arbitrageurs employ huge leverage to turn small pricing differences into substantial profits. Since arbitrageurs are often brokers or banks, they generally have a lower brokerage cost threshold and a lower fund cost to overcome than does the general public. Given their position in the marketplace, arbitrageurs can make a profit by exploiting even miniscule price differences between ADRs and ordinaries.

Settlement Time   Years ago, trades involving ORDs typically took considerably longer to settle than ADRs, sometimes up to 3 months. Now, settlement time for most ORDs is generally 2 to 5 days. More efficient markets worldwide have greatly reduced the settlement time benefits once linked to ADRs.

Convenience   Buying ADRs avoids some of the complexities of dealing directly in overseas markets such as different time zones, currency conversions, and language obstacles. Investors can deal with their regular broker, paying standard commissions for ADR purchases and sales. ADRs are issued by American banks, which can take physical possession of the non-U.S. securities and may be responsible for converting any dividends into U.S. dollars and deducting foreign withholding taxes for investors.

In addition, with depositary receipts, annual reports and other shareholder correspondence are printed in the language of the country in which they are issued. This allows U.S. investors, for example, to readily compare ADR holdings with U.S. investment alternatives. ADRs offer other benefits. With respect to the collection of dividends, it can be a confusing process with ORDs as regulations differ from country to country. In Japan, for example, investors must present certificates of ownership to the company or its agent prior to receiving dividends. And in some markets, particularly in Asia, ORDs may only trade in blocks of 500 or 1000 shares. ADRs typically can accommodate smaller investments.

On a related point, the sheer price level of an individual ORD compared to its ADR may be a factor, depending on how much the investor can afford. For example, in early 2003, NTT ORDs were trading at $3600 per share. Because an NTT ADR represented a claim to only 1/200th of an ORD, the value of a single ADR was merely $18. For investors who want to invest in round lots (or blocks of 100 shares), ADRs may be a more practical alternative.

Access to Information   In some cases, the information flow associated with ADRs is better than ORDs and eliminates the need for costly international communications. A minority of the companies with ADRs that trade on U.S.-listed exchanges must file 20-F reports. These reports are similar to annual reports required of all U.S. companies.

The 20-F includes a balance sheet, profit and loss statement, and a statement of cash flows, reconciled to U.S. generally accepted accounting principles (GAAP). In some cases, a cash flow statement may not even be required in the company's home market. This in-depth reporting of fundamental traits such as total sales, revenue, and pretax operating income is an important part of evaluating the investment prospects of individual companies.

Non-U.S. companies without ADRs may not produce the extensive financial reports described above. Even if they do, they may not publish them in English, and they may be difficult to obtain.

Even companies with non-listed ADRs usually publish an English-language version of their annual reports. Some companies choose not to list their ADRs on U.S. exchanges. Non-listed ADRs often trade OTC. Reporting requirements for OTC ADRs are less stringent and company financials may not conform to U.S. GAAP. In the United States, listing is mandatory for any non-U.S. company that seeks to raise capital, but not every firm seeks money from U.S. investors. Some firms may instead only seek to raise awareness or attract analyst coverage.

> *Many ADRs trade on the New York Stock Exchange, providing ample liquidity.*

One additional point to consider: Smaller companies often attract less analyst coverage than larger firms and may hold significant opportunity for diligent value investors. However, ADRs are usually not available for small companies in the early stages of their existence. Most companies that have ADR listings are already mature entities.

Liquidity   Liquidity refers to how quickly an asset can be converted to cash. Many investors mistakenly believe ADRs provide insufficient liquidity. In other words, when you want to buy or sell ADRs, it will be difficult to find buyers or sellers to accommodate your transaction. Some U.S. fund managers may contend that they have to buy ordinaries because the ADR market does not have sufficient transaction volume to support major buy and sell orders. This is not necessarily true. In fact, many ADRs trade on the New York Stock Exchange, providing ample liquidity.

While ADRs are generally not as liquid as typical blue chips, for example, there are generally enough ADR market participants to ensure the smooth execution of buy and sell orders. The market in which the ORDs trade will usually be the most liquid market, but sometimes it's more difficult for individual investors to access. To enhance liquidity, most ADRs can be converted into ORDs and sold in the issuing company's home country, usually within a day or two. If you are an active trader—and not a serious owner—and want to move in and out of the market fast, you might insist on the hour-by-hour liquidity that ORDs provide. Otherwise, what's the hurry? If you are a patient, value-oriented investor, you will be more concerned with tracking long-term business trends than responding to short-term, irrational blips in stock price.

Price Quotes   At one point, the degree of difficulty in obtaining current price quotations for ADRs and ORDs ranged from very easy to very difficult. The availability of data on the Internet has generally made getting reliable pricing information far easier. Finding quotes for exchange-listed ADRs always has been relatively easy. They are often printed in the business section of your local newspaper or in national business publications such as *The Wall Street Journal*. You can also find them online using various Internet search engines with the ADR's three- or four-letter trading symbol. Among the Web sites that offer ADR-related information, including pricing, are www.adr.com and the Bank of New York's Web site, www.bankofny.com.

Finding prices for unlisted ADRs that trade over-the-counter used to be more difficult. In the past, you had to call your stockbroker for an instant quotation or consult the Foreign Markets section of *The Wall Street Journal* for the approximate market value of an ORD share. However, prices were quoted in their domestic currency. To convert the value into U.S. dollars, you had to find the *Journal*'s listing of currency exchange rates, then multiply the foreign stock quote by the currency rate. You also had to know the correct ratio. As cited earlier, one ADR may not equal one ordinary share. Thanks to the Internet, such tasks now occupy the same place in history as using a slide rule and typing with a manual typewriter.

Years ago, obtaining accurate quotes for ORDs was the most difficult of the security types discussed here. In the past, you could obtain an approximate value by checking *The Wall Street Journal* or the Foreign Markets table in *Barron's*, a financial newspaper published weekly. Today, many Web sites provide pricing information for ORDs. For example, check out the finance section at www.yahoo.com.

ADRs versus ORDs: A Moot Point?

Ultimately, the fewer overseas stocks you own, and the smaller the total value or the proportion of your portfolio in overseas companies, the more you may prefer ADRs. Like many other things in life, it's a trade-off between cost and convenience. If it's too inconvenient for you to hold ORDs, then perhaps you're not going to find the costs associated with ADRs excessive.

ADR issuance may continue to increase in coming years. However, eventually, the choice between ADRs and ORDs may become moot. Increasingly, the world's stock exchanges are becoming electronically linked. Advances in communications and standardized record keeping could make ADRs obsolete. Tangible stock certificates are being replaced with electronic records, eliminating the need for physically transferring and storing stock certificates. Competition among ADR custodial banks is driving down processing fees. Ultimately, the benefits of ADRs, especially convenience and shorter settlement times, may erode as the world's markets migrate to universally accepted standards. Such an evolution would enhance the attractiveness of trading in ORDs.

PACKAGED OVERSEAS INVESTMENTS

Unless you have the time and inclination to research international companies, you might want to bypass ADRs and ORDs in favor of prepackaged overseas investments such as mutual funds. The latter fall into four broad categories: (1) global funds, which invest in all countries, including an investor's home country—for example, for a U.S. investor, a global fund would include stocks of U.S.-based companies; (2) international funds, which generally invest in all countries *except* the investor's home country—for example, for a U.S. investor, an international fund would *not* include U.S. stocks; (3) regional funds, which invest in particular areas of the world such as Europe or Asia or Latin America; and (4) single-country or sector-specific funds, which invest in one particular country or sector, such as Japan or Mexico or telecommunications or utilities.

Generally, global funds provide a broad, "one-stop" alternative for investors who do not wish to actively manage their domestic and international exposures. In other words, global fund investors might be content to allow the fund manager to decide what percentage of assets should be invested in Japan, for example, versus Europe and the United States.

For investors who already may have domestic exposure and seek to more actively control their allocation to international markets, an international stock fund may be more appropriate. Although a global fund's proportion of domestic versus international holdings may vary over time, an international fund's domestic allocation should always be zero. Thus, investors can more easily gauge the percentage of their assets invested domestically and internationally.

Regional, country, and sector funds offer an even *higher* degree of control for investors who may have great familiarity with a certain part of the world or sector or wish to make a conscious decision to concentrate their holdings in a particular area, a specific country, or certain industry or sector. Generally, such decisions are made by more sophisticated investors. One caveat to remember about regional, single-country, or sector funds:

They are often not segmented by style. In other words, it may be difficult to tell exactly what types of stocks—value, growth, or other—are purchased for a Japan equity fund or global telecommunications fund, for example.

Overall, depending upon your investment objectives, time horizon, risk tolerance, and diversification goals, one or more of these four types of funds may be appropriate for your needs. If you have specific questions, I suggest consulting your financial advisor.

OPEN- VERSUS CLOSED-END FUNDS

Many investors likely are familiar with open-end mutual funds. Today, open-end funds dominate the landscape, accounting for the vast majority of all available funds. When you invest money in an open-end fund, you receive units or shares. Open-end funds have no set number of outstanding shares; as more money comes in, the fund issues more shares (at the *net asset value*, a term I'll explain in a moment) and the fund manager buys more securities with the new money. The value of all outstanding shares is roughly equal to the value of the securities in the portfolio. When you wish to sell your shares, the open-end fund will always repurchase them at the portfolio's net asset value (NAV).

But what about *closed*-end funds? What are they? How do they work? Originally, all mutual funds were closed-end funds, forming the foundation of what was known as the investment trust industry. While closed-end funds provided a method for participating in the stock market, investors sought greater benefits (such as better liquidity) and fewer restrictions. In response to their demands, open-end funds were created. Today, closed-end funds typically are offered for less liquid or specialty investments.

A closed-end fund is both a company and a fund, with a *fixed* number of outstanding shares that trade either on an exchange or over-the-counter—not through the fund company itself. The value of the shares is set by the market. Like an open-end fund, the share price is closely related to the value of the fund's underlying net assets. However, with a closed-end fund, there usually is a deviation between these two figures—the price of the shares and the underlying value of the assets. That difference can create opportunity for a value investor.

Shares of a closed-end fund can trade at either a discount from the underlying value (NAV) of the stocks in the fund, or at a premium. Value investors should avoid paying a premium for shares of a closed-end fund and investigate opportunities where shares are trading at a discount.

Good sources of information on closed-end funds include *Barron's*, whose weekly listing indicates the amount of each fund's current discount or premium to net asset value, and *The Wall Street Journal*. Also consider Morningstar Mutual Funds, which includes detailed individual summaries of both open- and closed-end funds. For additional information on closed-end funds, you may wish to visit the Closed-End Fund Association online at www.cefa.com. This Web site offers information and tools devoted to closed-end funds. Your financial advisor also may be a good source of information on closed-end funds.

Before diving into the fund selection process, there are a few terms that you should understand.

Net Asset Value   The net asset value (NAV) represents the price at which investors may sell a share of the fund. Technically, it's the market value of fund holdings (after deducting liabilities) divided by the number of shares outstanding.

Loads   Also known as sales charges, loads generally are applied in one of two ways. Some funds impose front-end loads, in which a charge to purchase the shares is deducted from the initial investment. For example, a fund with a 4.5 percent front-end load deducts $45 for every $1000 invested. Back-end-loaded funds may assess a deferred sales charge, with the amount of the load dependent on the length of time the shares are held. You can think of this as a type of penalty for early withdrawal. For example, a back-end-loaded fund might impose a 5 percent sales charge on shares sold within the first year after purchase, 4 percent on sales within the second year, and so on until liquidations made after year five are free of charge. Funds that don't impose a front- or back-end load are known as no-load funds.

Loads versus No-Loads   Usually, financial advisors offer funds with a sales charge. They receive all or a portion of the charge as payment for the guidance, information, and service they provide for their clients. No-load funds typically are purchased by do-it-yourself investors. Some financial advisors will offer no-load funds, but charge clients a management fee for their service. There have been many articles written about the benefits and drawbacks of load versus no-load funds. To me, the debate boils down to this: If you seek guidance from an investment professional, you should expect to pay for it, whether it's through a front-end or back-end sales charge on a mutual fund, a commission on a stock trade, or a quarterly fee based on the total amount of assets an advisor helps you manage. To expect a professional investment advisor not to charge you for his or her experience, knowledge, and skill is unrealistic.

For those investors who are comfortable managing their own portfolios, they may not want professional guidance. In these cases, a no-load fund, for example, is often an appropriate decision.

As I mentioned earlier, this book is designed to give individuals a better understanding of value investing. It is not intended to be a guidebook that offers advice on what to do in every situation an investor may face over many years. It is intended to provide some insight on how attractively valued stocks can be purchased and how a portfolio of value stocks can be managed.

In Chapter 12, when I address the importance of strict adherence to an investment process, I'll show how working with a financial professional can be beneficial in helping you stick with the value-investing disciplines described in this book. However, whether you choose to invest on your own or in partnership with a financial advisor is your decision.

Operating Expenses   An open-end mutual fund has a variety of day-to-day expenses including costs for administration, legal counsel, operations, and client service. These costs are passed along to shareholders and deducted directly from fund earnings. The amount of a fund's operating costs varies based on diverse factors including the type of asset being managed, overhead, and where the fund operates. For example, stock funds with all or a portion of their holdings invested overseas usually have the highest expenses. Stock funds that invest only domestically tend to have lower expense ratios. Published track records for mutual funds reflect deductions for operating expenses.

While closed-end funds also have expense ratios, generally their expenses are lower than open-end funds because they provide no client service for shareholders. The expenses also tend to be small relative to the fund's discount or premium.

Value Tips on Choosing a Closed-End Fund

As a value investor, you may uncover attractive bargains among discounted closed-end regional and single-country funds. In some cases, you may find discounts of 15 percent or more, particularly when global sentiment about a market or region becomes unfavorable. Remember—closed-end funds can trade below NAV (discount) or above NAV (premium), depending upon supply and demand. Any time capacity is rationed and the investment is in demand, you may see a premium. Investors should always ask themselves if they believe both of these conditions (the limited capacity and strong demand) are likely to continue.

Note that in most cases, buying an underwritten, closed-end fund at the time of the initial underwriting is generally not a good idea as you are paying a premium to cover the costs of the underwriting. This could be thought of as something similar to the front-end sales charge on an open-end fund.

There are important exceptions, however, such as in the case of the Brazil Fund in 1991 and 1992. The Brazilian equity market at that time was essentially closed to foreign investors, and the only viable means of participation was through the closed-end Brazil Fund. But when a market is trading at a mere three times earnings (as Brazil was during those years), value investors could decide that paying a small premium is acceptable if the closed-end fund is the only viable means for investing in a market that offers compelling value.

EXCHANGE-TRADED FUNDS

Exchange-traded funds, or ETFs, were introduced in 1992. They are baskets of securities that trade like individual stocks. The most visible ETFs include SPDRs, or "Spiders" (which attempt to track the S&P 500 Index), Diamonds (designed to track the Dow Jones Industrial Average), and QQQs, or "Qubes" (designed to track the largest 100 Nasdaq firms, as measured by market capitalization). Like closed-end funds, ETFs offer investors high liquidity. However, ETFs and closed-end funds have several notable differences.

While closed-end funds may trade at wide discounts or premiums, ETFs usually trade at, or very close to, net asset value. Closed-end funds are mostly actively managed, while ETFs are passively managed. By maintaining passive and transparent portfolios, the ETFs can rely on arbitrage to help keep the trading price close to the net asset value. If a notable premium or discount were to develop, an arbitrageur could purchase ETFs and sell the share holdings individually to exploit any price differential. Closed-end funds do not offer this option, often resulting in wide premiums or discounts of shares to net asset value.

ETFs may provide an investor with low annual expenses and increased tax efficiency (though they may incur capital gains to rebalance a portfolio if they are tied to an index). Though ETFs can be traded throughout the day, minute-to-minute liquidity is not a concern for the long-term investor.

ETFs also present a costly drawback—investors incur trading costs for each purchase and sale of ETF shares, potentially making it expensive to invest in ETFs through dollar-cost averaging or multiple purchases of shares. Many ETFs are linked to indices, which present other dangers (as described in Chapter 8): Indices are often arbitrary; an index may be disproportionately composed of stocks trading at lofty levels; and the rebalancing of an index can trigger capital gains and reduce exposure to a portfolio's most undervalued holdings. In short, ETFs combine the drawbacks of passive funds with a layer of trading costs.

One final note: As this book went to press in 2003, new funds were being introduced that represented steps toward actively managed ETFs. One firm launched two ETFs that will update their holdings every quarter.[3] With the likelihood of less portfolio transparency to investors than passively managed ETF portfolios, actively managed ETFs could result in wider premium and discount pricing, much like closed-end funds.

CONCLUSION

Over the previous two chapters, I have explained why diversifying your portfolio to include a healthy sampling of international stocks can be a wise decision. I also have talked about how to get involved, addressing everything from ADRs to ORDs to various types of mutual funds. Regardless of how you choose to invest overseas, however, there are certain aspects that are unique to the process. These will be described in Chapter 10, "Unique Aspects of Global Investing."

Notes

1. Eric Uhlfelder, "Big International Fish in Shallow U.S. Waters," *Registered Representative*, January 1, 2003.

2. Alison Beard, "Global Investing: ADSs a Hit Among the Acquiring Classes. More and More Overseas Companies Are Using Their U.S.-Listed Stock to Finance M&A Activity," *The Financial Times,* April 16, 2001.

3. Yuka Hayashi, "Ex-Nuveen Exec Launches New ETFs with Active Element," *The Wall Street Journal,* April 28, 2003.

10

UNIQUE ASPECTS OF GLOBAL INVESTING

C hapters 8 and 9 described the benefits of global investing, as well as how to purchase international securities. It is important to keep in mind, however, that while international investing creates the potential for enhanced returns and diminished volatility over time, there are unique factors associated with international stocks. These factors include currency fluctuations, differences in accounting practices, and vastly different political environments. This chapter provides explanations of each of these factors to bolster awareness, better manage expectations, and assist in making more informed investment decisions.

CURRENCY FLUCTUATION

Changes in currency exchange rates are a double-edged sword. Taking U.S. investors as an example, sometimes fluctuations in the exchange rate between the U.S. dollar and another currency can be a disadvantage. At other times, it can help.

The basic situation is very simple. The value of any security you may own in a currency that's not your own will vary according to two things: (1) movements in the security price and (2) changes in the currency measured against your own "base" currency. Suppose you're a U.S. investor who owns Toyota shares in Japan and the yen strengthens against the U.S. dollar. If there's no change in Toyota's stock price, the value of your investment in dollar terms has gone up in the same proportion as the change in the foreign exchange rate. This is very straightforward and, of course, works the same way if the yen weakens against the dollar. One very practical point of terminology: if your currency (the dollar, in this example) strengthens against the other (the yen), then the value in dollars of your investment has gone down (and vice versa, of course).

The currency "market" is the biggest and most heavily traded in the world. While there is no physical marketplace (transactions are made electronically), more than $5 trillion change hands *daily*. Should you be an "investor" in this market? My recommendation is a firm no. The definition of *investor* shared in Chapter 1 does not apply to currency trading. Let me explain why. In my view, currencies should not be treated like stocks. They are not securities, that is, an ownership interest in a single business enterprise. In an era when currency funds are sometimes offered to investors as if they are mutual funds, let's be clear. Currencies are not an "investment." I believe they are merely a *measure* of wealth unlike an investment in a stock, which reflects ownership in a business designed to be a way of *creating* wealth.

The characteristic of currencies that best illustrates this is that the currency market is a zero-sum game. In such a game, no additional value is created. Value is transferred from one player to another. In currencies, by definition, when one goes down, another one goes up against it. For example, one currency can only be measured against another. You may read about the "dollar-yen rate" or hear on the news that the dollar "rose against the euro." Currency measurement is relative to other currencies.

Why Exchange Rates Fluctuate

Many factors influence the value of a country's currency. A currency doesn't necessarily move in simultaneous lockstep—or even in the same direction— against the monetary units of every nation. As we saw in Chapter 8, currency movements have tended to exhibit diverse patterns in the post-war era of floating exchange rates.

Essentially, the price of a nation's currency relative to another is set by supply and demand. While speculators and central banks can distort these trends over short periods, economic factors tend to prevail in the long run. For example, in the 40 years from the 1950s to the mid-1990s, the yen and deutsche mark appreciated in price against the dollar as the Japanese and German economies saw rapid growth, low inflation, and trade surpluses.

Currencies experience bull and bear phases. Since the U.S. Federal Reserve Board established its trade-weighted dollar index in the early 1970s, the U.S. dollar has experienced more than a dozen moves of 15 percent or more in either direction. Similar short-term movements can be observed in most other major currencies. Given the dynamic nature of the world's currency markets and the various factors at work within them, what should the global value investor do?

Currencies and the Value Investor

In my view, there's a strong and rational argument to do nothing. In a globally diversified portfolio, exposure to a range of currencies adds another layer of diversification. Not only are you diversified by stock, by industry, and by geography, you are also diversified by currency.

Even if you believed it was important to control the currency exposure in your portfolio, managing your true currency exposure is virtually impossible. For example, you can certainly increase or decrease your yen *positions*, but it's difficult to assess the underlying *exposure* to the currency. Let me illustrate. You can easily calculate what proportion of your portfolio is in Japanese stocks and currency balances. You can, with some effort, analyze how much of the revenue of each company (Japanese or not) in the portfolio is derived in yen. But you often don't know what every company's treasurer is doing in the currency markets to manage his or her own company's yen exposure. Without this knowledge, you don't have a complete grasp of the true exposure in your portfolio.

Currency Hedging

Up to now, I have not addressed the notion of currency hedging. That was deliberate. Value investors, in my view, don't need this technique. Currency hedging seeks to eliminate or reduce the impact of underlying currency movements while retaining exposure to the related investment. It is beyond the scope of this book to delve into details regarding currency management and its pros and cons. Just as background information, understand that tools such as forward contracts, futures contracts, and currency options are available for those who wish to manage their currency exposure. There are trading costs associated with using each of these tools. But ultimately, the question investors should ask themselves before reaching for these tools is, "If I attempt to hedge currencies, what is the *real* cost, that is, the cost if I do it wrong?"

As cited, because currency exposure can be difficult to measure in the first place, it's very difficult to manage. Given the costs associated with hedging, the technicalities of currency markets, and the possibility for doing more harm than good, I urge long-term value investors not to experiment with currency hedging. The only thing I suggest is observing the same level of diversification precautions you would with any other aspect of your portfolio: Don't allow yourself to get overconcentrated.

POLITICAL RISK

We all have seen how quickly an ideal political scenario can sour, and vice versa. In an extreme case, political upheaval can wipe out an entire portfolio. Anyone who happened to be fully invested in Chile when Salvador Allende began nationalizing major industries in 1971 could have lost everything.

But this scenario is rare and easily avoidable. Throughout this book, I have stressed the benefits of individual security selection: a bottom-up, company-by-company approach to investing worldwide. So why even address political risks? Do political considerations even matter for an investor who focuses on individual business fundamentals and builds a well-diversified portfolio? In short, yes— to a degree.

Consider how concerns of an economic crisis surfaced in Brazil in 2002 as the country's unemployment rate spiked and the inflation rate surpassed 20 percent in neighboring Argentina. Its debt crisis also raised fears of a contagion spreading across Latin American economies. But it was in the *political* arena that many investors raised the most serious doubts about the countries.

By July of 2002, investors were voicing concerns over the presidential election polls that showed a lead for left-wing candidate Luiz Inacio Lula da Silva. While outgoing President Fernando Henrique Cardoso's government paid careful attention to the market, da Silva's social issue agenda left many worrying about the country's debt obligations and economic health. As da Silva's

I believe one of the best defenses against political risk is diversification.

lead in the polls widened prior to October's election, Brazil's stock market tumbled. In the third quarter alone, the market lost 39.4 percent, as measured by the MSCI Brazil Index.

Investors fled in hopes of averting a political and economic crisis, citing:

- The country's debt had ballooned to $260 billion.

- Brazil's inflation rate reached an 8-year high, and its currency lost 40 percent against the U.S. dollar at one point in 2002.

- Both da Silva and a fellow left-wing candidate stretched their lead over the government-backed candidate.

- The Central Bank of Brazil failed to place all of the public debt offered during the summer of 2002.

- Brazil's debt rating was downgraded by Moody's Investor Service on June 4, 2002; by Fitch on June 20, 2002; and by Standard & Poor's on July 2, 2002.[1]

- Brazil more than doubled its inflation target for 2003 and 2004.

While the headlines focused on dramatic scenarios, investors who carefully weighed the factors could see several hints of opportunity. For instance:

- Brazil's companies were largely insulated from Argentina. According to Bloomberg, they sold $5 billion of goods to their neighbor—8.6 percent of exports, or less than 1 percent of GDP in 2001.

- Da Silva appointed a Princeton economist with free-market credentials to reassure investors.

- In August, the International Monetary Fund (IMF) announced a $30 billion loan program to Brazil.

- Brazil's economy registered third-quarter GDP growth of 2.4 percent as the weakened currency helped stimulate exports.

- Brazil posted a consolidated primary budget surplus of 52.4 billion reals (US$14.7 billion) for 2002, exceeding the level needed to fulfill the terms of its accord with the International Monetary Fund.

And how did Brazil fare with its *political* crisis? The crisis never seemed to materialize. Just months after election, da Silva was lauded by investors around the globe for his commitment to controlling inflation, luring investors—and rationality—back to Brazil's markets. The situation illustrates how markets can suffer even in the absence of an overt political crisis. As Fitch noted in its decision to lower the country's credit rating:

> [Our] argument takes into account the country's political transition. It is based, therefore, on what might or might not happen. In its declaration, however, the agency itself recognized its incapacity to form a judgment regarding the situation.

When broader market participants perceive political uncertainty and act impulsively, investors often may find extremely compelling bargains. I encourage investors to consider a country's political climate *after* they've identified a solid business in a country in which they want to invest.

I believe an evaluation of political terrain can affect the assessment of a company's underlying business value and help investors decide at what price shares should be purchased. When evaluating political risks, the value investor should consider the attitude of opposition political groups, the level of stability in the labor market, the country's economic sensitivity to energy costs, and the government's policies toward foreign investment and private enterprise. I also think political factors can influence how large of a position the security should occupy in a well-diversified portfolio. I certainly would not suggest an assessment or forecast of a country's political environment as a starting point for individual stock selection. I don't believe anyone possesses superior predictive abilities regarding political developments that could produce consistent benefits for investors.

I believe one of the best defenses against political risk is diversification. I suggest limiting investments in a single country to the greater of 20 percent of portfolio assets or 150 percent of that country's weighting in a comparable index. I believe this provides both diversification benefits and flexibility. By limiting exposure to any one country, only a portion of the total portfolio is exposed to particular political risks.

In addition, the value investor is a long-term holder of a stock and is willing to endure temporary drops in a country's stock market. For example, after the Tiananmen Square massacre in 1989, Hong Kong stocks fell substantially. But the ever-patient value investor eventually saw stock prices gradually surpass their original values.

Some value investors even view political risk in a positive light, since the resulting uncertainty can create good buying opportunities. As was the case with Tiananmen Square, political developments can involve tragic consequences. I'm not suggesting that investors ignore such tragedies or develop a callous nature. I am suggesting that in the wake of such occurrences, speculators may be motivated by emotional impulses. As always, the value investor should remain focused on the objective evaluation of businesses and the prices being paid for their shares. Sometimes, the best time to buy is after stocks have plunged and a market is selling at a relatively cheap price. Long-term investing likely will span periods that include events that could be described as shocking, bewildering, or horrifying. Investors—as opposed to speculators—need to retain their discipline in *all* market environments.

DIVERSE ACCOUNTING SYSTEMS

In sports, all teams play by the same set of rules. Scoring a goal in soccer is the same whether the game is played in Africa, Asia, Europe, or North or South America. Keeping score is a lot more confusing in the international investment arena, where each country has its own set of accounting rules and corporate disclosure practices. And even when the terms are the same, they don't necessarily mean the same thing. For example, an interesting comparison of price-earnings ratios was cited in a 1992 study. At that time, the Standard & Poor's Industrial Index was selling at 25.6 times earnings, compared with 36.7 for the Tokyo equity market. But Andrew Smithers of Smithers & Co., a London research firm, argued that Tokyo's real P/E was 20.2, or just 57 percent of the stated ratio.

The reason? Roughly 45 percent of the shares on Tokyo's market were owned by another quoted company, a system known as *cross-ownership*. To own the entire market, Smithers reasoned, an investor would only have to buy 55 percent of the Tokyo market. Confusing? You bet. But that same confusion creates opportunity for those who understand the differences in global accounting methods. In this chapter I offer general accounting guidelines for comparing equities across international borders.

The Challenge of Diversity

With some notable exceptions, the international investment arena remains a confusing world of diverse accounting practices. Any non-U.S. company with a listing on U.S. exchanges must satisfy reporting standards that conform to U.S. generally accepted accounting principles (GAAP). Some multinationals, such as Honda and Matsushita, fulfill this requirement by issuing two sets of accounting statements, one to meet local standards, and a second for purposes of U.S. GAAP. Other companies use a single report to publish results in accordance with their own national accounting requirements. Within the framework of that same report, numbers are converted into U.S. GAAP terms.

The challenge for international stock pickers is to compare the earnings of companies on a worldwide basis, despite national accounting discrepancies. It's a challenge we welcome as value investors because it gives us a leg up on the competition in the hunt for bargain stocks. If uncovering the bottom-line truth about a company's financial status were a quick and easy task, less diligent investors would do it too.

Uniformity Coming?

International accounting uniformity is an idea whose time appears to be coming—slowly. In October 2002, the International Accounting Standards Board (IASB) and Financial Accounting Standards Board (FASB) announced an agreement to work together to combine international and U.S. accounting standards. If successful, the organizations' efforts could make it easier to compare accounting statements from companies worldwide.

Based in London, the IASB began operations in 2001, taking over from the International Accounting Standards Committee (IASC), which was formed in 1973. Also formed in 1973, Norwalk, Connecticut–based FASB has been the designated organization in the private sector for establishing U.S. standards of financial accounting and reporting. According to FASB, these standards govern the preparation of financial reports and are officially recognized as authoritative by the Securities and Exchange Commission and the American Institute of Certified Public Accountants.

Not Better or Worse . . . Just Different

Until accounting practices are more standardized, it is important to realize that reporting rules around the world are not necessarily better or worse than U.S. GAAP, they are just different. Financial accounting is a somewhat subjective process. Accountants often make assumptions about the future that understandably differ from country to country.

In the United States, reporting profit margins on product lines is viewed as standard accounting procedure. In Germany, corporations equate such disclosures with giving away important secrets to competing firms. The New York Stock Exchange has barred German companies from trading as exchange-listed American Depositary Receipts (ADRs) until these companies agree to report profit margins on a line-by-line basis.

How to Compare Apples and Oranges

In comparing the real prices of worldwide equities, here are some points to consider:

- Compare cash flows rather than reported earnings. Although cash flow per share requires adjustment for differing accounting methods, the statistic is generally more comparable than earnings.

- Comparing international book values is meaningless unless you interpret the underlying accounting principles in each case. Even under U.S. GAAP, accounting book values rarely reflect true market asset values.

- Dividends tell the real story. If you compare a U.S. company with a non-U.S. company in the same field and both have similar business fundamentals, the non-U.S. company with a 6 percent dividend yield could be a better buy than the U.S. company yielding 3 percent. Dividends are paid in hard, cold cash, leaving no room for accounting interpretations.

- Some countries, such as Switzerland, Germany, and Japan, are more conservative than others when it comes to reporting earnings.

- Some overseas companies, particularly when reporting extraordinary earnings from sales of subsidiaries or real estate, may report these earnings less conservatively than they would under U.S. GAAP standards.

- Tax considerations affect the way in which non-U.S. companies report their earnings. In Germany and Switzerland, tax authorities do not permit businesses to maintain two sets of books. The shareholders and the tax authorities receive identical earnings reports. Therefore, reports to shareholders minimize earnings to avoid a heavier tax bite.

- Under U.S. GAAP, net income before taxes as reported to shareholders often differs from net income as computed on the company's tax return. A U.S. company could, for instance, use one depreciation schedule for reporting to its stockholders and a different set for reporting to the Internal Revenue Service.

To illustrate the last bulleted item above, consider this example. Suppose Company ABC buys a $100,000 piece of equipment. In reporting to stockholders, the company may opt for "straight-line depreciation" over a 20-year period. Using this approach, reported earnings are reduced by a mere $5000 during the first year and in subsequent years. For tax reporting purposes, on the other hand, Company ABC may elect the "double-declining-balance" method of depreciation.

First-year depreciation would be $10,000, which temporarily reduces the profit by an additional $5000, as compared with the straight-line method. The result is a temporary reduction in the amount of earnings reported to the IRS, thereby reducing the tax bite.

Regardless of the method used, over the life of the asset, the amount of depreciation will be the same. But by using accelerated depreciation in its reporting to the IRS, Company ABC can conserve more of its cash during the early years of an asset's useful life. And by using straight-line depreciation in its reporting to stockholders, Company ABC can present a more favorable earnings picture.

When comparing companies' results on an international basis, keep in mind that diverse depreciation methods produce diverse earnings reports. Cash flows, on the other hand, are less affected by different depreciation expenses. Therefore, in assessing corporate performance, international stock pickers should take a hard look at cash flows as well as reported earnings.

Comparing Goodwill

Goodwill is the term applied to a company's intangible assets such as the value of its product or service brands, customer relations, experience of employees, and management. In the United States, firms tend to pump up book values by their method of accounting for goodwill, especially relative to their non-U.S. cousins. At the end of September 1996, the stated U.S. GAAP accounting book value for Philip Morris, now Altria, was $17.65 per share. However, the company had $18.7 billion, or the equivalent of $23.05 per share, listed under goodwill.

Over the years, Philip Morris had acquired several leading brand names, including Kraft cheeses, Miracle Whip salad dressing, Sanka and Maxwell House coffees, and Post cereals. These brand names, which possess intangible economic value, were categorized as goodwill by the Philip Morris accounting staff.

Under Swiss accounting principles at that time, the book value for Philip Morris would most likely look quite different. Instead of $17.65, the company would have a negative book value of −$5.40 ($17.65 − $23.05). The Swiss did not begin to ascribe value to purchased goodwill until around 1995, so acquisitions consummated before that date at a premium to the worth of the assets generated no goodwill.

A straight comparison between the rates of return on equity for Philip Morris and Nestle, a comparable Swiss firm would have been meaningless. The value of such companies is determined in large part by the earning power generated by their brand names, advertising, and distribution clout. An investor has to look behind the numbers and understand what accounting principles are being used. In comparing these companies, asset value analysis is, candidly, a waste of time; you need to analyze their earning power instead.

You might start by comparing the treatment of goodwill on the income statements for the two firms. In the United States, goodwill is revalued at least annually and written down to market, if necessary. In the past, goodwill could be amortized over up to 40 years. That practice changed in 2002. Even if the Kraft name endures forever, its goodwill value for accounting purposes has a finite life span.

Swiss accounting practices handle goodwill differently. With no goodwill recorded during acquisitions until about 1995, no amortization took place. From that point forward, standards changed and became more consistent with International Accounting Standards (IAS), which required that Nestle book acquisition goodwill and amortize it over a period not to exceed 20 years. These variances between countries' accounting pronouncements over time create difficult, but necessary, reconciling items that analysts must evaluate before comparing returns on equity and book value across countries.

I don't think writing off accounting goodwill for a prestigious brand name reflects the true economics of the situation. In my opinion, the most recent goodwill pronouncement is more reflective of economic reality, even though it affords management an additional level of flexibility when it comes to how to account for goodwill and related amortization.

A Tale of Two Phone Companies

In 1991, Telefónica, Spain's major phone company, was a better buy than Pacific Telesis, a large U.S. exchange. But you wouldn't have known it from a cursory glance at the firms' accounting statements. The stated P/E ratio for Telefónica in the Spanish accounting report was nearly equivalent to the P/E ratio for Pacific Telesis in U.S. GAAP figures.

In reality, Telefónica was trading at half the price of the U.S. company, based on earnings. In 1989, the earnings per share, as stated in Telefónica's annual report, were $2.03. In 1990, earnings rose to $2.56, and in 1991 to $2.92. Converted to U.S. accounting, the earnings for the 3 years would have been $4.46, $5.50, and $5.70, respectively.

The primary reason for these discrepancies is that Spanish accounting mandates the use of relatively rapid depreciation rates for plants and equipment. At the time, these depreciation write-offs were particularly large and reflected Telefónica's substantial investments in new plants and equipment. Under U.S. accounting codes, depreciation schedules could be extended for longer periods of time, and Telefónica's earnings would look higher.

The Spanish accounting rationale goes something like this: By rapidly writing off very large investments in state-of-the-art phone equipment, you are acknowledging the speed of innovation in the telecommunications industry. Equipment becomes obsolete rather quickly, as new technology comes on line.

Proponents of U.S. accounting practices might counter by saying: Rapid write-off of equipment that is not yet obsolete or even close to it does not fairly reflect business dynamics or the profitability of an expanding company.

For investors, the issue isn't which accounting method is right or wrong. What's more important is being aware of these discrepancies and focusing on understanding how different points of view affect the bottom line, in this case, U.S. and non-U.S. earnings. At the end of 1991, Telefónica was trading at 12 times earnings in Spanish accounting terms. If the earnings were translated into U.S. terms, the company would be selling at a bargain P/E ratio of 6.5.

At the same time, Pacific Telesis Group, the large California telephone company, was trading at 15.5 times earnings. Telefónica, therefore, was a potential bargain, compared to Pacific Telesis.

EXAMPLES OF COUNTRY ACCOUNTING DIFFERENCES

As you can see from the saga of the phone companies, investors must be cognizant of country-by-country differences in accounting practices. The following country-specific examples underscore some of the key differences in accounting procedures across the globe.

Japan[2]

Accounting practices in Japan are so heavily influenced by tax regulations that earnings and asset values are often understated. Any item that is claimed for tax purposes must be included in the financial statements that shareholders receive.

Real Estate   Revaluation of property is not permitted. Therefore, when land prices soared in the 1980s, land assets remained at book values that were far below current market price.

Depreciation   Whereas U.S. companies employ straight-line depreciation, the Japanese use double-declining depreciation, thus often understating fixed assets and earnings. If Japanese companies employed the straight-line method, current earnings would increase on average between 10 to 15 percent. As cited earlier, straight-line depreciation reduces the value of an asset in equal annual increments.

Goodwill   Goodwill arising from consolidation is normally amortized over a 5-year period by the Japanese. With goodwill in the United States revalued at least annually and written down to market, if necessary, asset values for U.S. firms could be understated compared to those in Japan. Of course, U.S. GAAP numbers now may become overstated relative to comparable Japanese companies if no impairment is seen in the goodwill over a period of years.

United Kingdom[3]

In many respects, financial statements prepared in the United Kingdom are similar to those prepared according to U.S. GAAP. However, U.K. companies have a broader choice of accounting methods. The use of alternative accounting methods under U.K. accounting standards (Statements of Standard Accounting Practice or SSAPs) opens the door to a variety of interpretations.

Inventory   The major difference between U.K. and U.S. inventory accounting is that the LIFO (last in, first out) method is not permissible for tax purposes in the United Kingdom and is seldom used. LIFO is used by a large percentage of major U.S. firms. During periods of rising prices, a U.K. firm's reported cost of sales would be lower than it would be for a U.S. company using LIFO, and net income would be higher for the U.K. firm.

Germany

German tax and reporting books are one and the same. It is a system that encourages the overestimation of certain contingent liabilities or accruals that can be reversed into income in the future. This has the effect of reducing current-year tax burdens. By overestimating losses, German firms understate earnings by as much as 50 to 100 percent compared with U.S.

GAAP. Unlike U.S. companies, German firms are not required to provide earnings per share information.

Inventory Inventories in Germany are typically understated for tax reasons and not revalued when prices go up. Mergers and takeovers are reported on the balance sheet based on book value rather than the actual transaction price.

Brazil[4]

In Brazil, where high inflation has often rendered financial statements meaningless, restatement of accounts is used to reflect changes in price levels. This indexing practice, typically employed when inflation climbs above a certain threshold, requires marking most balance sheet accounts, including fixed assets and equity, up by the level of inflation seen over the course of the year and running gains and losses through either the income statement or directly through the equity account. Since World War II, the United States has never experienced the type of inflation witnessed in Brazil, and U.S. GAAP has never required inflationary adjustments in the financial statements, although during the 1970s certain inflation disclosures were required in the footnotes. Brazil's inflation rate in the past few years has declined and firms are no longer using inflationary accounting. However, if higher inflation rates were to surface, the practice likely would be revitalized.

In countries where high inflation prevails, governments often attempt to control the exchange rate. If the government sets exchange levels that are not consistent with a nation's inflation rate, accounting distortions may occur in the reports of global companies doing business within that particular country. These are particularly difficult to sort through but may materially distort the accounting financials from economic reality.

The Netherlands[5]

Dutch accounting is more flexible than U.S. GAAP. Although Dutch Civil Code standards are similar to U.S. standards, the former stipulates that accounting methods should be acceptable to the business community. This phrase provides considerable accounting leeway.

Asset Revaluation In the Netherlands, fixed assets may be revalued and stated in excess of historical cost. Replacement value is recalculated based on general price indices. When fixed assets are revalued, depreciation expenses in the income statement are based on replacement value. These increased depreciation expenses may not be used for tax purposes.

Clearly, the revaluation of fixed assets can significantly increase a company's reported net assets, particularly during periods of inflation. Net income will be lower under Dutch Civil Code standards than under U.S. GAAP. In the United States, only historical cost amounts may be used for depreciation purposes. This upward revaluation of assets could conceivably allow a Dutch company to borrow more than a company in the United States.

COMPARING COMPANIES ON A WORLDWIDE BASIS

As I suggested earlier in this chapter, cash flows rather than reported earnings are a good yardstick for comparing company earnings around the globe. National accounting differences tend to distort the earnings picture for various companies.

Exhibit 10-1 compares cash flow with reported earnings, relative to stock prices, in Japan and the United States since 1990. Although P/E ratios vary from country to country, this variation is reduced when you look at price-to-cash-flow multiples. Japan is a case in point. In P/E terms, Japan looks very expensive. But if comparisons are made on a cash flow basis, the valuations look more reasonable.

Cash flows rather than reported earnings are a good yardstick for comparing company earnings around the globe.

FINANCIAL ACCOUNTING: AN INEXACT DISCIPLINE

For the value investor seeking a sound business at an attractive price, financial statements are a vital element in the decision-making process. As we have indicated, however, financial accounting is an inexact discipline at best. Attaching hard numbers to dynamic and perpetually changing business circumstances is a difficult task.

The reams of estimates and assumptions that are part of an accountant's stock-in-trade are invariably subject to uncertainty and interpretation.

EXHIBIT 10-1   P/E versus P/CF: The United States and Japan

Quarter Ended	MSCI Japan		MSCI U.S.	
	P/E	P/CF	P/E	P/CF
12/31/92	38.9x	8.1x	22.7x	10.2x
12/31/93	67.8x	9.8x	22.1x	10.4x
12/31/94	98.2x	11.6x	16.9x	9.1x
12/31/95	105.2x	12.9x	17.2x	10.0x
12/31/96	108.7x	12.1x	19.3x	11.2x
12/31/97	41.9x	9.5x	22.9x	13.7x
12/31/98	185.2x	9.7x	30.2x	18.1x
12/31/99	−295.4x	16.2x	30.7x	19.5x
12/31/00	57.5x	11.4x	26.1x	15.7x
12/31/01	39.8x	8.5x	33.3x	16.0x
12/31/02	−126.2x	8.8x	22.6x	12.1x

Source: RIMES Technologies Corp., as of December 31, 2002.

Some accountants obviously display a great sense of humor when they attempt to report asset values and earnings down to the last dollar! In addition to being humorists, some accountants seem to be in the beauty makeover business. As investors, we must be wary of accounting techniques that massage corporate results to make them look better. These practices, while strictly legal, can confound readers of financial statements.

Watch out for sticky wickets such as flexible depreciation rules, off-balance-sheet financing, accounting for currency movements, treatment of costs and when to recognize them, acquisition and disposal accounting, and treatment of goodwill.

Accounting for Growth,[6] a book on "creative" British accounting, produced shock waves in the investment community. The author's conclusion—that investors should shun companies that frequently resort to "creative" accounting—is probably well taken. Companies that use liberal accounting gimmicks to hide their weaknesses are more likely than conservatively managed enterprises to spring unwelcome performance surprises in the future. Value investors beware: These accounting sleights of hand raise troubling questions as to management's truthfulness, its grasp on reality, and its long-term concern for shareholder interests.

As we saw with companies such as Enron, WorldCom, and Adelphia, creative accounting techniques are by no means the exclusive province of companies outside the United States. *Unaccountable Accounting*,[7] a popular and enlightening exposé on creative U.S. accounting techniques by Professor Abraham J. Briloff, suggests that U.S. managers are no slouches when it comes to "positioning" the truth. In the wake of bankruptcies that surfaced in 2002, this may not surprise U.S. investors. What *may* surprise them, however, is that Briloff's book was published in 1972—30 years before accounting concerns derailed companies such as Enron and WorldCom.

LONG-RUN REPORTING SMOOTHS OUT THE BUMPS

Over the long term, disparities in financial reporting, caused either by creative accounting or by accounting standards that differ from country to country, tend to disappear. Reported international earnings that are higher one year than they would be under U.S. GAAP tend to be lower in subsequent years under those same, non-U.S. GAAP accounting standards.

Value investors, whose decision making depends on fundamental business analysis, should keep in mind that 1-year results are essentially meaningless. This is true not only in terms of market prices, but also as far as evaluating the intrinsic worth of businesses.

CONCLUSION

Global markets offer tremendous opportunities for value investors. Keep in mind that when you look into companies around the world, it's important to evaluate all factors, such as currency fluctuations, political risk, and diverse accounting systems, that may influence your investment decisions. You may need to make adjustments to financial statements when evaluating company fundamentals in various countries to create a more "apples-to-apples" comparison. Be cognizant of the political climate in countries where you may invest, but don't let negative sentiment deter you from investigating promising individual companies in emotionally charged regions. While all of these factors may involve more work and research than you're used to in the domestic market, I believe the potential rewards make the effort very worthwhile.

LOOKING AHEAD TO PART 4

Through the first three parts of this book, I've covered why value investing works (namely, the combination of *rational* fundamental analysis and *irrational* market prices), how to find value stocks, and how to broaden investment horizons to include international opportunities. In Part 4 (Chapters 11 to 14), I'll address some of the psychological skills necessary to *maintain* a value-investing strategy, reiterate my conviction in stocks as an excellent means toward long-term financial goals, and stress the need for conviction and patience.

Notes

1. Web site: pages.stern.nyu.edu/~nroubini/asia/countries/ brazil_news.html.

2. Gary S. Schieneman, *Understanding Japanese Financial Statements: A Guide for the U.S. Investor,* New York: Arthur Young and Co. for Morgan Stanley, 1986.

3. Gary S. Schieneman, *Understanding U.K. Financial Statements: A Guide for the U.S. Investor,* New York: Arthur Young & Co. for Morgan Stanley, 1987.

4. Gary S. Schieneman, *Brazilian Accounting Practices and Principles,* New York: Arthur Young & Co. for Morgan Stanley, 1986.

5. Gary S. Schieneman, *Understanding Dutch Financial Statements: A Guide for the U.S. Investor,* New York: Arthur Young & Co. for Morgan Stanley, 1986.

6. Terry Smith, *Accounting for Growth,* Pomfret, VT: Trafalgar Square, 1992.

7. Abraham J. Briloff, *Unaccountable Accounting,* New York: Harper & Row, 1972.

4

Value Investing and You

Throughout the first three parts of this book, I've defined value investing and cited reasons why it has worked. I've focused on how to identify good investments and stressed the benefits of looking worldwide for opportunities. Now I turn my attention to maintaining a portfolio of value stocks. In Chapters 11 to 14, I'll explore the different skills you'll need to manage your portfolio—skills that complement those used to select businesses. I'll also address the inevitability of bear markets, how to cope with them, and why I believe stocks remain an excellent choice for long-term appreciation.

Psychological or emotional weaknesses that may adversely affect your long-term success are pinpointed with the hope of diminishing or eliminating their influence. In essence, this part of the book is largely about risk—what it is and how to handle it.

I'll look at aspects of investor psychology at the individual level (versus the macro level addressed in Chapter 2), including the effects of the Information Age, and make a comparison of an individual's investment process with that of groups, such as investment clubs or professional money managers. I'll underscore the importance of establishing and adhering to a dispassionate investment philosophy and process. I'll also challenge you to follow the lessons you'll learn here. I'll address the role of financial consultants and what they can and cannot do for you. And lastly, I'll stress the importance of patience.

11

MANAGING RISKS AND YOUR VALUE PORTFOLIO

The concept of the "portfolio" is perhaps as old as the adage "Don't put all your eggs in one basket." And still as useful.

A portfolio is designed to limit risks—namely, the risk of losing money—when investing in stocks. In this chapter, I examine the topic of risk—how value investors define it and how it can be managed but never completely eliminated. I'll look at different types of risk measurement, such as standard deviation, and why such gauges may not be appropriate for value investors. And when it comes to managing risk, I'll closely examine the "portfolio," the primary tool investors have in risk management, and a diversified portfolio's benefits and limitations. I'll also review and challenge tenets of "modern portfolio theory."

WHAT *IS* RISK AND HOW TO LIMIT IT?

Within the investment world, academics and theorists often have defined risk in terms of volatility, standard deviation, or beta. I'll address these concepts in a moment. But for most investors, risk simply means losing money. While stocks have been an excellent means for accumulating wealth over the long term, there are *always* risks when investing. I have worked in the investment industry during five different decades. Based on my experience, investors generally lose money for one of four reasons:

1. Payment of more than the intrinsic worth of the security
2. Significant deterioration in a company's position
3. Loss realized through actual sale
4. Straying from fundamental investing disciplines

In Part 2 of this book, I addressed important considerations value investors make prior to purchasing shares of a company. I discussed the essence of value investing, weighing the *value* of a business against the *price* of its stock. As Benjamin Graham pointed out, paying too great a price for a stock—a price beyond a company's underlying worth—eliminates the margin of safety and, thus, can be very risky. Always keep the relationship between business value and stock price in mind, especially when a stock has shown strong, short-term gains or during bull markets, when widespread euphoria can lead to overconfidence and a less diligent approach. This caution supports the first point cited above. Expanding on this notion, Graham wrote, ". . . the risk of paying too high a price for good-quality stocks—while a real one—is not the chief hazard confronting the average buyer of securities. Observation over many years has taught us that the chief losses to investors come from the purchase of low-quality securities at times of favorable business conditions. The purchasers . . . assume that prosperity is synonymous with safety."[1]

With respect to point two above, let's look at cases in which a company's fundamental strengths deteriorate. In other words, what happens when the reasons that prompted your first purchase of a company's shares are no longer valid? Let's say a company's products or services are shown to be inferior, management guides the company down an unwise path, or a natural disaster destroys the company's sole manufacturing plant. In these examples, value investors may reevaluate the company and revise their estimate of a company's intrinsic value.

If developments at a company do indeed prompt a revision of a company's underlying worth, value investors may wish to sell shares if they are trading *above* the revised estimate of the company's intrinsic value.

In this case, the investment no longer offers a margin of safety, and by selling your shares you may lose money. However, I believe it is wiser to realize the loss and reallocate the proceeds of the sale to another, more attractively valued opportunity. At the same time, if the share price is still significantly *below* your revised estimate of the business's intrinsic value and, thus, continues to offer a significant margin of safety, I recommend holding it. Again, the relationship between business value and stock price should be the primary factor in your decision to buy, sell, or hold.

Value investors, like any other investor, lose money when they sell shares at prices below what they paid for them initially. Sounds simple enough. If you do the opposite of buying at a low price and selling at a higher price, you aren't likely to make much money investing. So why, as outlined in point three above, would an investor do such a thing? Why would anyone buy a stock at $25 per share, for example, and sell it later for $10? I offer two explanations. First, as I already addressed, the business fundamentals underpinning the purchase decision might change and taking a loss reflects a prudent, long-term decision. And second, the investor succumbs to the lure of "Mr. Market."

I'll address the parable of Mr. Market in Chapter 13. Developed by Benjamin Graham, the story of Mr. Market helps explain the potential risks for value investors when they succumb to the fourth point: straying from their disciplines. First, however, let's explore various notions of risk and a primary way to mitigate each of them—diversification.

RISK APPLIED TO VALUE INVESTING

In Chapter 2, I looked at efficient market theory—the notion that stock prices always accurately reflect everything known about a company's prospects—and offered countering opinions. Here, I'll follow a similar approach in addressing the concept of risk, especially as defined by modern portfolio theory, or MPT. MPT, introduced by Harry Markowitz in the 1950s, asserts that risk can be reduced through asset allocation: building a portfolio composed of asset classes (such as stocks, bonds, and cash) with low "correlations." As noted in Chapter 8 when I addressed the benefits of international diversification, correlation refers to how closely returns for one asset class (large-cap, U.S. stocks, for example) mirror returns for another asset class (such as small-cap, non-U.S. stocks). In short, if part of your portfolio is "zigging" when another part is "zagging," the gains help offset the losses. While this theory seems logical (and helped earn Markowitz a Nobel Prize), it is vital to recognize how "risk" in this sense is defined. Over the years, investors have adopted MPT's mantra, "risk

MPT is based on the notion of redefining risk as share price fluctuation, or price volatility. But the value investor would find this definition unacceptable.

reduction through asset allocation," without perhaps giving much thought to what risks are being reduced by following this strategy.

MPT is based on the notion of redefining risk as share price fluctuation, or price volatility. But the value investor would find this definition unacceptable. Value investors do not lose money just because share prices decline, even if they temporarily drop below the original purchase price. Commenting on the redefining of risk as volatility at the heart of MPT, Malcolm Mitchell, the managing director of the Center for Investment Policy Studies, wrote, "That unsupported and unexplained redefinition confounds what all investors previously thought of as risk—and what non-professionals still think it is—that is, the possibility of losing money."[2]

Mitchell adds that, "Markowitz did not find a way to measure the risk that investors care about: the risk that arises from an uncertain future, the risk that things will turn out to be worse than we expect. He simply ignored that kind of risk and focused instead on variability—or, to take the term more commonly used today, volatility. Instead of measuring risk, Markowitz demonstrated how to measure volatility in a portfolio. Why volatility? One obvious reason is that volatility is measurable, whereas uncertainty is not. In sum, . . . defining risk as volatility is irrelevant to investors' real experiences, and worse, it obscures the true definition of investment risk as the possibility of losing money."

VOLATILITY AND THE VALUE INVESTOR

As cited above, volatility is the tendency of a security's market value to fluctuate sharply up or down in the short term. For traders who want to sell off their portfolios at a moment's notice, volatility and risk are roughly equivalent. But for value investors, who don't have the urge to liquidate their portfolios any time soon, volatility has limitations as a measure of risk. In the long term, I consider volatility less significant than the values of the businesses in your portfolio and the prices you paid for those businesses. Despite my reservations about the usefulness of volatility as a risk measure, I think it merits addressing in this chapter for the following reasons:

- Many investors are volatility-averse and cannot tolerate significant short-term price fluctuations in their portfolios.

- In the academic community, volatility is the only quantifiable measure of risk and is extensively cited in studies of risk analysis.

- Empirical studies also may use *beta* as a yardstick for risk. Beta measures a portfolio's relative volatility against overall market movement rather than against its own historical returns.

Understanding terms such as *standard deviation* and *beta* can help investors put them in the proper context when evaluating investment opportunities and monitoring their portfolios. Let's look in greater detail at the concept of beta.

BETA WATCH OUT

By definition, beta is a measurement of volatility relative to the market. For example, a beta of 1.0 means a stock has about the same volatility as the overall market. A beta of 1.7 indicates that when the market has risen 1 percent, the stock has historically climbed 1.7 percent. Conversely, when the market has fallen 1 percent, the stock has historically declined 1.7 percent. According to the academic theory of capital markets, the higher the beta, the greater the risk and the greater the potential reward. Conversely, the lower the beta, the lower the risk and the lower the potential reward. Risk-averse investors have contributed to the Wall Street myth that supports avoiding high-beta stocks. This notion has oversimplified good investment practice, as noted by many, including author John Train. Train takes the beta theory to task in *The Midas Touch*, an excellent book that provides considerable insight into the investing philosophy of Warren Buffett.[3]

According to Train, Buffett offered the example of being able to buy $1 worth of stock in the market for 75 cents. Suppose the price declined so the same $1 worth of stock could be had for 50 cents. At the same time, prices for the general market remained unchanged. Here, because the price of the $1 worth of stock fell while prices for the broader market remained flat, the stock's beta increased. Beta theorists see this as a negative development. However, the price drop also creates opportunity and a larger margin of safety. To avoid this opportunity simply because of the stock's high beta would be absurd.

Consider Buffett's purchase of stock in the Washington Post Company in the mid-1970s when its market capitalization was about $80 million. (Market capitalization represents a company's total number of shares of stock outstanding multiplied by the price of one share.) For the Washington Post Company, the whole company could easily have been marketed and sold in the mid-1970s for $400 million.

At the time, what if the company's market value had dropped even further—from $80 to $40 million. The additional downside volatility would have made the stock's beta increase, but it also clearly would have made it a better value. Should investors have been frightened by the high beta? Obviously not. By 1997, the Washington Post Company had a market capitalization of $3.6 billion, up nearly 45-fold since 1973.

Beta is used primarily by those who are looking at the whole market (or large numbers of stocks within it) and who don't look in detail at the fundamentals of specific companies. As I've shown, for value investors, this concept is irrelevant at best and downright dangerous at worst.

While short-term volatility may be reduced by purchasing only low-beta stocks, I believe long-term returns will likely be diminished and investors may fall short of their goals. Not having enough money to fund a child's college education or not being able to enjoy the lifestyle in retirement to which you aspired represent far greater risks, in my mind, than the bumps of short-term volatility. For long-term investors, short-term price fluctuations are of little importance. As Warren Buffett wrote in the chairman's letter of the 1996 annual report to shareholders of Berkshire-Hathaway, "I would much rather earn a lumpy 15% over time than a smooth 12%."[4]

STANDARD DEVIATION AND "LUMPY" RETURNS

When discussing how to measure the volatility of returns, you'll often hear the phrase *standard deviation*. What does this term mean? Standard deviation is the dispersion of returns around an average return. So what does *that* mean? In short, it means that the *greater* the standard deviation, the *greater* the volatility of a particular investment, portfolio, or market. Earlier in this chapter, I stated that high volatility (or high standard deviation) is not necessarily bad. Let's go back to your days in high school to illustrate this point.

Among all your high school classmates, most probably got Cs and Bs on their report cards. Before the onset of the recent phenomenon of "grade inflation," Cs and Bs were indeed average grades. For the purpose of this example, think of those grades as average "returns," if you will. A smaller number of students might have gotten all Ds or all Bs. And at the extreme ends of the scale, an even smaller number of students probably got all Fs or all As. You can think of the range of grades your classmates earned as similar to the range of returns for an investment such as stocks or bonds. And based on historical precedent, you might be able to draw a reasonable estimate of how a student might perform during a semester or year. For example, you'd expect a typical C student to get Cs. Occasionally, he might do really well and get an A in one class. He might do poorly and get an F. But for the most part, you'd expect him to get Cs.

Applying this approach to each of your high school classmates, you could quantify how much their grades fluctuated from their historical average and come up with a standard deviation. This would measure the variability of their grades—or to what degree they fluctuated around their average. Thus, a student with a high standard deviation of grades might have erratic performance: for example, getting Cs one quarter, As the next, Bs the next, and Fs the next. His performance would be characterized as more unpredictable, and thus, he might be considered a "higher risk" student.

A student who got As virtually all the time would have a low standard deviation—there's little variability in her performance. But a student who consistently got Fs would *also* have a low standard deviation. For a failing student who regularly got poor grades, a low standard deviation wouldn't necessarily mean he's a "low risk" student. It would simply mean he's a consistently bad performer. The same logic applies to investing. A low standard deviation in and of itself isn't necessarily good or bad. You have to look at it within the context of actual performance.

DIVERSIFICATION: ITS ADVANTAGES AND LIMITATIONS

Even in a well-structured value portfolio, risk (as defined by volatility or losing money) cannot be eliminated. But risk can be limited through diversification. Purchasing shares of only one company, for example, or investing in only one industry, suggests a certainty that the choice will outperform all others. That is a gamble, and while it may prove correct, such a decision likely represents excessive risk for most investors. Diversification (the concept of *not* putting all your eggs in one basket) can save you a good deal of trouble down the road. The benefits of diversification are impressive. For example, owning five stocks in different industries can reduce portfolio risk by 80 percent. If an investor owns 10 stocks, portfolio risk is reduced by 90 percent.[5] Notice how quickly risk declines when the number of stocks in a portfolio increases to 10.

Given the data, should value investors consider 10 stocks to be the limit for their portfolios? No. Many of the top-performing value portfolios contain hundreds of stocks. Some people mistakenly believe that returns are diluted by an increased number of portfolio holdings. As long as strict value criteria are followed, more stocks in your portfolio may not prove counterproductive to long-term results. Be advised, though, that more stocks in your portfolio will affect your *relative* returns, or your returns in relationship to a benchmark such as the S&P 500 Index or the MSCI World Index. It becomes increasingly difficult to achieve performance results that are significantly *different* than an index when you hold more and more stocks that are already *in* the index.

Effective Diversification

To minimize the consequences of a single holding's poor returns adversely affecting the entire portfolio (this is known as *stock-specific risk*), I suggest limiting exposure to any individual company to no more than 5 percent of the entire portfolio at cost. I also suggest limiting exposure to individual industries and countries to a maximum of 20 percent of the portfolio at cost or 150 percent of an appropriate index weighting in these areas. These guidelines are designed to provide a broad degree of flexibility in constructing portfolios while limiting potentially unwise concentrations in individual companies, industries, or countries. You may wish to develop similar guidelines when building and maintaining your own portfolio of value stocks. I'll discuss maintaining your portfolio in greater detail in Chapter 13.

While diversification is important, some investors believe that diversification not only limits risk but also *enhances* returns over the long term. This may or may not be true, especially with respect to diversifying a portfolio across different asset classes. A portfolio that is diversified among stocks, bonds, and cash, for example, can indeed reduce short-term volatility, but it may also *reduce* long-term results relative to an all-stock portfolio. Based on historical precedent, stocks have delivered the greatest returns over the long term. Mixing bonds and cash (whose long-term returns have tended to lag those for stocks) in with an all-stock portfolio can have a diminishing effect. Keep in mind there is no "proper" portfolio mix. A portfolio composed wholly of stocks may not be appropriate for you. It largely depends upon your individual goals and tolerance for volatility.

While diversification is important, some investors believe that diversification not only limits risk but also enhances *returns over the long term. This may or may not be true.*

If you are a volatility-averse investor, a run of dismal prices in the short term could be hazardous to your long-term financial health. If your fear of fluctuating market values or need for short-term cash could push you into selling at low prices, it might make sense for you to dampen the volatility in your portfolio. Recognize your own tolerance for volatility, and structure your portfolio accordingly. That's preferable to making multiple selling errors based on fear. A financial consultant may be able to help evaluate your risk tolerance and build a portfolio suited to your specific temperament. If you want to work with a financial consultant, I'll offer some guidance on what to expect and how to work together in Chapter 13.

Diversification Is Not Free

Naturally, diversification costs more in terms of commissions, spreads, and taxes. Commissions on 200 shares each of two stocks, for example, cost more than commissions for 400 shares of a single stock. By not diversifying, however, the investor has placed an inappropriate reliance on skill (or luck) to determine investment results. I believe paying slightly more up front to lower your risk is well worth the cost over the long term.

LIQUIDITY

Some people believe *liquidity*, which is the extent to which the market can accommodate purchases or sales of a stock without large price changes, can pose a risk for investors. Some may wonder, for example, if a problem develops in a certain company, is the door big enough for everyone to get out at the same time? In other words, how quickly can I sell my holdings in a crisis? Often, you may hear of a stock that's "thinly traded" or trades in "low volume." This means that on a typical day, not many shares of the company's stock are traded. The company may have fewer shares outstanding than others and/or there is limited interest in its shares.

Concerns about liquidity are largely a waste of time and may limit investment opportunity. In extreme cases, liquidity can become an issue for large money management firms that hold huge amounts of an individual company's shares. For the most part, however, institutional and individual value investors who buy good, undervalued businesses and hold them for the long term minimize the significance of a stock's day-to-day trading capacity.

The following case illustrates how allowing liquidity concerns to impede an investment decision can lead to a costly oversight.

Delaware Trust Company, a small bank, was just one of many companies that Wall Street consistently overlooked in the late 1970s, perhaps because analysts considered the stock to be illiquid. Yet, the company was clearly undervalued. In 1978, the company had $500 million in total assets and the following fundamental traits:

- P/E ratio: 4

- Price-to-book value: 35 percent

- Return on equity: 8 percent

- Return on assets: 0.5 percent

- Loan loss, as a percent of reserves: 15 percent

At the time, the book value for Delaware Trust was over $120 per share and the stock, which traded by appointment only, was priced at $45. After investigating every aspect of the company's financial health, an astute value investor could have acquired shares of Delaware Trust even though it traded "by appointment only." In other words, sometimes shares would not trade for 3 months at a time. Note in Exhibit 11-1 that for the first few years after this hypothetical purchase, very little progress would have been made. In 1984, however, the stock price surged dramatically.

Delaware Trust Company was purchased in 1987 by Meridien Bank, which paid shareholders $853 per share. This would have been a 33 percent annualized rate of return on the initial investment. Clearly, liquidity is not always important for long-term value investors. It is important only for short-term speculators. Warren Buffett, a long-term investor who recognizes the limitations of focusing on daily changes in stock prices, said, ". . . only buy a stock that you'd be comfortable owning if they closed the stock exchange for three years tomorrow."[6]

EXHIBIT 11-1   Delaware Trust Company's Share Price History

End of February	Share Price
1979	$56
1980	$61
1981	$66
1982	$79
1983	$92
1984	$128
1985	$200
1986	$260
1987	$475
1987 (May)*	$853

*buyout
Source: Brandes Investment Partners.

DOLLAR COST AVERAGING

Before closing this chapter, I'll share a few comments on the investing strategy known as *dollar cost averaging*. If you're not already aware of this approach, it's designed to build wealth over the long term by continuously investing a fixed dollar amount in securities regardless of fluctuation in the prices of those securities. Dollar cost averaging is most often associated with mutual fund investing. Beyond building wealth, this approach may deliver another benefit. Because of short-term share price fluctuations for funds, more shares can be purchased when prices are low and, of course, fewer shares when prices are high. Overall, as investors make additional investments, the average *cost* for purchasing shares could be less than the average share *price*.

In theory, this appears to be a sound approach—getting a good cost for shares while regularly investing a fixed amount of money to build long-term wealth. In fact, many investors establish dollar cost averaging programs by linking mutual fund accounts with their checking accounts to ensure automatic investing into the fund, often every month. Benjamin Graham extolled the virtues of dollar cost averaging. "The monthly amount may be small, but the results after 20 or more years can be impressive and important to the saver," he wrote in his book *The Intelligent Investor*.[7]

Certainly, a long-term bull market can make dollar cost averaging successful. But what about applying this tactic during a *declining* market? Investors should consider their ability to continue purchasing through periods when prices are low. The emotional pressure to cease a dollar cost averaging plan tends to escalate when stock prices fall. Investors may feel they are "throwing good money after bad" if prices decline over a protracted period.

When stock prices fall over a long period, the average *cost* per share may *not* prove to be less than the average *price* per share. In fact, there are no guarantees that a dollar cost averaging plan can assure a profit or protect against loss in declining markets. Yet, I believe it is often precisely at the moment when investors are tempted to abandon dollar cost averaging that maintaining commitment to such a plan is essential.

Graham addressed dollar cost averaging in commenting on business executive John J. Raskob's article, "Everybody Ought to Be Rich," published in the *Ladies Home Journal* in 1929. Extrapolating the stock market's rise during the 1920s two decades into the future, Raskob had contended that a $15 investment each month in good common stocks (with dividends reinvested) would grow to $80,000 in 20 years. How did his theory pan out in reality?

Based on Graham's calculations—assuming investment in the Dow Jones Industrial Average (DJIA) between 1929 and 1948—an investor's holdings at the beginning of 1949 (20 years after embarking on the program) would have been worth about $8500. "This is a far cry from the great man's promise of $80,000, and it shows how little reliance can be placed on such optimistic forecasts and assurances."[8] However, Graham makes an important counterpoint: ". . . the return actually realized by the 20-year operation would have been better than 8% compounded annually—and this despite the fact that the investor would have begun his purchases with the DJIA at 300 and ended with a valuation based on the 1948 closing level of 177."[9] (That's a decline of 41 percent.)

While dollar cost averaging may deliver benefits for some (namely, establishing a disciplined method for investing), I think it's also important that long-term investors are aware that this strategy precludes a core tenet of value investing: consideration of *price*. Systematic investing programs eliminate any comparison between business value and stock price when making purchase decisions. Perhaps money can be made in this way, but the strategy doesn't qualify as value investing. True value investors buy only when the price is right.

CONCLUSION

In this chapter, I have addressed risk—how it's defined and how effective diversification plays an important role in reducing it. I have listed salient reasons why modern portfolio theory and risk statistics such as standard deviation and beta have limited usefulness for value investors. I also addressed liquidity concerns and why they do not play a significant role for the value investor.

In essence, investing in stocks always contains an element of uncertainty. Nobody knows what the future holds, and there is always the risk that tomorrow may not live up to our expectations. However, by carefully selecting and maintaining a diversified portfolio of value stocks, you can pursue your long-term investment goals with the confidence of knowing you have intelligently addressed these risks. Next, I will ask a question that goes to the heart of portfolio construction: Why should you invest in common stocks at all? For the answer, turn to Chapter 12.

Notes

1.   Benjamin Graham, *The Intelligent Investor: A Book of Practical Counsel,* 4th rev. ed., New York: Harper & Row, 1973, p. 280.

2.   Malcolm Mitchell, "Is MPT the Solution—or the Problem?" *Investment Policy*, July 2002.

3.   John Train, *The Midas Touch,* New York: Harper & Row, 1987, p. 55.

4.   Warren E. Buffett, Berkshire Hathaway Inc. Chairman's Letter, February 28, 1997. Available online at www.berkshirehathaway.com/letters/1996.html.

5.   Thomas Rorro, *Assessing Risk on Wall Street,* Deerfield Beach, FL: Liberty Publishing Co., 1984.

6.   Charley Ellis, "Living Legends," *CFA Magazine*, January–February 2003, p. 26.

7.   Graham, *The Intelligent Investor*, p. 57.

8.   Ibid., p. x.

9.   Ibid., p. x.

12

ARE STOCKS AN INTELLIGENT INVESTMENT?

S tocks can be viewed as the bricks that build strong economies.
Individual businesses seek to raise money by selling stock. The money they raise might help build new factories, develop new products or technologies, or expand their market share. In short, businesses seek to create wealth through valuable products or services that contribute to a healthy economy built on accessibility, opportunity, and exchange. Individual businesses generate the wealth that fuels the capitalistic economic system. Within this system, all assets—whether they are stocks, bonds, real estate, commodities, collectibles, and so on—maintain their value only if companies are viable. Many investors lose sight of the fact that asset values arc interrelated. If businesses falter, many other areas will be negatively affected.

Today's economies share similar challenges as they did 50, 100, or 150 years ago: inflation, interest rate fluctuations, unemployment, trade imbalances, war, natural catastrophe. All these developments can cause economic uncertainty. Amid weakened confidence, people in the past have looked to alternative markets such as art, precious metals, bank deposits, and bonds. While these assets may help preserve capital, they may also lead to an irreparable loss of purchasing power.

Over the long term, capitalism has endured, economies have survived, and stocks have continued to offer opportunities for substantial capital appreciation. In this chapter, I present arguments in favor of equities as an investment—a long-haul commitment—along with insights into inevitable stock market ups and downs. I'll make comparisons between equities and other financial alternatives and highlight the positive effect time has had on investment portfolios.

STOCKS AS AN INVESTMENT

Are stocks a worthwhile investment? If history is the ultimate judge, the answer is an overwhelming yes.

According to data from Ibbotson Associates, a Chicago-based investment consulting and research firm, U.S. common stocks (as measured by the Standard & Poor's 500 Index) averaged a compounded annual return of 10.2 percent over the 75-year period through 2002, compared to 5.5 percent for U.S. government bonds and just 3.8 percent for cash equivalents (U.S. Treasury bills).

Are stocks a worthwhile investment? If history is the ultimate judge, the answer is an overwhelming yes.

While those figures may not seem drastically different from one another, consider the ultimate difference in returns over time. Investors who put $100 into common stocks in 1927 would have seen their nest eggs grow to $177,500 by 2002; that same $100 invested in U.S. government bonds would have been worth just $5970, or nearly 30 times less. The $100 invested in cash equivalents would have grown to even less: just $1748.[1]

Jeremy Siegel, a noted professor at the Wharton School of Business at the University of Pennsylvania, commented on his research of historical returns of U.S. asset classes.

> The long-term stability of [stock] returns is all the more surprising when one reflects on the dramatic changes that have taken place in our society during the last two centuries. The U.S. evolved from an agricultural to an industrial, and now to a post-industrial, service- and technology-oriented economy. The world shifted from a gold-based standard to a paper money standard. . . . *Yet despite mammoth changes in the basic factors generating*

wealth for shareholders, equity returns have shown an astounding persistence.[2] (Emphasis added.)

Global equities, as measured by the MSCI World Index, also have proved resilient and rewarding for investors, returning a compounded annual return of 8.3 percent over the past 30 years.

WHAT ABOUT MARKET DECLINES?

Just as people sometimes catch a cold or flu, economies and markets also get aches and pains from time to time. From the end of World War II to the end of the twentieth century, U.S. markets have experienced 12 market declines of 15 percent or more. In these periods, which averaged 12.5 months in length, the S&P 500 Index fell by an average of 26.8 percent.

But people recover from their short-term illnesses, and so do markets. In fact, the average price rise during the first year following each of these 12 market declines was nearly 31 percent. (These figures do not include the S&P 500's thirteenth bear market, which began in 2000.)

These recoveries from adverse market levels may present exciting opportunities to value investors. Often, quality businesses can be bought at temporarily discounted prices. While bear markets can test discipline and try patience, value investors recognize their impermanence and the opportunities they can create.

In the summer of 1973 after the stock market had plunged 20 percent in 2 months, a friend of Warren Buffett asked the renowned value investor how he felt. "You know," Buffett replied, "some days I get up and I want to tap dance."[3] The oracle of Omaha was even more candid a year later, when the Dow had just dipped below 600. A *Forbes* interviewer asked how he contemplated the market. "Like an oversexed guy in a harem," Buffett quipped. "This is the time to start investing."[4]

While post–bear market recoveries have tended to be strong, astute investors may uncover and profit from equity investing even *during* bear markets. Bear markets are often defined as declines of 20 percent or more from a major market index's peak. Although they may be indicative of sluggish returns among equities in general, index declines can mask strong performance from a large portion of individual stocks in a given universe.

As shown in Exhibit 12-1, the S&P 500 Index as a whole shed more than 30 percent over the 2 years ended June 30, 2002—a foray into bear territory by almost any investor's standards. For the same period, though, S&P

500 constituents registering gains actually outnumbered declining S&P 500 members by a count of 279 to 210. In addition, 39 of these gainers posted returns of more than 100 percent during the period.

A key factor behind these seemingly contradictory numbers is the methodology used to construct the S&P 500. As I mentioned when addressing active and passive investment approaches in Chapter 8, a number of popular indices are capitalization weighted. This means larger companies represent larger portions of the index than their smaller counterparts. As a result, bigger companies have a bigger influence on the index's returns. When the S&P 500's larger members post declines, which was generally the case over the 2 years ended June 30, 2002, these declines can overshadow gains from smaller-sized stocks.

I believe this evidence helps highlight the veiled opportunities that bear markets might offer. Select equities may deliver strong performance, even as major market indices post declines. Similarly, active investment managers can earn solid returns for investors even when the broad market remains relatively flat.

ACTIVE MANAGEMENT CAN ADD VALUE—EVEN IN BEAR MARKETS

Between 1965 and 1982, the price level for the Dow Jones Industrial Average advanced at an annualized rate of 0.6 percent. Including dividends, returns

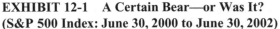
EXHIBIT 12-1   A Certain Bear—or Was It?
(S&P 500 Index: June 30, 2000 to June 30, 2002)

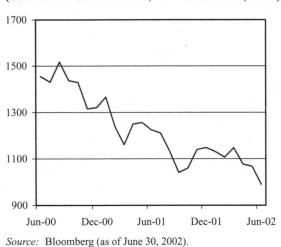

Source: Bloomberg (as of June 30, 2002).

EXHIBIT 12-2   Actively Managed, Large-Cap Mutual Fund Performance, 1965 through 1982

	Annualized Performance	Growth of $100,000
Dow Jones Industrial Average	5.7%	$271,214
S&P 500	7.1%	$344,332
Average of 47 mutual funds	10.2%	$577,265

Note: This is a hypothetical example and is not representative of any specific portfolio or mutual fund. Reinvestment of dividends and capital gains are assumed. Your actual results will vary.
Source: Bloomberg, Morningstar (as of June 30, 2002).

were better. The Dow gained 5.7 percent per year. Over the same 18-year period, the S&P 500 Index climbed at an annualized rate of 7.1 percent. Could investors have done better with active managers during this tough stretch?

To answer this question, I searched the Morningstar database, which includes performance history for thousands of mutual funds going back several decades. The search focused on actively managed, large-cap funds with track records that spanned the entire 1965–1982 period. These criteria yielded a sample of 47 funds. As shown in Exhibit 12-2, the funds tended to outperform the Dow and S&P 500 by substantial margins.

To put these annualized return figures into perspective, consider that a $100,000 investment in the Dow or S&P 500 would have grown to $271,214 or $344,332, respectively. The same investment in the average fund would have appreciated to $577,265 over the same 18-year period.[5] Because this study excluded funds that may have ceased operating between 1965 and 1982, the results may be biased. At the same time, I believe it demonstrates that, even when the overall market is not charging upward, some active managers can deliver strong returns.

Periods of weak stock market performance may deter investing in equities and prompt a search for alternative methods of building wealth. Next, I'll look at a number of these alternative assets.

HARD ASSETS

The historical evidence regarding the superiority of stocks relative to other financial assets is unambiguous: Stocks have outperformed bonds, commodities, real estate, and gold by a wide margin over the long term. See Exhibit 12-3. Still, amid adverse markets, many give in to fear and abandon stocks for investment alternatives. What are the relative returns from hard assets?

Gold

Gold has been touted as a reliable inflation hedge, but take a closer look. From 1900 to 2000, the yellow metal appreciated by a mere 2.6 percent annually.[6] U.S. inflation averaged 3.2 percent per year between 1900 and 2000.[7] Some inflation hedge! Even if you were fortunate enough to bail out at the top of the metal's spectacular bull run in 1980, your returns still would have been subpar relative to equities over the same period. Between 1926 and 1981—gold's glittering period—its price rose by just 5.8 percent per year, or barely half the annualized return of the S&P 500 Index.

Nearly all of the appreciation in gold prices during the twentieth century occurred over the 10 years ended in late 1980. Gold prices have gone mostly nowhere both before and after that relatively brief period.

EXHIBIT 12-3   Stocks, Commodities, Real Estate, and Gold 1982–2002

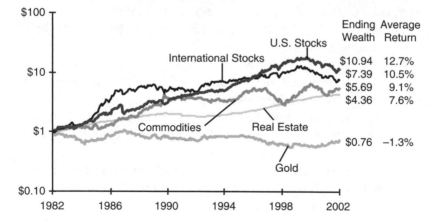

Note: Hypothetical value of $1 invested at year-end 1982. Assumes reinvestment of income and no transaction costs or taxes. Indices are unmanaged. Performance is historical. An investor's actual results will vary.

This is for illustrative purposes only and not indicative of any investment. Past performance is no guarantee of future results.

Source: Copyright © 2003 by Ibbotson Associates, Inc., March 1, 2003.

Commodities

Many investors pick commodities as their ticket to instant wealth. In reality, however, a lottery ticket might provide better odds. Even professional investors, armed with sophisticated trading techniques and the latest software programs, have difficulty consistently making money in the commodity pits.

A commodities advisor in *Money* magazine observed that 90 percent of small investors lose money in commodities, and cited the potential to lose several times the original investment.[8] Small wonder! Given the speed, volatility, leverage, and pressure inherent in the commodities business, the asset class offers no margin of safety advantage to bank on.

Fine Art

Fine art may provide enjoyment, but it falls short as an investment asset. A 2001 study examined art as an investment for the 1900–1999 period and found art "significantly underperform[ed] stocks in the U.S,"[9] even before accounting for often-sizable transaction costs. The mean annual return on art was 5.2 percent between 1900 and 1999, while the Dow Jones Industrial Average gained 7.4 percent.

Real Estate

Even during the postwar period—a time considered by many to be the golden age for land values—unleveraged real estate generally has been only a mediocre long-term investment.

Unlike businesses, real estate does not *create* wealth. Values are based on whatever real estate revenue streams can be generated, and those cash flows are a direct result of overall business health. For example, the cost of owning a single-family home is covered by money earned through a business. Consequently, businesses have to be more profitable than real estate (as an investment) or else rents couldn't be paid or houses purchased.

If real estate has been a relatively pedestrian performer over time, why do many people believe it to be so profitable? The answer is simple: leveraging, that is, the potential to make money with borrowed money. Most excess real estate profits are the result of extreme leveraging, particularly when real estate prices are rising rapidly. The downside, of course, is that while paper profits often go up by borrowing, so do potential losses. Many investors have forgotten that real estate prices also tend to be cyclical.

Whenever you are tempted to see real estate as an investment panacea, remember the U.S. real estate market in Texas in the 1980s or in California in the 1990s. Those markets took major hits, bursting leverage-driven bubbles. If businesses don't do well, neither does real estate. And if businesses are doing well, I believe there is no better way to build your wealth than by owning a diversified portfolio of stocks.

THE IMPORTANCE OF TIME

The most important commodity in your investment toolbox is time. Yet time and the power of compounding are often undervalued in our fast-paced culture.

The most important commodity in your investment toolbox is time.

Consider the effects of time on growing your financial nest egg. Exhibit 12-4 shows how a hypothetical $100,000 investment grows over various time periods at different compounding rates. Over a typical 45-year working lifetime, the difference between a $100,000 investment compounding at 5 percent and at 10 percent (the long-term average for common stocks) is $6.4 million. And the difference between earning 10 and 15 percent—an ambitious target for value investors—is *$46.5 million* over those 45 years. Yes, equity prices will fluctuate, but, as addressed in Chapter 11, perhaps tolerating short-term uncertainty is well worth the long-term results.

TIMING THE MARKET: SPECULATIVE GROUND

Trying to time one's exposure to the stock market can be futile, regardless of the theory or indicator employed. Bear market low points are impossible to predict and spending time trying to identify them distracts one from prudent financial decisions.

Charles Dow, cofounder of *The Wall Street Journal,* expressed a similar sentiment in 1902. "In dealing with the stock market," Dow said, "there is no way of telling when the top of an advance or the bottom of a decline has been reached until some time after such a top or bottom has been made."[10]

EXHIBIT 12-4   Investing $100,000: The Power of Compounding

	Compounding Rate		
Years	5%	10%	15%
5	$127,628	$161,051	$201,136
15	$207,893	$417,725	$813,706
30	$432,194	$1,744,940	$6,621,177
45	$898,501	$7,289,048	$53,876,927

Note: This is a hypothetical example and is not representative of any specific portfolio. Reinvestment of dividends and capital gains are assumed. Your actual results will vary.

Trying to time the market presents two dangers to an equity investor. First, any time out of stocks presents the risk of missing out on significant appreciation. As shown in Exhibit 12-5, $100,000 invested in the S&P 500 Index over the 5050 trading days from the beginning of 1983 through 2002 grew to $625,583. However, missing just the 10 best days of those 5050— that is, the 10 biggest daily gains of the S&P 500 over the 20-year stretch— reduces the final value of that $100,000 investment to $365,750, a difference of more than $250,000. And as the number of days missed increases, of course, the value erosion increases. With the index's 40 best days excluded, for example, a $100,000 investment in the S&P 500 over the 20 years ending in 2002 grew to only $129,447—an annualized return of just 1.3 percent.

Second, by moving out of equities, you're sacrificing an advantage (the margin of safety) to invest in asset classes that have lower historical returns, a disadvantage to those seeking *long-term* appreciation. Based on historical evidence, it appears that the longer you stay invested in stocks, the more you diminish your potential for losses. Ibbotson looked at returns for stocks between 1926 and 2002. During that span, there were 77 one-year periods (1926 to 1927, 1927 to 1928, 1928 to 1929, and so on). Of those 77 one-year periods, stocks registered gains 70 percent of the time. If the investment period is stretched to 5 years, (1926 to 1931, 1927 to 1932, 1928 to 1933, and so on), stocks posted gains during 89 percent of the 73 five-year periods between 1926 and 2002. And during the 63 fifteen-year periods over the same time, stocks never failed to appreciate. Patience—rather than attempting to time the market—has proved beneficial.

EXHIBIT 12-5   Timing the Market Can Have Consequences

S&P 500 Index, 1983–2002	Trading Days				
	All 5,050	Less 10 Best	Less 20 Best	Less 30 Best	Less 40 Best
Cumulative gain	525.6%	265.8%	147.7%	75.4%	29.4%
Annualized gain	9.6%	6.7%	4.6%	2.8%	1.3%
Growth of $100,000	$625,583	$365,750	$247,699	$175,355	$129,447

Note: This is a hypothetical example, assuming a $100,000 initial investment. It is not representative of any specific portfolio. Reinvestment of dividends and capital gains are assumed. Your actual results will vary.

Source: Brandes Investment Partners, Bloomberg (as of December 31, 2002).

EFFECTS OF INFLATION

Remember 1982, when U.S. economists assured us that Paul Volcker had killed the inflation dragon once and for all? That belief proved greatly exaggerated. As long as households, corporations, and governments borrow and spend excessively, inflation and high interest rates remain threats.

Inflation has always been present, though at certain points in the business cycle it usually remains discreetly out of sight. While inflation, as measured by price increases for consumer goods, remained benign for much of the last decade in many developed nations, other costs, including housing, surged. Has the problem disappeared entirely? I don't believe so. I *do* believe investing in stocks may help maintain living standards or help meet long-term investment objectives, such as a down payment on a home.

Jeremy Siegel examined the effects of inflation in *Stocks for the Long Run.* "It is clear that the growth of purchasing power in equities not only dominates all other assets but is remarkable for its long-term stability. . . . In contrast to the remarkable stability of stock returns, real returns on fixed income assets have declined markedly over time . . . since 1926, and especially after World War II, fixed income assets have returned little after inflation."[11]

CONCLUSION

This chapter presented evidence supporting the superiority of common stocks as a long-term investment vehicle. I also described how businesses (represented by common stocks) create the wealth of an advanced economy. All other values flow from that wealth. Corporate bond interest is paid by the cash flow of businesses; government bond interest is paid by taxes on business wealth. Real estate rents are paid by business cash flow. Art, commodities, and precious metals are purchased with wealth produced by businesses. It follows that businesses, over the long term, should produce higher returns than other asset classes, such as bonds, art, commodities, and real estate.

Some of the greatest opportunities in decades currently await diligent and patient investors. These opportunities don't rely on timing the market. They depend on investigative acumen and a long-term investment horizon. The value investor should constantly keep these concepts in mind when mingling with Wall Street.

Notes

1. Of course, U.S. government bonds and bills are backed by the full faith and credit of the U.S. government. Common stocks have no such backing and have tended to exhibit greater short-term price volatility. This is a hypothetical example and is not representative of any specific portfolio. Reinvestment of dividends and capital gains are assumed. Taxes and other expenses not applied. Past performance is no guarantee of future results. Your actual results will vary.

2. Jeremy J. Siegel, *Stocks for the Long Run,* New York: McGraw-Hill, 1998, p. 13.

3. Janet Lowe, *Value Investing Made Easy,* New York: McGraw-Hill, 1996, p. 123.

4. "Look At All Those Beautiful, Scantily Clad Girls Out There!" *Forbes,* November 1, 1974, p. 41.

5. This is a hypothetical example and is not representative of any specific portfolio or mutual fund. Reinvestment of dividends and capital gains are assumed. Taxes and other expenses not applied. Past performance is no guarantee of future results. Your actual results will vary.

6. Gold Information Network, www.goldinfo.net/yearly.html.

7. Elroy Dimson, Paul Marsh, and Mike Staunton, *Triumph of the Optimists: 101 Years of Global Investment Returns,* Princeton, N.J.: Princeton University Press, 2002, p. 63.

8. Prashanta Misra, "Trust Us: Forget Commodity Trading," *Money*, October 1994, p. 19.

9. J. Mei and M. Moses, Art as an Investment and the Underperformance of the Masterpieces: Evidence from 1875–2000, New York University Stern School of Business, 2001, p. 1.

10. Lowe, *Value Investing Made Easy*, p. 118.

11. Siegel, *Stocks for the Long Run*, pp. 11–12.

13

STAYING THE COURSE

In Chapter 2, I described various reasons why value investing works. Namely, there are numerous irrational biases inherent in human nature that impair decision making. These biases, which have been explored by psychologists for years, are being increasingly studied in the context of investment decisions. Reflecting the growing popularity and acceptance of such principles, the 2002 Nobel Prize winners in economics were Daniel Kahneman and Vernon L. Smith, two researchers who integrated psychological factors into their studies of economies and financial markets.

The Royal Swedish Academy of Sciences cited Kahneman for applying psychological factors to "human judgment and decision-making under uncertainty." His experiments showed a "shortsightedness in interpreting data that could explain large fluctuations on financial markets."[1]

The growing recognition of psychological factors that influence our actions in economic and investment markets validate what many value investors have known for years. There are profits to be made in the stock market for patient investors who do two things: conduct thorough, fundamental analysis and have the fortitude to act rationally in an often-irrational environment.

In this chapter, I offer suggestions on how you can avoid the irrational quirks that tend to plague investment decisions as well as ideas on how to keep yourself from succumbing to the very behaviors you seek to exploit in the market. These suggestions are designed to help you avoid the "why we won't be able to do what we've learned" problem that sometimes characterizes value investors, especially novices. I want to help you stay focused on your long-term objectives, not day-to-day fluctuations in share prices. Consider this chapter a personal challenge—one that I'm confident you can meet if you adhere to certain guidelines and remain disciplined.

In addition to offering guidance on "staying the course," I'll also share my thoughts on "doing it yourself" versus hiring a professional financial advisor, and the different skills necessary for *maintaining* your portfolio versus *creating* it. But first, let me introduce you to Mr. Market.

MR. MARKET

As I mentioned in Chapter 11, Benjamin Graham developed the parable of Mr. Market to help explain the stock market's often irrational behavior when pricing individual stocks. This parable also helps explain the risks that value investors invite when they fail to *remain* value investors.

Graham suggested imagining that you own a $1000 stake in a business. Think of Mr. Market as one of your business partners. Every day, "he tells you what he thinks your interest is worth and furthermore offers either to buy you out or to sell you an additional interest on that basis."[2] Be warned, however, Mr. Market has a personality quirk. Years ago, we might have described his condition as manic-depressive. More recently, we've adopted the term *bipolar*.

Regardless of what it's called, you need to know that Mr. Market often does not act rationally. At times, he is extremely optimistic and may try to entice you to buy an additional interest in the business at a very high price.

Remember, amid any market swings, you remain in control. You decide the true value of the companies you hold, not Mr. Market.

At other times, he can be extremely pessimistic. He may tempt you to sell your holding at a very low price because he is convinced it will fall to zero. The important thing to remember about Mr. Market is that *you choose how to interact with him.*

As Graham wrote, "You may be happy to sell out to him when he quotes you a ridiculously high price, and equally happy to buy from him when his price is low. But the rest of the time you will be wiser to form your own ideas of the value of your holdings. . . ."[3] Graham wrote that investors who hold shares of common stock share a similar relationship with the broader market. An investor "can take advantage of the daily market price or leave it alone, as dictated by his own judgment and inclination."[4]

The fickleness of Mr. Market underscores yet again the fundamental tenet of value investing. Value investing works by capitalizing on the difference between business values and share prices. The fluctuating share prices that Mr. Market presents you each day have very little or nothing to do with the underlying value of businesses. Always be vigilant to guard against confusing business value with stock price.

Remember, amid any market swings, you remain in control. *You* decide the true value of the companies you hold, not Mr. Market. *You* decide when, and at what price, you want to purchase or sell shares. Because of his irrational mood swings, Mr. Market can tempt you to sell holdings at a loss or purchase suspect businesses at high prices. Trust *your* judgment. Trust *your* research. Don't be swayed by the siren song of an overly emotional marketplace. Being aware of Mr. Market and his mood swings can help you be patient and help you make rational investment decisions.

In Chapter 1, we looked at what appears to be escalating share price volatility in the markets. In 1998, for example, the number of days in which the S&P 500 Index fluctuated more than 3 percent was higher than in each of the previous 8 years combined. This trend toward more volatile markets may or may not continue. Either way, you need to be prepared mentally and emotionally for swings in share prices. Let's look at some specific means of preparation.

BOLSTERING YOUR DEFENSES

"Know thyself."

Ah, the wise counsel from Socrates. Although I'm sure the Greek philosopher wasn't talking about global stock markets when he shared this advice around 400 B.C., his words are particularly relevant for investors.

This two-word statement is deceptively complex. As previously discussed, we, as humans, have inherent biases and tendencies to act irrationally. Ben Graham described the individual investor as his own worst enemy. How can we protect ourselves from ourselves? Following Socrates' advice, let's get a better handle on who we are.

Author Rich Tennant developed a humorous test[5] to help assess your risk tolerance when investing:

Which one of these phrases best describes how you retrieve toast?

1. Wait for toast to pop up even though it's burning
2. Go after toast with wooden toast prongs
3. Go after toast with an all-metal butter knife
4. Go after toast with metal butter knife wearing wet swimsuit and stainless-steel colander on head.

Match the number of your answer to the following risk profile:

1. Low Risk
2. Moderate Risk
3. High Risk
4. Ultra High Risk

While your toast-gathering technique may not necessarily provide an exact script for how you will act when managing a portfolio of value stocks, this fun quiz may provide some insight on who you are. Namely, how aggressive are you? How patient are you?

On a more practical note, think back to the technology stock boom of the late 1990s. Did you have money invested in stocks at that time? If so, how did you feel? And more importantly, what did you do? Did you follow the crowd and load up on technology shares? Did you maintain a diversified portfolio? When stocks began their descent in March 2000, how did you respond? Did you sell all your stocks? How about nearly 3 years after the top? Were you still selling? Were you being patient—perhaps waiting for a modest rebound so you then could sell your holdings? Or were you purchasing select bargains? Aside from this barrage of questions about the tech stock bubble, the most important ones you can ask yourself are these: Looking back on how I've managed my money, what have I learned about myself? How do I really respond when stock prices rise or fall? Is it different than how I *thought* I would respond?

Successful value investors are patient investors. I'll touch on this more in Chapter 14. How patient are you? How willing are you to trust your judgment and swim against the often irrational current of the market? To gain clearer insight on what motivates you, I suggest searching the Internet for different tests that can help you assess your investment profile. Use key words such as "risk tolerance quiz" or "risk tolerance profile" in your search.

Keep in mind that the objective is to help you gain a better understanding of yourself so you can build the necessary defenses against your own potentially self-defeating tendencies. Often, it's difficult to be objective. It's difficult to look at our behaviors for what they really are. This is why we're often our own worst enemies.

One way to help you get an objective point of view is by working with a professional financial advisor. Credible advisors have years of experience in working with investors similar to you. By having a frank discussion with an advisor, he or she may be able to detect areas of weakness in your approach, unrealistic expectations, or misperceptions that could get you into trouble. I'll touch on aspects of working with a financial advisor later in this chapter. Whether you work with a professional or do it yourself is your decision. Either way, I'll share a few examples here of cognitive errors to guard against, as well as suggestions designed to bolster your mental edge and emotional mettle.

FRAMING

Look at the lines in Exhibit 13-1. Which horizontal line is longer? The one on top or the one underneath? Look closely. Things are not always what they *appear* to be. This illustration underscores a key point for investors: We cannot always trust our perceptions. As we saw in Chapter 4 when we looked at the differences between a good company and a good investment, value investors need to be diligent. We need to be skeptical. And most important in

Look at the lines in Exhibit 13-1. Which horizontal line is longer? The one on top or the one underneath? Look closely. Things are not always what they appear *to be.*

EXHIBIT 13-1   The Dangers of Framing

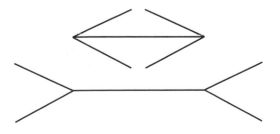

EXHIBIT 13-2   Objective Analysis versus Perception

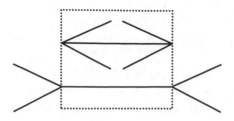

this context, we need tools and rules to help us distinguish opportunity from empty promises. As we see in Exhibit 13-2, the lines actually are equal in length.

Think of the lines in Exhibit 13-2 as stocks in which you could invest. Think of your eyesight as the evaluation tool most investors use when analyzing stocks. Then think of the ruler as your value investment discipline. By applying a disciplined approach to evaluating opportunities, you limit guesswork, emotional influence, or cognitive errors. You force yourself to trust objective analysis, not your emotions or the opinions of others. The goal is to make more informed decisions based on facts.

REGRET

How often have you given someone a lottery ticket as a gift? If you said never or rarely, you're in good company. Most people don't want to regret giving away a potentially winning ticket.

This mindset also influences how we manage portfolios. As discussed in Chapter 11, if developments at a company lower its intrinsic value to less than what you paid to purchase shares, effectively eliminating the margin of safety, it's not a bad decision to sell that stock at a loss. Our aversion to regret, however, may prevent us from executing a trade in which we lose money. We don't like to lose and may hold out hope that the stock will rally. We don't want to "give away" what could turn out to be a "winning" investment. But our hopes, likes, and dislikes have no place in an investment process. Stay focused on value-investing disciplines. Strive to manage your portfolio without emotion. Stick to analyzing business fundamentals and comparing the relationship between business value and stock price.

WHICH WAY TO INVEST?

Whether you choose to manage your money yourself or hire a professional advisor, value investing can be approached through a variety of methods; none is necessarily better than any other. The choice of method simply reflects personal preference in the way a value strategy is executed. Generally, there are a few ways to carry out your strategy:

1. Do It Yourself

- Research and select individual stocks and manage your own portfolio.

- Invest in mutual funds.

- Try a combination of the two.

2. Hire a Financial Advisor

- He or she may research and select individual stocks and manage a portfolio for you.

- He or she may recommend mutual funds.

- He or she may recommend a separate account, or "wrap account," to be managed by an investment management firm.

- He or she may recommend a combination of all of the above.

MANAGING YOUR OWN PORTFOLIO

If you decide to manage your own value portfolio, be aware that it could become an extremely time-consuming process. Serving as your own money manager requires that you conduct research, conduct trading, and evaluate investment performance. Ideally, do-it-yourself value investors should have considerable experience in finance and accounting. While managing money requires a high degree of dedication and commitment, a value investor with sufficient time and expertise could realistically expect to improve on the returns earned by many professional managers. You *can* do it. As we've addressed, many of the larger institutional managers fall prey to the same irrational behaviors discussed in this book. I believe avoiding these traps can give you quite an edge over the so-called pros.

The value investor acting independently should plan to spend at least 30 hours a week managing a portfolio. The investor also should be familiar with the resources described in Chapter 3. Once you have selected a value company for purchase, there are typically three ways to execute your trades. You could use a discount broker, a full service broker, or an online broker. Discount and online brokers tend to charge less for transactions than full-service brokerages. At the same time, they tend to offer less (if any) guidance. As discussed in the excerpt on load versus no-load mutual funds in Chapter 10, if you seek guidance from an investment professional, you should expect to pay for it, whether it's through a front-end or back-end sales charge on a mutual fund, a higher commission on a stock trade, or a fee based on the total amount of assets an advisor helps you manage. To expect a professional investment advisor or broker not to charge you for his or her experience, knowledge, and skill is unrealistic.

VALUE MUTUAL FUNDS

Value mutual funds provide diversification and professional money management that is difficult to obtain for the smaller or average-sized account. What should an investor look for in a fund? I suggest searching for offerings with a well-defined long-term value philosophy, continuity of management, and a good, long-term performance record.

This type of information is relatively easy to find. Two sources are Morningstar and the *Value Line Mutual Fund Survey*. Morningstar information is available online at www.morningstar.com. Value Line also offers information at its Web site, www.valueline.com. Both sources include long-term track records, managerial histories, and style boxes, which quickly reveal whether a fund uses a value approach to securities selection. In addition to these online sources, you also may want to visit your local library for Morningstar or Value Line publications.

The main drawback of fund investing is the lack of the personal touch. Value portfolios in a mutual fund format can't be tailored to special preferences and needs. And since the holdings are essentially blind pools, some individuals feel distanced from the businesses in which they are investing.

INVESTMENT CLUBS

Sometimes, do-it-yourself investors join others to form investment clubs. In general, I don't believe this is a good idea. Why not? Professor Meir Statman, a pioneer in the field of behavioral finance, wrote about the dangers of "camaraderie." These dangers apply to investment clubs. Citing research by Walter Goodman, Statman compared the mindsets of individuals in investment clubs to that of gamblers entering a casino. "Camaraderie is what we see in the busloads of anticipation that roll up to the casinos every morning and what we hear in the cheers when the dealer goes bust against the whole blackjack table. It's not just the joy of winning," according to Goodman, "but winning as part of a team."[6] There are plenty of "teams" to join. According to the National Association of Investors Corporation, there were more than 30,000 investment clubs in the United States in 2003.

Similar to casino gambling, there is a social aspect to investment clubs that can prove detrimental. Like gamblers, investment club members may feel united as a team against a common foe—the house or the market. This team mentality can lead to overconfidence, illusions of control, and decisions that reflect a follow-the-herd mentality. "Investment clubs serve many useful functions," according to research by Brad Barber and Terrance Odean, professors at the University of California, Davis. "They encourage savings. They educate their members about financial markets. They foster friendships and social ties. They entertain. Unfortunately, their investments do not beat the market."[7]

The professors studied returns for 166 investment clubs between February 1991 and January 1997. The clubs were randomly drawn from the account data of a large discount brokerage firm. According to Barber and Odean, "These clubs tilted their common stock investments toward small-cap growth stocks with high market risk. They turned over 65 percent of their portfolios each year, which implies that the average holding period for a club's stock investment was approximately 18 months. These clubs earned an average annual net return of 14.1 percent; during the same period, the S&P 500 returned 18 percent."[8]

This research supports my conviction that individual investors can achieve better-than-market returns by thinking for themselves and following a course of action that may differ from their peers. Doing what everyone else is doing—even everyone else in your investment club—means you'll likely get the same returns as everyone else. Based on my experience, if you want to achieve solid results over the long term, you often have to go against the grain. Conduct your own research and act upon it.

Based on my experience, if you want to achieve solid results over the long term, you often have to go against the grain.

HIRING A PROFESSIONAL

Managing a value-investment program requires considerable time, experience, hard work, and attention to detail. In this regard, it is no different from other professional endeavors where superior long-term results are demanded.

Individuals can and do succeed in managing their own money, given proper training and experience. But in many cases, the skills of a teacher, doctor, lawyer, or other nonfinancial professional, for example, do not necessarily translate to portfolio management. In other words, the specialized skills that build wealth in one profession are not necessarily the same as those needed for successful investing.

Because of the highly specialized nature of portfolio management, many investors might do well to consider the services of a professional financial advisor. The advisor carries out the day-to-day work, following a philosophy and plan agreed to by the client.

If you decide to partner with a financial advisor, I echo the advice offered by the Association for Investment Management and Research (AIMR). AIMR describes itself as "the leading global nonprofit professional association in the investment industry." It administers the Chartered Financial Analyst designation, a widely accepted professional qualification in the investment industry, and provides leadership in "investment education, professional standards and advocacy." You can learn more about AIMR at www.aimr.com.

AIMR offers five "Ps" when selecting an advisor with whom to work:

1. Preparation
2. Professionalism
3. Philosophy
4. Performance
5. Professional designations

In essence, prepare questions for potential advisors and interview them as if you were selecting an employee for your own business. Ask for referrals. Research candidates' backgrounds: their employment history, education, and professional affiliations. Ask about advisors' investment philosophies, how they intend to work with you, and frequency of communication. Ask to see samples of reports you would receive. Analyze the long-term performance of his or her recommendations. Ask how he or she gets paid. Ask about his or her involvement in any ongoing educational programs. Ask about the advisor's investment process: What can you expect in working with him or her. For more guidance on selecting an advisor, you may want to search the Internet for online resources using key words such as "selecting a broker," "choosing a financial advisor," or "advisor relationship."

HOW TO GET THE MOST FROM AN INVESTMENT ADVISOR

Once you have selected a competent advisor, the investor still has a job to do. A good client can help an advisor to function efficiently. How can a value investor become a good value client? Above all, understand how implementing the value investment philosophy will impact your returns over the short and long terms.

For example, as you know, the value approach entails the purchase of unpopular securities. Bargain levels are difficult to find in securities whose prices are actively moving up, or are already widely recognized as superior businesses.

Therefore, an initial value portfolio, whether created by the advisor or established through a mutual fund portfolio or a separately managed "wrap" account (to be discussed in a moment) may take time to show gains. Unpopular securities do not become market leaders overnight; often it takes up to 3 years before a value portfolio begins to demonstrate its initial intrinsic worth. Being patient, however, doesn't mean being passive. While you are waiting for the more emotion-based segment of the marketplace to recognize your portfolio's intrinsic value, make certain your advisor is sticking to the value approach. Do not, however, get caught up in such minutiae as short-term quotes, or monthly, quarterly, or even yearly portfolio evaluations. If questions arise about particular holdings, focus on how the company fits the chosen philosophy and whether the advisor is still on track.

The investor's second responsibility as a client is to communicate. Tell the advisor how much money is available for equity investments, how much will be available in the future, and your time horizon. Keep the advisor informed of any changes that might affect your plans. Be aware that large and unexpected capital withdrawals can disturb investment strategies, especially during market lows. Finally, let the advisor know of any concerns or problems.

Doing your part to make an advisory relationship work can save time, money, and frustration. Also remember that changing advisors increases the amount of time required for an investment plan to prove itself all over again. Additionally, switching advisors usually results in significant transaction costs as one advisor's positions are sold and another's purchased.

As cited previously, a professional financial advisor likely will suggest one of three approaches to managing your money: He or she may research and select individual stocks and manage a portfolio for you; he or she may recommend mutual funds; or he or she may recommend a separate account or "wrap" account to be managed by an investment management firm. I've addressed aspects of the first two options. Let's focus on the last option a bit more closely.

SEPARATELY MANAGED OR "WRAP" ACCOUNTS

Separately managed accounts are similar to mutual funds in that money is managed by a professional investment advisory firm and typically well diversified over a variety of holdings. In addition, individual investors do not have to worry about day-to-day details of their account or administrative issues. What's different? Namely, with a separate account, investors actually own shares of individual companies. They do not share ownership with a pool of investors. Instead of owning mutual fund shares that may represent dozens or hundreds of companies, separate account investors own the actual shares of each company in their portfolios. What's the benefit? Primarily, investors have greater control.

This enhanced control can be especially important with respect to taxes. Unlike a mutual fund, separate account investors can execute a number of tax-related strategies, including focusing on long-term gains, harvesting losses through tax-loss swapping, doubling up, and considering individual tax lots when selling. Investors pay capital gains taxes only when stocks are sold at a profit, not on gains accrued by a mutual fund in which an investor may or may not have participated. In addition, separate accounts offer greater flexibility, often accommodating investor restrictions or preferences, such as avoiding stocks that profit from gambling or sales of tobacco products. (Keep in mind, when it comes to the advantages and potential pitfalls of executing tax-aware strategies, I urge you to consult with your tax advisor before acting.)

Typically, investors do not pay a commission for each trade executed in a separate account. Instead, they pay a management fee that combines, or "wraps" together, costs for professional management, custody, trading, administration, and individual service provided by the financial advisor.

When investing through a "wrap" account, your financial advisor becomes your "chief financial officer." He or she may develop rules for selecting, monitoring, and evaluating money managers responsible for investing your assets. These rules might include step-by-step actions for evaluating individual managers, dismissing those who are not doing what they were hired to do, and identifying and hiring new ones. Reputable advisors routinely send out teams of analysts to monitor the investment firms responsible for the day-to-day management of wrap accounts. Good, long-term performance, of course, is part of the picture. Equally important are the quality of the investment firm's professional staff, the consistency of the firm's investment strategy, and the nature of the strategy itself. I believe that the most effective investment management firms specialize in a particular approach: value, growth, large-cap, small-cap, domestic, nondomestic, or some combination. Look for a firm whose philosophy most closely conforms to your own. Work with your advisor in selecting the philosophy first and the investment manager second.

Financial advisors also should monitor the managers' performance and remain on the lookout for red flags, such as a sudden shift in investment style, runaway growth, or changes in key personnel. For example, value-style investment managers who start chasing growth stocks because that style happens to be hot at a given moment are not doing what they were hired to do. And sometimes firms can become victims of their own success, taking on too many clients too quickly and losing control of the quality of the portfolios they manage. For more information on separately managed accounts, I suggest talking with your financial or tax advisor.

Now that you're familiar with the primary methods in which your money could be managed, let's turn our attention to retaining your long-term focus.

STAYING THE COURSE

For individuals who want to stick to a disciplined value-investing approach, I offer four suggestions:

1. Write it down.
2. Rebalance your portfolio.
3. Pause to reflect.
4. Work with a professional.

Write It Down

Institutional investors have "investment policy statements." I think individual investors should too. This statement (sometimes called an IPS) is a detailed plan that outlines specific objectives. It may include guidelines for asset allocation, time horizons, and how you may work with a financial advisor. Your IPS also may include more specifics, such as restrictions on certain stocks that you don't want to own. Regardless of the level of detail included in your plan, your IPS should help you do at least three things:

- Set realistic objectives

- Outline your asset allocation strategy

- Establish procedures for managing your portfolio

If you work with a financial advisor, the IPS might also include procedures for communicating with your advisor. The IPS will outline how your investment process and objectives will be communicated to all parties involved with the investments, for example, advisors, beneficiaries, and current and future fiduciaries, and who is responsible for implementing what aspects of the plan.

Setting objectives can help avoid the tendency to constantly compare short-term returns for your portfolio against an index, or that brother-in-law who likes to brag about how much money he's making in stocks. It might make you feel better to have owned the best-performing stock each quarter, but it is far more important to evaluate periodically how your overall portfolio is doing compared to the specific goals you have set.

In addition to assessing your risk tolerance and gauging your time horizon, there are other factors to consider when creating your objectives, including return requirements, income and liquidity needs, tax considerations, and legal and regulatory concerns.

Here's a sample investment objective for a doctor: "To make his job optional by the age of 55; to have an annual income from his investments of at least $100,000 (after taxes and in today's dollars, with an inflationary factor of 4.0%), beginning in the year he turns 55; to leave a substantial legacy to his two daughters; to minimize potential tax liabilities; to periodically monitor and revise his portfolio, as required."[9]

I suggest putting a lot of time into developing your plan and far less time into tinkering with it.

With respect to developing your asset allocation strategy, balance your long-term goals with any short-term needs. Consider your tolerance for volatility and time horizon. Again, a financial advisor may be able to assist you in coming up with a mix of different asset classes.

When it comes to procedures for managing your portfolio, you might want to include specific, step-by-step guides for purchasing or selling shares and rebalancing. Having a written game plan for buying or selling a stock greatly reduces your potential for making emotional decisions and can be an excellent defense against the kinds of psychological pitfalls addressed here and in Chapter 2. A written action plan also brings greater consistency to your approach. Instead of winging it or wondering if you're considering all the angles before making a decision, you've got a checklist to follow. Think of it as a recipe designed to bring success. You can build and maintain a portfolio from scratch with each step outlined along the way.

As for reviewing progress toward your goals, establish how often you plan to do this. You may want to examine your portfolio every 6 months or once a year. I suggest putting a lot of time into *developing* your plan and far less time into tinkering with it. Unless your long-term goals or objectives change, you probably will make few adjustments to your IPS once it's established.

Rebalance Your Portfolio

When examining your portfolio periodically, one aspect to consider is rebalancing. That's a fancy word for making any necessary adjustments to keep your portfolio's asset allocation in line with your goals. Adhering to a sound rebalancing strategy often forces you to make decisions in your portfolio that run counter to the crowd. For example, when stocks surge, you may sell a portion of your holdings to prevent them from becoming too large a piece in your portfolio. Conversely, when stock prices fall, you may purchase *more* shares to bolster their diminished allocation.

Many investors add to their stock positions when the market climbs and sell shares when the market declines. Value investors see market declines as short-term events that create opportunities to purchase attractive businesses at bargain prices. Keeping a long-term perspective and rebalancing your portfolio periodically can deliver important benefits down the road.

Pause to Reflect

Often, we tend to get swept up in our day-to-day activities. Responsibilities for work, family, and friends may divert our attention from longer-term goals we have set for ourselves or the people we care about. The same can be true of investing. I encourage you to pause periodically to reflect on your investment approach, to review your goals and how you've set about achieving them, and refresh your conviction for the value approach. In addition to the book you're holding, I suggest purchasing *The Intelligent Investor* by Benjamin Graham and reading a chapter or two at least once each year. You may not learn anything new in reading excerpts from Graham's book, but hopefully you will fortify your defenses against making irrational investment decisions. From *The Intelligent Investor,* I highly recommend Chapter 8, "The Investor and Market Fluctuations," and Chapter 20, " 'Margin of Safety' as the Central Concept of Investment."

Work with a Professional

As I described earlier, a professional financial advisor may provide valuable objectivity in working with you to create and monitor a long-term investing plan. Advisors can also address questions you may have regarding specific developments in your life and their influence—if any—on implementing your plan. If you choose to hire a financial advisor, remember the five "Ps," maintain realistic objectives, and communicate honestly. Together, you and your advisor can build a relationship based on mutual respect and trust.

CONCLUSION

When it comes to investing, typically there are no guarantees. But I am almost certain about one thing for value investors: If you strictly adhere to value-investing principles, you will likely question the merit of this approach at some point. You likely will second-guess your decisions. You will have doubts. By investing in out-of-favor stocks, you may look foolish in the short term. Your portfolio may decline when the rest of the market is surging. You may read negative comments about your portfolio holdings in the financial press and wonder why you ever purchased them. I'm telling you this now to prepare you. In the last chapter of this book, I'll encourage you to stick to your value disciplines, trust your independent analysis, and avoid the temptation to abandon value principles. Above all, I urge you to be patient.

Notes

1. Matti Huuhtanen, "Two Americans Win Nobel Prize for Economics," *The Seattle Times,* October 9, 2002 (pulled from the Internet on December 2, 2002, at seattletimes.nwsource.com/html/businesstechnology/134551407_webnobe109.html).
2. Benjamin Graham, *The Intelligent Investor: A Book of Practical Counsel,* 4th rev. ed., New York: Harper & Row, 1973, p. 108.
3. Ibid.
4. Ibid.
5. This test was excerpted from a press release announcing the availability of the book *Mutual Funds for Canadians for Dummies* written by Andrew Bell and published by CDG Books Canada in 2001. The press release, distributed by Canada News Wire, was retrieved from www1.newswire.ca/releases/April2001/04/c1583.html.
6. Meir Statman, "Lottery Players/Stock Traders," *Financial Analysts Journal*, January/February 2002, p. 17.
7. Brad M. Barber and Terrance Odean, "Too Many Cooks Spoil the Profits: Investment Club Performance," *Financial Analysts Journal,* vol. 56, no. 1 (January/February 2000), p. 24.
8. Ibid., p. 23.
9. Taken from this Web site:
www.physiciansnews.com/finance/399.html.

ABOVE ALL,
BE PATIENT

T humb through the table of contents of most investment books. You'll
likely find chapters on selecting, purchasing, and trading securities.
Investing often sounds like action and more action. More often than
not, it's just the opposite: Patience is a key discipline for the value investor.

Don't expect to achieve financial success overnight. There will be periods when stocks aren't performing well. That is when patience becomes especially important to your long-term success. Don't fidget, don't fuss, don't bail out, don't let your emotions get the better of you, and don't be concerned with day-to-day market fluctuations. The business cycle hasn't been conquered. The preceding pages have described the basic value tools and principles, but knowing and understanding those principles won't be enough unless you practice patience and self-discipline.

How critical is patience and discipline for the successful investor? Benjamin Graham makes the argument for restraint in *The Intelligent Investor*:

> For indeed, the investor's chief problem—and even his worst enemy—is
> likely to be himself. . . . We have seen much more money made and *kept*
> by "ordinary people" who were temperamentally well suited for the

investment process than by those who lacked this quality, even though they had an extensive knowledge of finance, accounting, and stock-market lore.[1]

Long-term objectives, not short-term price fluctuations, should determine investment decisions.

Patience helps turn disadvantages into advantages. As addressed in Chapter 11, consider the common perception of risk as the possibility of a market or equity decline. For the investor with a time horizon of 3 to 5 years (or longer), this definition of risk is invalid—true risk is measured in the context of the long-term appreciation potential of a business or portfolio of stocks. An investor does not suffer a loss because a stock declines, only when deciding to sell such a security. Long-term objectives, not short-term price fluctuations, should determine investment decisions.

When it comes to patience, financial media and investment advertisements may lead investors astray. The media often encourages sentiments of panic and greed, constantly offering stock and investment recommendations and predictions. Investment ads often portray affluent investors making trades or checking stock prices while on the ski slopes, in a cab, or at the airport. Both portray knowledge as power, convenience as essential, and rapid trading as investing. Unfortunately, these amenities can undermine an investor's patience and selectivity. The only thing frequent trading and price monitoring likely guarantee are increased trading costs.

When authors Thomas Stanley and William Danko surveyed millionaires for their book *The Millionaire Next Door*, they found that fewer than 1 in 10 millionaires are what they termed "active investors." In fact, 42 percent of the millionaires they interviewed had made *no* trades whatsoever in their stock portfolios in the year prior to the interview.[2] So much for the media's image of investing.

Another fallacy the financial media promotes is the illusion of market prediction. Once a market participant believes prices and patterns are predictable, it's hard to suppress speculative instincts and remain patient.

For example, hindsight bias is rampant in the financial media. Within minutes after the market closes, market analysts are busy explaining the exact reasons why the Dow was up 90 points or why the Nasdaq Composite was down 2 percent. Events that even the best-informed experts did not predict seem to have been inevitable immediately after they occur. However, the truth is that people can rarely reconstruct, after the fact, what they thought about the probability of an event before it occurred.

Patience is certainly a tougher order today than it was even 10 years ago. Financial media, including cable television channels, magazines, Web sites, radio stations, newspapers, and newsletters promote apocalyptic headlines, inconsistent recommendations, suggestions for short-term market trades, superficial explanations, and a fixation on short-term market performance. Investors will find their patience tested by the media, whose messages are produced for mass consumption. Practicing patience and discipline demands tuning out the media's incessant prattle.

At my firm, there's a television in the lunchroom. We placed a placard atop this TV as a reminder of the dangers of watching certain financial news channels. Designed to sound similar to the warning on a pack of cigarettes sold in the United States, the placard states that such channels, " . . . contain significant amounts of speculative materials, known to Graham & Dodd investors to cause overreaction to short-term market events, diminished focus on company fundamentals, including the relationship between stock price and underlying value, and other harmful effects on long-term portfolio performance. If tuned to stations such as these, changing the channel now greatly reduces serious risks to your financial health."

I already have stressed the consequences of following the market's orientation toward short-term results and instant gratification. Successful value investors must stand apart and defy group thinking.

Consider the patience demanded of investors of two U.K.-based spirits companies, Guinness and Grand Metropolitan. Both traded at attractive multiples in 1996, owned solid balance sheets, and their businesses were defensive and generated much cash. During this speculative period, few investors appreciated the value of these companies, and those who did found their patience tried by a series of criticisms and developments.

The two companies announced a plan to merge in 1997 as Diageo, with the goal of strengthening the spirits businesses and exploiting cost savings and new marketing power. The financial press questioned the formation of a conglomerate (Grand Metropolitan also owned several nonspirits businesses), labeled the companies as slow growers, and pointed out the new company had to sell some solid brands as a condition of Federal Trade Commission (FTC) approval. Selling nonspirits divisions would take time and would be subject to FTC approval.

A patient investor might have reevaluated the intrinsic value of the combined business to determine if it were still undervalued. In the case of Diageo, this was true. In addition, the company continued to reward investors with a generous dividend. Management consistently added to shareholder value. The sale of its Pillsbury food business to General Mills reduced Diageo's debt by $4.5 billion, provided another $4.5 billion in cash, and freed up substantial borrowing capacity. When Seagram was purchased by the French media company Vivendi, the spirits divisions of Seagram were put on the market. Flush with cash from the Pillsbury transaction, Diageo teamed with another spirits company (Pernod Ricard) to purchase these brands and expand their spirits businesses.

At the time, Diageo boasted twice the level of sales of its nearest competitor and was able to exert influence on wholesalers and retailers to negotiate better purchasing terms. The company began a substantial share repurchase program, and in late 2002, the company announced the sale of its Burger King division to a private group. Diageo's attractive returns for the period rewarded investors who waited more than 5 years for the firm's stock price to approach fair value. Investors who did not sell the business in reaction to media criticisms or headlines also enjoyed generous dividends along the way.

While the rest of the world rushes to buy great concepts or the latest high flyer, the successful value investor must hang tough and stick to basics. If you maintain a disciplined approach, the courage of your convictions, and patience, I believe you will find investing in undervalued businesses throughout the world a rewarding pursuit.

Notes

1. Benjamin Graham, *The Intelligent Investor: A Book of Practical Counsel,* 4th rev. ed., New York: Harper & Row, 1973, p. xv.
2. Thomas J. Stanley and William D. Danko, *The Millionaire Next Door,* Atlanta: Longstreet Press, 1996, p. 100.

EPILOGUE

Throughout this book, I have stressed that it is the combination of *rational* fundamental analysis and *irrational* market prices that creates opportunities for value investors. Here I recap the highlights of *Value Investing Today*.

Early in the book, I emphasized the importance of purchasing shares of a business that offer a margin of safety: a healthy difference between the price of the stock and the value of the underlying business. I cautioned against short-term thinking and succumbing to speculative impulses. I addressed reasons *why* value investing works by drawing attention to emotional overreactions in everyday life and comparing these behavioral flaws with stock market investing, using examples such as extrapolation, faulty intuition, and optimism. I touched on my acquaintance with Benjamin Graham, the father of security analysis, and his enduring investing principles. I shared historical returns for other value-investing practitioners to illustrate the approach's long-term effectiveness.

I provided guidance on how to identify value stocks and build a portfolio by examining key aspects of companies' financial statements. I shared suggestions on where to find promising investment candidates, what types of businesses generally to avoid, as well as elements of sound corporate governance. I stressed the importance of a global perspective when investing, shared various methods for participating in the world's diverse markets, and highlighted unique aspects of investing worldwide, such as accounting differences and the similarities and differences among ADRs and ORDs.

In the final chapters, I summarized the lessons I shared, offered a framework for managing expectations regarding the rewards and risks of investing in the stock market, and investigated investor psychology at the individual level. I challenged you to adhere to the guidance I offered—to ignore the influence of the media and its incessant obsession with short-term developments—and to maintain your long-term perspective.

Value investing is not easy. It is not glamorous. I believe, however, that it is "intelligent investing," an effective method for identifying solid investment opportunities and building wealth over the long term. I appreciate your interest in my views on value investing and wish you success in your endeavors.

Index

AAA bonds, long-term, 63–65
Accounting for Growth, 154
Accounting practices, 56
  "creative," 154–155
  and fraud, 86–87
  international variations in, 145–155
  and stock options, 87–89
Accrual accounting, 75
Active management, 113–116
  during bear markets, 176–177
  benefits of, 116
  and ETFs, 137
Activism, shareholder (*see* Shareholder activism)
Additional shares, issuing, 57
Adelphia, 155
ADRs (*see* American Depositary Receipts)
ADSs (American Depositary Shares), 123
Advisors, financial (*see* Financial advisors)
AIMR (Association for Investment Management
  and Research), 194
Airbus, 104
Allende, Salvador, 142
Altria, 148
Amazon.com, 55
American Depositary Receipts (ADRs), 72–73,
  121–132
  access to information about, 129–130
American Depositary Receipts (ADRs) (*Cont.*):

bank's role in, 123–124
convenience of, 129
exchange-listed, 124
and German companies, 146
history of, 122–123
and international mergers, 125
liquidity of, 130
market for, 124–125
ORDs vs., 126–132
"over-the-counter," 130
and price quotes, 130–131
pricing of, 128
settlement time of, 128
sponsored vs. unsponsored, 124
American Depositary Shares (ADSs), 123
American Institute of Certified Public
  Accountants, 146
Amoco, 125
Annual earnings growth, 65
Arbitrageurs, 128
Argentina, 142, 143
Art, 179
Asian stock markets, 99, 101
Asset allocation, 161–162
Assets:
  on balance sheet, 74
Assets (*Cont.*):
  current, 64, 65

hidden, 74
intangible, 75
net asset value, 133, 134
net current, 64, 65
revaluation of, 152–153
undervalued, 74
Association for Investment Management and
    Research (AIMR), 194
Auditor's letter (in financial statements), 77
Australasia, 99

Balance sheet (statement of financial position),
    73–75
Balance sheet debt, 63–64
Bank of New York, 131
Barber, Brad, 193
Barron's, 131, 134
Bear markets, 175–176
Behavioral bias(es), 17–29
    and behavioral finance, 18–19
    and efficient market theory, 26–28
    exploiting, 24–26
    extrapolation as, 20–21
    faulty intuition as, 19–20
    optimism as, 21–23
    problems resulting from, 22–23
Behavioral finance, 18–19
Benefits of value investing, 32
Benetton Group, 127
Berkshire Hathaway, 35, 36, 66, 164
Beta, 163–164
Black, Bernard, 82–83
Bloomberg, 143
BMW, 24–25
Board of directors, 84–86
Bogle, John, 91
Bonds, long-term AAA, 63, 64, 65
Bonuses (for company executives), 56
Book value (shareholder's equity), 65, 74
    of foreign companies, 147
    tangible, 64
Bottom-up investors, 52, 109
Brandes Institute, 33, 53
Brandes Investment Partners, 41
Brazil, 142–144, 152
Brazil Fund, 136
Briloff, Abraham J., 155
British Airways, 124
British Petroleum, 125
British Telecom, 127
Brokers/brokerages, 192
Buffett, Warren, 41

and Berkshire Hathaway, 35
and beta theory, 163–164
on forecasting, 116
on intrinsic value, 66
on liquidity, 168
on market declines, 175
on skill, 36
on stock options, 88
Burger King, 206
BusinessWeek, 22
"Buying straw hats in winter" analogy, 10

California, 180
Canadian stock markets, 101
Capital-intensive companies, 57
Carabell, Christopher, 116
Cardosa, Fernando Henrique, 142
Cash flows, 76–77, 147, 148, 153
CBSMarketWatch, 55
Central Bank of Brazil, 143
Character (of company), 57
Chartered Financial Analyst (financial advisor
    designation), 194
Chief executive officers, 85
Chile, 142
China, 126
Cisco Systems, 58, 59
Citigroup, 111
Classes of stocks, 57
Closed-End Fund Association, 134
Closed-end funds, 133–136
    choosing a, 135–136
    ETFs vs., 136
Clubs, investment, 192–193
CNOOC, 126
Commodities, 179
Companies:
    board of directors of, 84–86
    capital-intensive, 57
    chief executive officers of, 85
    control of vs. ownership of, 81–82
    finding (see Finding value companies)
    foreign, 57
Competition, 112–113
Conglomerates, 11
Coombes, Paul, 84
Corporate governance, 79–94
    and accounting practices, 86–89
    and control vs. ownership, 81–82
    focus of, 80
Corporate governance (Cont.):
    importance of, 82–86

and shareholder activism, 89–93
warning signs about, 84
Correlation, 104
and asset allocation, 161–162
cycles of, 105–106
and diversification, 105
Cost-reduction programs, 57
"Creative" accounting practices, 154–155
Cross-ownership, 145
Currency:
and ADRs, 127
fluctuations in, 107–108, 139–142
hedging, 141–142
trading, 140
Current assets, 64, 65
Current liabilities, 65
Cycles, economic, 105–106

da Silva, Luiz Inacio Lula, 142–143
DaimlerChrysler, 122
Dalbar, Inc., 12
Danko, William, 204
Day traders, 11
Debt:
on balance sheet, 63–64
long-term, 74
short-term, 74
total, 65, 74
Debt-to-equity ratio, 65, 66, 74
Declines, stock market, 175–176
DeLalla, Elizabeth, 116
Delaware Trust Company, 168
Depositary receipts (see American
    Depositary Receipts; Global
    Depositary Receipts)
Depreciation:
"double-declining balance" method, 148
Japanese method of accounting for, 151
straight-line, 147–148
Deutsche Telekom, 125
Diageo, 205–206
Diamonds, 136
Dimson, Elroy, 102–103
Discount brokers, 192
Discount to intrinsic value, 5–6
Diversification, 165–167
benefits of, 102–103
and correlation of international stock markets,
    105
cost of, 167
Diversification (Cont.):
and currency fluctuations, 141

of emerging markets, 112
and investing abroad, 98–103
limiting risk through, 165–167
and political risk, 144
(See also Portfolio management)
Dividends, 63, 64, 147
DJIA (see Dow Jones Industrial Average)
Dodd, David, 13, 67
Dollar cost averaging, 169–170
Dot-coms, 8–9, 27–28, 51
"Double whammy," 39
"Double-declining balance" method of
    depreciation, 148
Dow, Charles, 180
Dow Jones Industrial Average (DJIA):
1929–1948, 170
1965–1982, 176–177
and Diamonds, 136
during Internet bubble, 8
in mid-1970s, 41
Dreman, David, 22, 41
Dutch Civil Code standards, 152–153

EAFE Index (see Europe, Australasia, and Far
    East Index)
Earnings:
decline in, 65
of foreign companies, 147
growth of, 65
strength of, 66
of value companies, 50
Earnings per share (EPS), 63, 66, 67
estimated, 69
sustainable, 68–69
Earnings yield, 63, 64, 65, 66
Economic cycles, 105–106
EDGAR (www.sec.gov/edgar), 73
EDS (Electronic Data Systems), 42–43
Efficient market theory (EMT), 26–28, 38
semi-strong version of, 27
strong version of, 27–28
weak version of, 26
Electronic Data Systems (EDS), 42–43
Emerging Markets Free (EMF) Index,
    110–111
Emerging markets, 110–112
EMF (see Emerging Markets Free Index)
EMT (see Efficient market theory)
Enron Corporation, 79, 85, 155
EPS (see Earnings per share)
Equity:
debt-to-equity ratio, 65, 74

tangible, 65
Estimated EPS, 69
ETFs (exchange-traded funds), 136–137
eToys, 55
Europe, Australasia, and Far East (EAFE) Index, 99, 105–107
European stock markets, 99, 101
"Everybody Ought to Be Rich" (John J. Raskob), 170
Exchange-listed ADRs, 124
Exchange rates, 107–108, 140–141
Exchange-traded funds (ETFs), 136–137
Executive compensation, 56
Expenses, 75, 135
Extrapolation, 20–21

"Falling knives," 53–54
Fama, Eugene, 38
FASB (Financial Accounting Standards Board), 146
Faulty intuition, 19–20
Federal Reserve Board, 141
Federal Trade Commission (FTC), 205
FIFO (first in, first out) accounting technique, 74
Financial Accounting Standards Board (FASB), 146
Financial advisors, 189, 191, 194–201
    benefits of working with, 200
    and developing investing objectives, 198–199
    getting the most from, 195–196
    selecting, 194–195
    and "wrap" accounts, 196–197
Financial Analysts Journal, 103
Financial health (of value companies), 50
Financial strength, 66
Financial Times, 125
Financing cash flows, 76–77
Finding value companies, 49–94
    characteristics to look for, 49–59
    financial statements as tools for, 73–77
    "five tests" method for, 64–65
    four-step test for, 65
    and good companies vs. good investments, 57–59
    Graham's net-net method for, 62
    Graham's second best-known method for, 62–64
    and information gathering, 71–78
    Internet tools for, 72–73
    and intrinsic value, 65–67
Finding value companies (Cont.):
    P/E ratio as metric for, 67–69

top-down vs. bottom-up approach to, 52
and warning signs of companies to avoid, 56–57
Fine art, 179
Finland, 104
First Call, 22
First in, first out (FIFO) accounting technique, 74
Fitch, 143, 144
"Five tests" for value, 64
Fixed prices, 57
Flexibility (of emerging markets), 111
Forbes, 175
Ford, 59
Foreign companies, 57
    (See also Investing abroad)
"Four-step" test for valuing stocks, 65
Framing, 189–190
Frank Russell Company, 34, 35
Fraud, 86–87
French, Kenneth, 38
FTC (Federal Trade Commission), 205
Full service brokers, 192
Funds:
    closed-end, 133–136
    global, 132
    index, 114–115
    international, 132
    loads, 134–135
    open-end, 133
    operating expenses, 135
    regional, 132–133
    sector-specific, 132–133
    single-country, 132–133
    value mutual, 192

GAAP (generally accepted accounting principles), 74
Gale, David, 85
Gavin Anderson & Company, 122
GDRs (Global Depositary Receipts), 121–122
General Electric, 107
General Mills, 205
Generally accepted accounting principles (GAAP), 74, 129, 145–146, 147, 155
Geographic hard times, 53
Germany, 146, 147, 151–152
Glamour (growth) stocks, 9, 33, 38–40, 42
Global Depositary Receipts (GDRs), 121–122
Global funds, 132
Global investing (see Investing abroad)
Global Investor Opinion Survey (McKinsey &

Company), 94
GNI (gross national income), 110
Golden parachutes (for company executives), 56
Goodman, Walter, 193
Goodwill, 75, 148–149, 151
Government regulations, 57
Graham, Benjamin, 41
    on behavioral biases, 187–188
    on dollar cost averaging, 169–170
    on estimating intrinsic value, 67
    and *The Intelligent Investor,* 200
    margin of safety concept of, 4–6
    and methods for selecting value companies,
        62–65
    and Mr. Market, 161, 186–187
    on patience, 203–204
    on price vs. value, 160
    on results, 25, 44
    on shareholder activism, 92–93
    on speculating vs. investing, 13–14
Grand Metropolitan, 205
Grantham, Jeremy, 108–109
Gross national income (GNI), 110
Growth:
    earnings, 65
    of emerging markets, 111
    of principal, 32
    value-destructive, 50–51
Growth (glamour) stocks, 9, 33, 38–40, 42
Growth investing, 7–9
Guinness, 205

Hard times, geographic, 53
Haugen, Robert A., 28
Hedging, currency, 141–142
Heinz, 28
Hidden assets, 74
"Hold and hope" (shareholder option), 90
Honda, 145
Hong, Harrison, 22
Hong Kong stock market, 104, 126, 127, 144
Hoover's Company Capsules, 72
Horizon (*see* Investment horizon)

IAS (International Accounting Standards), 149
IASB (International Accounting Standards
        Board), 146
IASC (International Accounting Standards
        Committee), 146
Ibbotson Associates, 34, 174, 181
IMF (International Monetary Fund), 143
Income, net, 76, 147

Income statement, 75–76
Index funds, 114–115
Indexing, 113–116
Industries, out-of-favor, 53
Inflation, 57, 182
Initial public offerings (IPOs), 8, 54–56
Intangible assets, 75
The Intelligent Investor (Benjamin Graham), 4,
        13, 169–170, 200, 203–204
Internal Revenue Service (IRS), 147, 148
International Accounting Standards (IAS), 149
International Accounting Standards Board
        (IASB), 146
International Accounting Standards Committee
        (IASC), 146
International funds, 132
International investing (*see* Investing abroad)
International Monetary Fund (IMF), 143
International stock markets, 99–100, 104
Internet stock bubble, 8–9, 27–28, 51
Internet stocks, 8–9
Intrinsic value, 4–6, 65–67
Intuition, faulty, 19–20
Inventory, accounting for:
    German method, 151
    United Kingdom method, 151
Investing abroad:
    and accounting system differences, 145–155
    active management vs. indexing approach to,
        113–116
    bargain hunting when, 108–109
    bottom-up vs. top-down approach to, 109–110
    closed-end funds, 133–136
    comparing international companies when,
        153, 154
    and competition, 112–113
    and correlation of international stock markets,
        104–106
    and currency fluctuations, 107–108, 139–142
    depositary receipts, 121–132
    in emerging markets, 110–112
    exchange-traded funds, 136–137
    investing in U.S. markets vs., 139–156
    methods of, 119
    opportunities in, 101–102
    ordinary shares, 119–121
    packaged overseas investments, 132–133
    and political risk, 142–145
    and portfolio diversification, 98–103
    reluctance about, 97–98
Investing abroad (*Cont.*):
    risk in, 102–103, 142–145

in small- and mid-cap companies, 103–104
  and U.S. multinationals, 106–107
Investing cash flows, 76
Investing in index funds, 113
Investing strategies, reevaluating, 160–161
Investment clubs, 192–193
Investment horizon, 13, 35–36, 40
Investment policy statement (IPS), 198
Investment strategies, 197–200
Investors:
  bottom-up, 52
  top-down, 52
InvestWorks database, 113
IPOs (see Initial public offerings)
IPS (investment policy statement), 198
IRS (Internal Revenue Service), 147, 148

Japan:
  accounting practices in, 150–151
  reporting earnings in, 147
  stock markets in, 99, 104, 108, 115, 127
The Journal of Finance, 33
J.P. Morgan Bank, 72–73, 122, 125

Kahneman, Daniel, 185
Kiplinger, 72
Kraft cheeses, 148
Kuala Lumpur Kepong, 124
Kubik, Jeffrey, 22

Ladies Home Journal, 170
Lakonishok, Josef, 33
  (See also LSV study)
Large-cap stocks, 38
"Last in, first out" (LIFO) accounting technique, 74
Liabilities:
  on balance sheet, 74
  current, 65
  of shareholder, 81–82
LIFO (last in, first out) accounting technique, 74
Limited liability of shareholders, 81–82
Liquidity, 167–169
  of ADRs, 130
  of emerging markets, 111
Loads (sales charges), 134
Long-term AAA bonds, 63, 64, 65
Long-term debt, 74
Long-term investment horizon, 13, 35–36
L'Oreal, 44
Lows, new, 53
LSV study, 33, 37, 40, 42
Lycos, 125

Margin of safety, 4–6
Market capitalization, 164
Market declines, 175–176
Market inefficiencies (of emerging markets), 112
Markets:
  bear, 175–176
  emerging, 110–112
Markowitz, Harry, 161
Marsh, P., 102–103
Matsushita, 145
Maxwell House coffees, 148
McDonald's, 101–102
McKinsey & Company, 83–84
Media, 54, 204–205
The Memoirs of the Dean of Wall Street
  (Benjamin Graham), 92–93
Mergers and acquisitions, 125
Meridien Bank, 168
Merrill Lynch, 59
The Midas Touch, 163
Mid-cap stocks, advantages/disadvantages of,
  103–104
The Millionaire Next Door (Thomas Stanley and
  William Danko), 204
Miracle Whip salad dressings, 148
Mitchell, Malcolm, 162
Modern Portfolio Theory (MPT), 161–162
Money, 179
Moody's Investor Service, 143
Morgan Stanley Capital International (MSCI)
  Brazil Index, 143
Morgan Stanley Capital International (MSCI)
  Emerging Markets Free (EMF) Index,
  110–111
Morgan Stanley Capital International (MSCI)
  Europe, Australasia, and Far East (EAFE)
  Index, 99, 105–107
Morgan Stanley Capital International (MSCI)
  World Index, 175
Morningstar, 101, 102, 177, 192
Morningstar Mutual Funds, 134
MPT (Modern Portfolio Theory), 161–162
"Mr. Market" (fictional character), 161, 186–187
MSCI (see under Morgan Stanley Capital
  International)
Multinationals, U.S., 106–107
Mutual funds, value, 192
  (See also Funds)
Myners, Paul, 90–91

Nasdaq, 136
Nasdaq 100, 8

Nasdaq National Market System, 120
National Association of Investors Corporation, 193
NAV (net asset value), 133, 134
Neff, John, 35, 36
"Negative surprise," 33
Nestle, 43–44, 104, 127, 149
Net asset value (NAV), 133, 134
Net current assets, 64, 65
Net income, 75, 76, 147
Netherlands, 152–153
"Net-net" method of valuing companies, 62
New Economy, 8, 9, 24
New lows, 53
New York Stock Exchange (NYSE), 120, 122, 127, 146
New Zealand stock market, 104
Nintendo, 127
Nippon Telephone & Telegraph (NTT) Corporation, 120, 122, 129
Nokia, 104
Northern Pipeline, 92–93
NTT (Nippon Telephone & Telegraph) Corporation, 120, 122, 129
Nucor, 110
NYSE (*see* New York Stock Exchange)

Odean, Terrance, 193
Old Economy, 8, 24, 28
Online brokers, 192
Open-end funds, 133
Operating cash flows, 76
Operating expenses, 135
Optimism, 21–23
Options, stock, 87–89
Ordinaries to ADR ratio, 127
"Ordinary" shares (ORDs), 119–121
    ADRs vs., 126–132
    in the OTC market, 120
    price quotes for, 131
OTC (*see* Over-the-counter market)
Out-of-favor industries, 53
Out-of-favor (value) stocks, 9, 33, 42
Over-the-counter (OTC) market, 120, 130, 131
Ownership, cross, 145

Pacific Telesis Group, 149–150
Passive management, 113
Patience, 181, 203–206
P/E ratio (*see* Price-to-earnings ratio)
Pension Management, 116
Perks (for company executives), 56

Pernod Ricard, 206
Pfizer, 107
Philip Morris, 148–149
Pillsbury, 205
Political risk, 142–145
"Popular" stocks, 40
Portfolio management, 159–171
    active vs. passive, 113–116
    and diversification, 165–167
    do-it-yourself approach to, 191–193
    and dollar cost averaging, 169–170
    by financial professionals, 194–201
    and liquidity, 167–169
    and rebalancing your portfolio, 199
    and risk, 159–169
    and volatility, 162–165
Portfolio managers, 40
Portfolios, value, 54
POSCO, 109–110
Post cereals, 148
Pratten, Clifford F., 27, 28
Price (term), 3–4
Prices:
    of ADRs, 128
    as critical factor in determining value of stock, 66
    and "five tests" for value, 64
    fixed, 57
    and "four-step" test for valuing stocks, 65
    mispricing of stocks, 37–38
    quotes for ADRs, 130–131
    of stocks in recent decades, 42
    underpriced stocks, 39
    of value stocks, 33
Price-to-book ratio, 38, 66
Price-to-earnings (P/E) ratio:
    comparing companies', 68
    and earnings yield, 63
    and five tests for value, 64
    for foreign companies, 145, 149
    and indices, 67–68
Principal, growth of, 32
Products:
    at fixed prices, 57
    of value companies, 50
Programs, cost-reduction, 57
Proxy statement disclosures (in financial statements), 77–78
"Prudent" stocks, 40
"Push and prod" (shareholder option), 90

QQQ ("Qubes"), 136
QUALCOMM, 21

"Quantitative Analysis of Investor Behavior
      (QAIB)" study, 12–13

Raskob, John J., 170
Real estate, 151, 179–180
Rebalancing your portfolio, 199
Reebok, 115
Regional funds, 132–133
Regret, 190
Regulations, government, 57
Revenues, 75
Risk, 37–41, 159–169
   and asset allocation, 161–162
   definition of, 102
   diversification as means of limiting, 165–167
   of investing abroad, 102–103, 142–145
   measuring tolerance for, 188
   stock-specific, 166
   volatility vs., 162
Risk tolerance, 188
Royal Swedish Academy of Sciences, 185
Ruane, William, 35, 36
Russell 3000 Growth Index, 34, 37
Russell 3000 Index, 34, 37
Russell 3000 Value Index, 34, 37

Safety, margin of, 4–6
Salaries (of company executives), 56
Sales charges (loads), 134
Sanford C. Bernstein & Co., 35
Sanka coffee, 148
Sara Lee, 28
Seagram, 206
SEC (see Securities and Exchange Commission)
Sector-specific funds, 132–133
Securities and Exchange Commission (SEC), 73,
      86, 146
Security Analysis (David Dodd and Benjamin
      Graham), 13, 67
Selfridge Stores, 122
"Sell and shrug" (shareholder option), 90
Separately managed ("wrap") accounts, 196–197
Sequoia mutual fund, 35, 36
Service Corporation International (SRV), 51
Services:
   at fixed prices, 57
   of value companies, 50
Settlement time (of ADRs), 128
Shareholder activism, 80, 89–93
   benefits of, 92–93
Shareholder activism (Cont.):
   reasons for lack of, 91–92

   tactics in, 90–91
Shareholder's equity (see Book value)
Shleifer, Andrei, 33, 82
   (See also LSV study)
Short-term debt, 74
Short-term thinking, 11–13
Siegel, Jeremy, 174–175, 182
Single-country funds, 132–133
Small-cap stocks, 38, 103–104
Smith, Vernon L., 185
Smithers, Andrew, 145
Socrates, 187
Sony, 104, 124
South Korea, 109
Spain, 102, 149–150
SPDRs ("Spiders"), 136
Speculation, 13–15
"Spiders" (SPDRs), 136
Sponsored ADRs, 124
SRV (Service Corporation International), 51
"Stagflation," 22
Standard & Poor's, 22, 143
Standard & Poor's Industrial Index, 145
Standard deviation, 164–165
Standard Oil, 92, 93
S&P 500 Index, 35, 36
   in early 2000s, 175–176
   and "falling knives," 54
   and historical returns for stocks, 174
   and index funds, 115
   and international stock markets, 104
   and MSCI EAFE Index, 99, 105–107
   from 1965 to 1982, 177
   and SPDRs, 136
   and U.S. multinationals, 107
Stanley, Thomas, 204
Statement of cash flows, 76–77
Statement of financial position (see Balance sheet)
Statman, Meir, 192–193
Staunton, M., 102–103
"Staying the course," 197–200
Stock Finder, 72
Stock market(s):
   bear, 175–176
   declines in, 175–176
   foreign, 99, 101, 104, 108, 115, 126, 127, 144
   timing the, 180–182
Stock(s), 173–183
   active management of, 176–177
   classes of, 57
Stock(s) (Cont.):
   and compounding rates, 180, 181

"five tests" for safety of, 65
"five tests" for value of, 64
and "four-step" test for valuing, 65
growth, 9, 33, 38–40, 42
and inflation, 182
Internet, 8–9
as investment, 174–175
large-cap, 38
and market declines, 175–176
mid-cap, 103–104
mispricing of, 37–38
options, 87–89
performance of, vs. other investments, 177–180
popular vs. prudent, 40
small-cap, 38, 103–104
underpricing of, 39
value, 9, 33, 38, 42
Stocks for the Long Run (Jeremy Siegel), 182
Stock-specific risk, 166
Straight-line depreciation, 147–148
Strategies, investment, 197–200
Sustainable EPS, 68–69
Switzerland:
    accounting practices in, 149
    reporting earnings in, 147
    stock market in, 127
Synergy, 11

Taiwan Semiconductor, 89
Tangible book value, 64
Tangible equity, 65
Taxes:
    and foreign companies, 147
    and "wrap" accounts, 196
Technical analysis, 20
Technology stocks, 8–9
Telefónica, 102, 125, 149–150
Templeton, Sir John, 12
Tennant, Rich, 188
Terra Networks, 125
Texaco, 59
Texas, 180
Thomas Weisel Partners, 55
Tiananmen Square massacre, 144
Time, importance of, 180, 181
Timing the market, 180–182
Tokyo equity market, 145
Tokyo stock exchange, 127
Top-down investors, 52, 109
Total debt, 74
Toyota, 140
Toys "R" Us, 55

Train, John, 163
20-F reports, 129

Unaccountable Accounting, 155
Undercapitalization (of emerging markets), 111
Undervalued assets, 74
Unilever, 122
United Kingdom, 151
Unsponsored ADRs, 124
U.S. Federal Reserve Board, 141
U.S. multinationals, 106–107

Value:
    discount to intrinsic, 5–6
    intrinsic, 4–6, 65–67
    net asset, 133, 134
    tangible book, 64
    as term, 3–4
    (*See also* Book value)
Value companies:
    characteristics of, 49–51
    finding (*see* Finding value companies)
    identifying, 53–56
Value investing:
    benefits of, 32
    and "buying straw hats in winter"
        analogy, 10
    growth investing vs., 7–9, 32–34
    historical results of, 34–36, 41–42
    long-term thinking and, 11–13
    and margin of safety, 4–6
    and risk, 37–41
    as skill, 36–37
    speculation vs., 13–15
    and volatility, 37–38
Value Line Mutual Fund Survey, 192
Value mutual funds, 192
Value (out-of-favor) stocks, 9, 33, 42
Value portfolios, 54
Value-destructive growth, 50–51
ValueLine Investment Survey, 72
Vanguard Windsor mutual fund, 35, 36
Vishny, Robert W., 33, 82
    (*See also* LSV study)
Vivendi Universal, 79, 206
VoiceStream Wireless, 125
Volatility, 32, 162–165
    beta as measure of, 163–164
    and investing in international stock markets,
        102–103
Volatility (*Cont.*):
    and MPT, 162

risk vs., 162
standard deviation as measure of,
    164–165
of stock market in recent decades, 42
of stocks in 1990s and 2000s, 14
Volcker, Paul, 182
Volume, 167–168
"Voting with your feet," 90

The Wall Street Journal, 85, 131, 134
The "Wall Street Walk," 90
Washington Post Company, 164
Web sites:
    investment, 72–73

of publicly traded companies, 73
Wellington Management, 35
World Bank, 110
World Trade Organization (WTO), 126
WorldCom, 79, 86, 155
"Wrap" accounts, 196–197
WTO (World Trade Organization), 126

Yale University, 105–106
Yield:
    dividend, 63, 64
    earnings, 63, 64, 65, 66

About the Author

Charles H. Brandes, CFA, is founder and a managing partner of Brandes Investment Partners, LLC, an investment advisory firm serving institutional and private clients with more than $50 billion under management as of December 31, 2002. A CFA charterholder for more than 25 years, Brandes had the tremendous fortune early in his career to meet and learn from Benjamin Graham, long considered the father of security analysis and value investing. He was able to learn firsthand the techniques Graham used to uncover bargain securities, and he has used those basic principles as the foundation to achieve consistently superior results for his clients.